# ASTANA

## ARCHITECTURE, MYTH & DESTINY

FRANK ALBO

The publisher gratefully acknowledges the support of the Canada Council for the
Arts and the Manitoba Arts Council for its publishing program. We acknowledge the support of
the Government of Canada through the Canada Book Fund and the Government of Manitoba
through the Publishing Tax Credit Program for our publishing activities.

Design: Hayden Sundmark
Editor-in-Chief: Joanne Therrien
Editor: Ben Vrignon
Copy Editor: Lynne Therrien

Legal deposit—2017:
Library and Archives Canada
Manitoba Legislative Library

**VIDACOM**

Vidacom Publications
P.O. Box 123 Winnipeg, Manitoba Canada R2H 3B4
admin@plaines.mb.ca
www.plaines.ca
www.vidacom.ca

Printed and bound in Canada

*To the munificent people of Kazakhstan,*
*the wayshowers of the twenty-first century.*

τίς ἂν οὖν ἡμῖν, ἦν δ’ἐγώ,
μηχανὴ γένοιτο τῶν ψευδῶν
τῶν ἐν δέοντι γιγνομένων,
ὧν δὴ νῦν ἐλέγομεν, γενναῖόν
τι ἓν ψευδομένους πεῖσαι
μάλιστα μὲν καὶ αὐτοὺς
τοὺς ἄρχοντας· εἰ δὲ μή,
τὴν ἄλλην πόλιν;

Socrates

Door detail, Khazret Sultan Mosque, Astana

Peaks of Tien Shan, including Khan Tengri, reflecting on the surface of Tuzkol, a salt lake in southeastern Kazakhstan.

Nurzhol Boulevard featuring Bayterek Tower, the House of Ministries' golden towers, and the Akorda Presidential Palace, Astana.

# ACKNOWLEDGMENTS

This work would not have been possible without the assistance of many collaborators. Firstly, I would like to thank the Ambassador of the Republic of Kazakhstan to Canada, His Excellency Konstantin V. Zhigalov, to whom I am indebted for his sage advice and direction. I am also beholden to the Kazakhstani Ministry of Foreign Affairs for its generous support, and to the Mayor's Office of Astana for supplying many of the stunning photographs used in this publication. My gratitude further extends to Kris Pikl, Michael Hancock, Rafis Abazov, Saulesh Yessenova, Dave Verbeeten, Aizhan T. Akhmedova, and Valeriy Loman, director of the Saryarka Archaeological Institute of the Buketov Karaganda State University, for being lured in at the eleventh hour to offer their pertinent insights and suggestions. I want to especially thank my designer, Hayden Sundmark, for his keen eye and attention to detail, as well as Esthée Freynet for recommending Vidacom's dedicated Joanne Therrien as a publisher. Acknowledgment is also rightly due to Korkyt Ata, the Turkic Orpheus who found the Earth's *axis mundi* through epic poetry and song, and to Cliff Johnson who was an indispensable resource in crafting the treasure hunt concealed in this book. However, my deepest appreciation is reserved for my family and my two Queens of Heaven and Earth.

**FIG 1** Pyramid ruins, Karaganda Region

# PREFACE

In the spring of 2013, I was preparing a graduate seminar on utopian urbanism that surveyed a chronology of paradisiacal cities from Plato's Atlantis to Nazarbayev's Astana. Laying the groundwork for this course, I was struck by the sheer number of popular misconceptions about Kazakhstan that proliferate on the Internet. A cursory search through websites and blogs suggested that rather than being some uncouth backwater of illiterate boors—a myth fabricated by Sasha Baron Cohen's outrageous mockumentary, *Borat* (2006)—Kazakhstan had been denominated the international command centre of the Illuminati, a nefarious secret society plotting to take over the world.[1]

I decided to perform a Google search using the terms "Astana + Architecture" and found myself plunged down a rabbit hole of connivance and conspiracy. I soon discovered that Astana is the sun-worship capital of Zionist Freemasons; that its principal buildings are connected to the pyramids at Giza by an energetic grid; and that the city's Master Plan is a coded "magical diagram" devised by a totalitarian world government.[2] Complementing these astonishing assertions has been the recent unearthing of the "world's first pyramid" in the Karaganda Region of central Kazakhstan (Fig. 1).[3] Although in substantial ruins today, the structure once resembled the famous Step Pyramid of Djoser at Saqqara (ca. 2667–48 BCE). A flurry of viral media reports proclaimed that the Sary Arqa pyramid had been constructed 1000 years before its Egyptian counterpart, but the archaeologists from Buketov Karaganda State University who investigated the site concluded it had been erected during the late Bronze Age (ca. 1570–1200 BCE).[4]

Having carved myself a niche career as a specialist on the architecture of Freemasonry, I must admit to being unapologetically hooked. Soon every tab in my browser linked to a morass of sinister machinations and arcane symbols associated with Kazakhstan, including an enormous "Devil Pentagram" etched onto the southern shore of the Upper Tobol Reservoir (Fig. 2). Concerning its purported occult origins, archaeologist Emma Usmanova seemed to have dispelled all speculation when she determined that the 1200-foot pentagram was merely the remains of an old Soviet summer camp. After all, the symbol of the Soviet Union was a five-pointed star—but this has not deterred Dan Brown-wannabes from mythologizing Kazakhstan as a hotbed of satanic activity.[5]

The New York Times furthered such fantasies upon the recent discovery of immense geoglyphs in northern Kazakhstan, presenting them as the architectural remains of Stone Age nomads dated over 8000 years old.[6] However, using advanced methods of dating, a team of international archaeologists led by Andrey Logvin have accurately pinpointed the construction of two of the earthen mounds to the Early Iron Age Period, ca. 800 BCE.[7] These Central Asian analogues to the Nazca Lines in Peru include a collection of nearly one hundred geometric earthworks. The so-called Ushtogaysky Square, which measures 287 metres in length, is a particularly compelling example of the magnitude of the site. But it was the enormous 90-metre "swastika" (or triskelion) that sparked a fresh rash of seditious theories in the popular press (Fig. 3). Though widely associated with Nazi ideology, the swastika was initially a benevolent symbol of Indo-European origin, and according to the *Mānasāra*, an ancient Sanskrit treatise on Vedic architectural theory, it constituted the ideal city plan for capital cities.[8]

Kazakhstan is a jewel of extraordinary splendour, and the culture of the region is full of unexpected surprises. With Russia to the north, China to the east, the Caspian Sea to the west, and Turkmenistan, Uzbekistan, and Kyrgyzstan to the south, it is the largest landlocked country on Earth. Kazakhstan is a vast expanse of untouched steppes, grand canyons, arid deserts, majestic mountain ranges, and breathtaking landscapes as lush as Peter Jackson's Middle Earth and as windswept as the Badlands of South Dakota (Figs. 4–6). Though this country gave the world apples, first domesticated horses, and may have begotten the legend of King Arthur (see pages 75–79), Kazakhstan remains in the West a veritable *terra incognita*, a derisive toponym for Borat, and a mecca of Internet conspiracy theories.[9] For most North Americans, contemporary Kazakhstan is shrouded in a collective sense of ignorance and exoticism.

As I groped my way through this labyrinth of myth and incredulity, I received a fortuitous call from the Protocol Office of Manitoba. It was Deputy Chief Karen Bryk, asking if I would be available to guide His Excellency Konstantin Zhigalov, Ambassador of the Republic of Kazakhstan to Canada, on a private tour of the Manitoba Legislative Building. For the last eight years, I have led regular guided tours of the building that identify the ingenious arrangement of Masonic symbolism concealed in its architecture, ranging from hidden hieroglyphic inscriptions to numerological codes so intelligently masked they have escaped historians and visitors for nearly a hundred years.[10] It is fair to say that my introduction to what would later become this book was tinged with a very palpable sense of serendipity and purpose. For what began as an impromptu meeting with Ambassador Zhigalov ultimately led to the opportunity to take an entirely opposite approach to all my previous scholarship on the history of Architecture. And in a flash of inspiration, my task became clear. Rather than *decode* genuine Masonic buildings of the past, I would *encode* an imaginary Masonic utopia of the future.

**FIG 2** "Devil Pentagram," Upper Tobol Reservoir, northwestern Kazakhstan.

**FIG 3** Kostanay Region geoglyphs, including the "swastika" (triskelion), northern Kazakhstan.

**FIG 4**  Ush Konyr plateau, Almaty Region, Kazakhstan.

**FIG 5**  Bozzhira, Mangystau Region, southwestern Kazakhstan

**FIG 6**  Aksu River canyon, southern Kazakhstan.

*Jupiter Pluvius* (detail) by Joseph Gandy (1771–1843), 1819.

# INTRODUCTION

Myths are not merely the fables of the gods; they are embedded in nearly every aspect of the human imagination. Psychology, art, literature, philosophy, film, architecture, and even science (according to Karl Popper), all encode some fabric of myth.[11] In today's parlance, myths are often synonymous with fiction, but for Freud, Jung, and Otto Rank, myths reflect our most primordial desires and provide us with a glimpse into the essential truths of the human condition.[12] For the Romantics of the nineteenth century, myths were believed to conceal higher wisdom and offered scientifically accurate descriptions of the cosmos and rationalizations of natural phenomena.[13] F.W.J. Schelling (1775–1854) placed mythology on equal footing with logical philosophy, while the pioneering iconoclast, Friedrich Nietzsche (1844–1900), went so far as to claim that "myth was higher than history" and constituted "a concentrated image of the world."[14]

The casual observer is often oblivious to the fact that even cities contain epic mythology about our cultural DNA. Nowhere is this more apparent than in Astana. While similar to other capital cities in that it serves national interests and political goals, a closer examination of Astana's buildings reveals a matrix of mythological connotations well beyond those intended by the state. Most of the literature on Astana has focused on the motivations of the first President of the Republic of Kazakhstan, Nursultan Nazarbayev (b. 1940), and has only offered rudimentary assessments of the capital's visual elements and design.[15] Some scholars have argued that Astana is little more than a sophisticated veneer fabricated by political elites.[16] This work departs from these trends. Instead, it uses symbolism and semiotics to provide an interpretative lens for positioning Astana as an ideal case study for a modern-day foundation myth about peaceful governance, religious tolerance, and environmental ethics.

My approach to the architecture of Astana is an urban tribute to The Inklings, a famous literary clique affiliated with Oxford University from the 1930s to the late 1940s. The core group consisted of the philosopher of consciousness, Owen Barfield (1898–1997), high-fantasy pillars J.R.R. Tolkien (1892–1973) and C.S. Lewis (1898–1963), and the prolific author of supernatural thrillers, Charles Williams (1886–1945). The Inklings were driven by the notion that we are all interconnected and part of a larger imaginal reality. Lewis himself, a onetime ardent atheist-cum-Christian-apologist, boldly conjectured that "reason is the natural organ of truth; but imagination is the organ of meaning."[17] The literature produced by The Inklings employed epic fantasy as an indictment against modernity and a panacea for the traumas of twentieth-century disenchantment, materialism, and alienation.[18] Lewis's *The Chronicles of Narnia* (1950–56) has been shown to contain a coded exegesis on the seven planets of medieval cosmology, while Tolkien's *The Lord of the Rings* (1954–55) provides a veiled commentary on Roman Catholicism.[19] In a similar manner, this book presents architectural mythmaking as a tangible roadmap for addressing the greatest challenges facing the twenty-first century—religious extremism, the sustainability of the planet, and the proliferation of nuclear weapons.

The inception of this book stemmed from my online webinar series called *The Eagle and Child*, a deferential nod to the pub in Oxford where The Inklings met, and around the common hearth of mythopoeia set alight the minds of the twentieth century. This three-part series was billed through social media as a reactivation of that celebrated intellectual hub, but with one major difference—I invited the global community to take part in co-authoring a foundation myth for Astana that did not yet exist. By all accounts, my methodology was controversial and unorthodox, since many of my premises derived from hermeneutical speculation, as opposed to conventional history, ethnographic fieldwork, and on-site research. At no point did I ever consult the citizens of Astana and ask for their views of the city or its architecture. But after several visits to Kazakhstan, what I discovered about the country, its people, and its culture fascinated and intrigued me all the more.

As a melting pot of global culture for thousands of years, the territory of Kazakhstan houses the cultural memories and traditions of the world. Civilizations and empires have risen and perished on its windswept steppes, leaving only traces of their existence and legacy. The people of Kazakhstan have embodied triumph in the face of overwhelming odds and the optimistic architecture of Astana presents an epic journey of courage, resilience, and solidarity that unites people across generational boundaries, ethnicities, and cultures. Behind the glistening façade of the capital's most cherished buildings is an underlying narrative that touches upon the entirety of human achievement and beckons us along a peaceful path toward a sustainable modern world.

Never before in the history of modern Central Asia has city planning played such a defining role in the ascent of a nation or its rise to industrial power.[20] Astana, with a population quickly approaching 900 000, is the third in line of post-Soviet capitals to receive a full-blown architectural facelift, but neither Ashkhabad in Turkmenistan nor Baku in Azerbaijan have blossomed to the same degree. Neither have Tashkent, Bishkek, or Dushanbe, due to their lack of necessary resources and economic outreach.[21] Even China is awash with failed utopias and pristine "ghost cities" that are eerily devoid of lived experience or latent culture.[22] What is uniquely different about Astana is that its urban programme reflects mythopoetic conceptions of design that run through the whole course of human history, from the paradise gardens at Pasargadae in ancient Persia to Walt Disney's unrealized concept for the Experimental Prototype Community of Tomorrow (EPCOT) in Florida.[23] In nearly all respects, Astana is the *ne plus ultra* of an indissoluble utopian enterprise to create a perfectly realized world in which fantasies and dreams are actualized.

## Methodology and Summary

This book leans on the giants of anthropology, architecture, archaeology, and genetics to locate a mythical subplot underlying the urban fabric of Astana. I make use of Maurice Halbwachs's proposition of *collective memory*, Mircea Eliade's analysis of *sacred space*, Jean Baudrillard's concepts of *simulacra* and *hyperreality*, Eric Hobsbawm's hypothesis of *invented tradition*, Claude Lévi-Strauss's *structuralism*, the semiotic theories of de Saussure, Peirce, Eco, and Preziosi, and Stephen Baehr's exegesis of Paradise Myths in secular Russian literature and culture. Four key elements of my interpretive methodology are borrowed from Ernst Cassirer's theories on how humans create a universe of symbolic meanings, Leo Strauss's notion of "reading between the lines," Vladimir Propp's *Morphology of the Folktale* (1958), and Susanne Langer's theory that we are hardwired to impose symbolic meanings on our environments.

I have also cribbed from Enlightenment mythographers Antoine Banier (1673–1741) and Thomas Blackwell (1701–57), who envisioned myth as a civilizing influence, and from English architects Joseph Gandy (1771–1843) and William Lethaby (1857–1931), who saw myth as the foundation of a new architectural language.[24] Another source of mythographic inspiration came by way of Johann Valentinus Andreae (1586–1654) and the "Tübingen Circle," a cadre of heterodox Lutheran intellectuals who concocted the myth of the Rosicrucian Brotherhood to bring about the "Universal Reformation of Mankind" (Fig. 7).[25]

By cloaking their utopianism in myth and then wrapping it in mystery, the Tübingen Circle engendered one of most effective publicity stunts of all time—a full-scale "Rosicrucian furore" that swept across seventeenth-century Europe and remains to this day an enduring subject of fascination and intrigue.[26] This book is therefore not a mere compendium of dates, facts, and figures; instead, it is a how-to manual for the invention of modern urban mythography—one that ascribes a library of coded meanings to the built environment of Astana. These messages range from the prehistoric migrations of ancient nomads into North America 15 000 years ago to the quest for Earth sustainability showcased at the World Expo 2017.

In recent decades, a new vanguard of scholars have begun to shift their focus from the Fertile Crescent to Central Asia as the fountainhead of early civilization.[27] In the third volume of his trilogy exploring the evolution of human consciousness, *Wandering God: A Study in Nomadic Spirituality* (2000), Morris Berman sheds new light on the *horizontal* worldview of Palaeolithic nomads in distinct contrast with *vertical* hierarchies of sedentary civilization. The latter, he claims, engendered rigid societies of inequality, warfare, and alienation. Ancient nomads, on the other hand, fostered egalitarianism, openness, tolerance, and "a kind of mature ambiguity" that "cathected the whole environment" and provided an alert "fluidity of mind."[28] Berman suggests reviving this ancient value system as an antidote to the disenchantment of contemporary society and as a prescription for the resacralization of the natural world.

In Chapter One, I introduce three ancient Indo-European innovations critical to the development of advanced society and show how the multiculturalism of the Silk Roads and the majestic landscape of the Great Steppe have been aestheticized in the architecture of Astana. After unpacking the problematic notions of Kazakh ancestry, ethnogenesis, and early forms of urbanity in Chapter Two, I move on to an exploration of foundation myths, epic poems, and folktales in the construction of national identity. Here, I show how urban semiotics provide an interpretive framework for decoding Astana's Palace of Schoolchildren and Khan Shatyr Entertainment Centre. In Chapter Three, I make the case for President Nazarbayev being both an obligatory "hero" of the foundation myth, as well as the Chief Architect of the capital, showing how his commitment to a nuclear-free world and his zeal for Kazakh folklore are emblemized by the Presidential Palace and the monumental Bayterek Tower.

In Chapter Four, I contextualize Astana in relation to the rebirth of Sary Arqa, a political toponym that relates to the romanticization of nomadic culture and Kazakh heroism. I then proceed to an evaluation of Soviet influences in architecture, including Russian Constructivism and socialist utopianism, which culminate in the Disneyland aspects of fantasy urbanism and hyperreality present in Astana. Chapter Five tackles Kisho Kurokawa's nature-inspired Master Plan for Astana and explores his organic philosophy of Metabolism, symbiosis, and abstract symbolism. In deconstructing the Eurasian design elements in the capital, ranging from Timurid Islamic

architecture to "Wagnerian Valhalla," I examine the geometrical symbolism of Astana's Central Concert Hall. In Chapter Six, I demythologize the supposed links between Astana and Freemasonry, showing how the design elements in the capital derive from the architectural language of Étienne-Louis Boullée (1728–99) and Claude-Nicolas Ledoux (1736–1806). The Pyramid of Peace is then symbolically analyzed as a beacon of religious harmony and transparency, while the House of Ministries is interpreted as a modern reconstruction of Solomon's Temple influenced by Bruno Taut's "City Crown." I conclude with a discussion of Astana's World Expo site as a catalyst for Jeremy Rifkin's theory about the fundamental reordering of Earth's ecology and human society.

In piecing together this complex jigsaw puzzle, a compelling pattern emerges — the design and layout of Astana does not reveal the headquarters of Luciferian Freemasonry and the Illuminati, but rather veils a pan-national epic that heralds a new era of global cooperation. Astana's glass and steel masterpieces, its luxury hotels, megamalls, national monuments, and public institutions, provide a blueprint of three basic solutions for the necessary betterment of civil society: religious tolerance, nuclear disarmament, and planetary sustainability.[29] These three messages form the basis of a foundation myth that is communicated through the most significant buildings in the Kazakhstani capital, from Bayterek Tower to the Monument of Independence. Together, these buildings provide the bedrock of a universal tale about the rise of civilization and the peaceful co-existence of the human family (Fig. 8).

**FIG 7** *Geheime Figuren der Rosenkreuzer (Secret Symbols of the Rosicrucians)*, ms. 1943, BPH M308.

FIG 8   Astana's central axis at night, featuring the Transport Tower, KazMunaiGas complex and Khan Shatyr Entertainment Centre.

Astana's glass and steel masterpieces, its luxury hotels, megamalls, national monuments, and public institutions, provide a blueprint of three basic solutions for the necessary betterment of civil society: religious tolerance, nuclear disarmament, and planetary sustainability.

The Great Steppe, Ushkonyr rural community, southeastern Kazakhstan.

# CHAPTER ONE

# Eternal Kazakhstan

*Myth is much more important and true than history.*
*History is just journalism, and you know how reliable that is.*[30]
Joseph Campbell

## *Mythic Migration*

Modern humans migrated into the territory of Kazakhstan approximately 100 000 years ago, replacing the first series of hominin expansions into Eurasia between 1 800 000 and 800 000 years ago. Human mitochondrial genetics (mtDNA) have provided tremendous insight into the dispersal of modern *Homo sapiens* into Central Asia, itself a crucible of genetic diversity, language, and culture during the Late Pleistocene period (ca. 12 000 years ago).[31] As Spencer Wells, the Director of the Genographic Project, summarized: "if Africa was the cradle of humankind, Central Asia was its nursery."[32] By carefully following biological clues and human migration patterns,

Wells identified a man living in southeastern Kazakhstan whose DNA begat all Europeans and even Native Americans. This "Kazakhstani Adam" answers fundamental questions about our collective past and helps unlock the genetic secrets behind one of the greatest odysseys in human history.

Archaeological and paleontological research have further established a definite link between the indigenous populations of North America and the peoples inhabiting the Altai region of Russia and Kazakhstan.[33] One prevailing theory is that between 16 500 and 11 000 years ago, a small clan of nomadic explorers crossed the Bering Strait and followed an ice-free corridor into the Great Plains of Canada and the United States. Lead by Sijia Wang at Harvard, a team of twenty-seven geneticists has shown that the Chipewyan populations (Na-Dene/Athabaskan) from northern Canada are the progeny of a single group of far-distant Siberian ancestors who entered the Americas together.[34] Specific single-nucleotide polymorphisms on the male-inherited Y chromosome allow us to track this ancient expedition and plot the geography and period where the first settlers may have emigrated from Central Asia to the New World. Studies at the Sorenson Molecular Genealogy Foundation and the University of Pavia have confirmed that up to 95 percent of all Native Indians trace their ancestry to six women who were initially inhabitants of Central Asia.[35]

These prehistoric wayfarers would have faced the Ice Age head-on, overcoming ferocious arctic conditions as the last glacial age was coming to a close. This journey required incredible endurance and their determination was rewarded upon their arrival on the game-filled plains of North America. The notion that linguistic relations also crossed the Bering Strait has been bolstered by the controversial research of linguists Joseph Greenberg and Merritt Ruhlen, who claim that the majority of languages spoken in the Americas derived from *Amerind*, a hypothetical superfamily indigenous to Central Asia.[36] In the Kazakhstani pro-nationalist magazine, *Mangi El*, Senator Adil Akhmetov has followed up these assertions by searching for the precise structural affinities between Native American and Turkic languages.[37]

Even more fascinating is that the totemic symbols that underlie the state emblems of Kazakhstan also reflect the wellspring of mythologems that similarly define many of the indigenous cultures of North America—the eagle, the sun, blue skies, nomadic tents, the Simurgh/Thunderbird, and the sacredness of trees.[38] According to ancient legend, the Turkic-speaking Uyghur people sprang forth from a sacred tree. Ever since the time of the groundbreaking investigations of the fêted naturalist, Alexander von Humboldt (1769–1859), ethnologists have come to recognize a common stock of beliefs and traditions linking Central Asia and America. This not only concerns the primary tools of early civilization, such as canoes, baskets, and the stone axe or *toki* (the same word is found in Melanesia, as well as North and South America), but also with regard to the complex conceptions of magic, divination, astronomical observations, and folklore.[39]

The custom of tying pieces of cloth to tree branches (*mata*) lies at the heart of religious observances connected with the ritual sanctuaries of Terekty Aulie and Tamgaly in Kazakhstan (Fig. 9). The renowned Kazakh scholar and explorer, Chokan Valikhanov (1835–65), was the first to examine Tamgaly, explaining the practice of rag-tying as a personal supplication to the will of ancestors.[40] For Valikhanov, "a single tree growing in the steppe ... serves as an object of worship."[41] His brilliant career, though short, propelled Valikhanov to the status of a national hero and the progenitor of an entire field of ethnography that explored the ways in which Islam intersected

**FIG 9** Mata cloth tied to a ritual pole at the Terekty Aulie petroglyph site, Karaganda Region, central Kazakhstan

FIG 10  Human effigy petroform at Tie Creek, southeastern Manitoba.

FIG 11  Solar-headed god petroglyph at Tamgaly Valley, eastern Kazakhstan.

with Inner Asian religious values, received wisdom, and shamanism.[42] In discussing the unorthodox mediations of Central Asian Folk Islam, Lymer, Tyson, and Hoppál have shown the custom of rag-tying to be widely observed throughout Central Asia, including in Kyrgyzstan, Turkmenistan, Uzbekistan, Tibet, and Afghanistan.[43] This procedure is also widespread among the Great Plains peoples of Canada, who perform a similar entreaty for spiritual guidance and prayer.

Tamgaly Gorge provides an excellent example of the cultural kinship southeastern Kazakhstan shares with the indigenous traditions of the Great Plains.[44] Set amidst the stunning Chu-Ili mountain range is an outstanding collection of rock art dated from 1400 BCE, which features several examples of the practice of tying prayer cloths. Correspondingly at Bannock Point, in Manitoba's Whiteshell Provincial Park, we find a "Tree of Life" decorated with swatches of coloured cloth surrounding dozens of petroforms arranged in configurations representing turtles, snakes, birds, and humans. Nearby at Tie Creek, similar ceremonial effigies from ca. 2000 BCE assume a variety of zoomorphic shapes used as astronomical calendars for marking out the rising of the midsummer sun (Fig. 10).[45]

The tradition may be analogous to the petroglyphs at Tamgaly, which include one of the earliest depictions of the motions of the heavens along with enigmatic images of "solar-headed gods" (Fig. 11).[46] Though many of these petroglyphs long predate the existence of Kazakhstani statehood, they illustrate an inherited Indo-European mode of expression reflected in the sun-glorifying artwork of the ancient Scythians (see pages 45–56).[47] While it is possible these figures allude to a shared shamanic heritage, it is worth noting that both Kazakh and Canadian First Nations folklore concentrate upon the same lexicon of astronomical phenomena, such as Ursa Major, Ursa Minor, the Pleiades, Orion, and the sidereal cycles of the Moon.[48]

## Mythic Origins

In his masterful book, *The Horse, the Wheel, and Language* (2007), David Anthony shows "how Bronze-Age riders from the Eurasian steppes shaped the modern world."[49] Building upon the works of Marija Gimbutas, Colin Renfrew, and Jim Mallory, Anthony reveals how the domestication of the horse, the use of the wheel, and the transmission of Indo-European language were the key factors in the development of early civilization.[50] From the first moment humans straddled a horse, moved a wheel, and spoke with a common tongue, the pace of human progress accelerated dramatically, setting in motion a technological revolution that would forever alter the historical destiny of the world.[51] Using breakthroughs in radiocarbon dating, metallurgy, archaeology, and comparative linguistics, Anthony makes a compelling case for Indo-European nomads being the unsung progenitors of advanced human society.

According to Alan Outram and others, horses were first domesticated in the villages of the Botai culture (ca. 3500–2500 BCE) in north-central Kazakhstan.[52] All known equine races originate from a single mother whose relics were discovered at this Neolithic settlement, located near modern-day Astana. The Botai archaeological site provides concrete evidence of advanced social organization, upending the notion that Kazakhstan lacks any kind of urban heritage. Horses remain an integral part of the social structure of Kazakh life and play a prominent role in farming, traditional racing, clothing, and food. For Mario Alinei, "overwhelming linguistic evidence" shows that the spread of equestrian terminology "in all the languages of Eastern Europe" derived exclusively from Turkic loanwords.[53] As remarkable as this may be, one should also bear in mind that it was the Turkic invention of the stirrup that enabled the Norman cavalry to handily defeat the Saxons at the Battle of Hastings in 1066, thereby irrevocably changing the history of the Western world.[54]

It is almost impossible to exaggerate the importance of the wheel. There are very few objects in the whole of history that have changed humanity more drastically than this pivotal invention.[55] The wheel is the central part of most machines, from turbines to pulleys, and it has become so ubiquitous in our daily lives that it is easy to overlook how profoundly it has shaped modern society. Proto-Indo-Europeans invented the wheel and axle sometime before the dawn of the fourth millennium BCE and devised at least five words that signified wheels or wagons. As evidenced from the Evdik kurgan near Kazakhstan (ca. 3500 BCE), the wheel was developed through trial and error and ultimately made its way to Egypt and Mesopotamia. There, amid the Cradles of Civilization, load-bearing wagons were transformed into formidable instruments of war that allowed chariot-riding kings to forge the first world empires (Fig. 12).[56]

Nearly half the world's population speaks a language that is a derivative of Proto-Indo-European—the progenitor of Greek, Latin, Sanskrit, and nearly all the languages of Western Europe, including English.[57] This ancestral mother tongue underwent differentiation in the fourth millennium BCE and its original speakers fundamentally changed the Eurasian steppes into a flourishing transcontinental corridor of commerce, communication, and exchange. The first waves of Indo-European migration had a direct impact in the development of Graeco-Roman, Celtic, German, Baltic, Persian, Indian, and even Chinese cultures.[58] Not only did they innovate significant advancements in language, mining, and warfare, but the ancient steppe nomads also marshalled in an era of dynamic social change.[59]

## Mythic Landscape

To the cartographers of Classical Greece, the territory of Kazakhstan was beyond the edge of the known world. According to the Greek historian Herodotus (484–25 BCE), the area was protected by fierce Amazon warriors, while Aeschylus (525–456 BCE) believed it was a hinterland of centaurs and one-eyed tribesmen who guarded an ever-flowing stream of gold (Fig. 13).[60] Having eluded Alexander

**FIG 12** Bas-relief of Tiglath-Pileser III (reigned 745–27 BCE), Nimrud, northern Iraq.

**FIG 13** *Battle between the Greeks and the Amazons,* marble sarcophagus, ca. 170–80 CE.

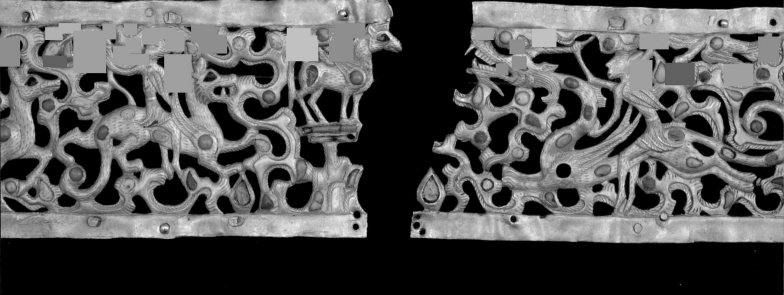

the Great (356–23 BCE) and even Marco Polo (1254–1324), Kazakhstan has long been perceived in the West as a land belonging more to myth than to reality.[61] Amid the high peaks of its Tien Shan Mountains, which also straddle the borders of neighbouring China and Kyrgyzstan, allegedly lies the mythical land of Hyperborea, a place of perfection, harmony, and perpetual youth.[62] According to local tradition, it is also the resting place of Noah's Ark and a cosmic axis between Heaven and Earth, which is illustrated today in the form of a model ship whose mast doubles as a tower for cellular communication.[63]

Closely associated with Kazakh identity is the Great Steppe, that vast belt of grasslands and savannahs linking Europe and China.[64] In Kazakhstan, the steppe is immutable and transcendent, a synonym for freedom and the archetype of nomadic existence. What the Mediterranean Sea was to ancient Greeks, the Great Steppe is to the descendants of Central Asia's nomads. The limitless horizons of the steppe command contemplation, wonder, and awe. Extending from the Pacific Ocean to the mouth of the Danube, they subsume both the majesty of the American Prairies and the Argentine Pampas combined.

The Eurasian Steppe Belt also encompasses the nerve centre of the world's first integrated transnational economy, the Silk Road(s). Often misunderstood as a single route, the Silk Roads—or *Seidenstraße*—were coined by the nineteenth-century scholar, Ferdinand von Richthofen (1833–1905).[65] This prodigious trade network brought together people and technology from across Eurasia and facilitated the spread of language and the continuous transmission of innovation, ranging from the philosophy of Classical Greece to Chinese decorative art. In contemporary Kazakhstan, the Silk Roads represent a politically stabilizing force and a means of restoring the country as the central artery of the global community. The Silk Roads contributed to the richness of Kazakh culture and were essential to the migratory flow of genes dating back to those of the earliest ancestors of modern *Homo sapiens*.

The Silk Roads also greatly contributed to the diffusion of the world's religions. There, Buddhism, Zoroastrianism, Confucianism, Manichaeism, Nestorian Christianity, and Islam mingled alongside an array of Central Asian traditions, including Siberian shamanism, Tengrianism, and ancestor worship.[66] This cross-pollination of beliefs is best evinced in the "Kargaly diadem," one of Kazakhstan's most precious ancient treasures, which dates back to the second century BCE. This gold masterpiece features mythological divinities and animals inlaid with semiprecious stones, intricate foliage, and an undulating cloudscape of latticework showcasing an assembly of world culture in a single composition (Fig. 14). It appears as though the creation of the world was equated with manufacturing a piece of art, and the diadem's spectacular details exhibit the degree to which ornamentation served as a foundational core of Kazakhstan's aesthetic psyche.

Astana has been criticized for urbanizing this mélange of ostentation and for introducing political pomposity and the notion of "superplace" within the context of a surreal cultural experience.[67] The imperial pomp and "ludic spaces of leisure, pleasure, and living" in Astana may seem gaudy and meretricious, but they also accurately represent Kazakhstan's native consciousness and traditional aspects of domestic space, in which all craftwork—from the simplest utensils and elegant jewellery to weapons and ceremonial clothing—constitute a specialized language of decorative art.[68] Every colour reflects a deeper meaning: red represents fire and blood; green, vegetation and spring; white, the celestial and purity; and gold, wisdom, knowledge, and the sun.

## Mythic Spirituality

Tengrianism is an ancient animist belief system from Central Asia characterized by the reverence for the Eternal Blue Sky, or Tengri—the supreme celestial deity in the Altaic world. The recurring imagery of the blue sky proliferates in the architecture of Astana, and the government has even put restrictions in place stipulating that building façades must reflect the national colours of blue (sky) and gold (sun). From the Kazakhstan Temir Zholy building to the Military History Museum, the Tengriist devotion to the blue sky is ever-present in the skyline of the Kazakhstani capital (Fig. 15).[69] The Azure Complex extends this symbolism further, as its slanted buildings lean nobly toward the golden-orbed Bayterek Tower. The blue-striped building complex surrounds the cylindrical

headquarters of Nazarbayev's Nur Otan party, thus forming a figurative link between the life-giving sun, represented by the Tower, and the President's indomitable political regime (Fig. 16).

An aestheticized Tengriist admiration for the landscapes of Kazakhstan permeates the architectural marvels in Astana. Khan Shatyr Entertainment Centre, for instance, doubles as both a giant yurt and an allusion to the highest point in Kazakhstan—Khan Tengri (6995 metres), the pyramidal peak of the Tien Shan mountain range. The name *Khan Tengri* does not translate easily in Kazakh, but some approximate renditions include "Sky God," or "King of Heaven." It is important to note that Tengri is neither anthropomorphic nor a personified god, but rather designates the celestial, ineffable clear sky above the world. Its symbolic significance is articulated most succinctly on the stele of the eighth-century Turk prince Kül-Tegin, where Tengri is the source of power that allows one to govern the state with legitimacy, integrity, stability, and equanimity.[70] The oldest dated monument of Turkic literature, the stele records the national epic of the ancient Turks, commemorating their legendary origins and hard-fought liberation from the Tang Dynasty of China (ca. 618–907). The inscription, which is written in verse, begins with an invocation to Tengri, who enabled the ancient Turks to be brought to life, rescued, and nourished.[71] A full-sized replica of the original stele stands in the atrium of the L.N. Gumilyov Eurasian National University in Astana.

ᛏᚤᛌᛄᛊᚸᛡᛡᚴᛄᛘᛁᛆᛏ

**FIG 15**   Concaved blue walls of the Shabyt Palace of Arts, Astana. Architect: Shokhan Mataibekov, 2009.

**FIG 16**   Slanted roofline of the Nur Otan Party Headquarters. Architects: Shokhan Mataibekov and Ramazan Aubakirov, 2010.

**FIG 17** Man praying in Nur-Astana Mosque, Astana.

Since the fall of the Soviet Union, some Kazakhstanis have turned to Tengrianism and its religious tenets have become pivotal to the renewal of a modern national identity.[72] For Marlène Laruelle, Tengrianism "is perfectly adapted to the contemporary world" in being highly individualistic, ecologically-minded, and tolerant of other faiths.[73] She further posits that in offering a direct "claim to modernity," Tengrianism advocates personal autonomy and a willingness to participate in globalization unimpeded by strict doctrines, clergy, or interdictions. This ancient spiritual tradition demands neither ritual observance nor blind devotion to a sacred text, but instead extols living in harmony with nature and the environment.[74]

In Kazakhstan, a growing interest in Tengrianism has helped spark a revivalist ideology in the areas of politics, religion, and nationalism. While the vast majority of modern Kazakhstanis identify as Muslims (approximately 70 percent), Tengrianism has emerged within the statecraft of Kazakhstan in much the same way that Zoroastrianism has re-emerged in Tajikistan, shamanism in Buryatia, and neo-paganism in Russia, the UK, and the United States. Many followers of Tengrianism in Kazakhstan proudly adhere to their Islamic heritage, but they are often in opposition to the kind of Islam introduced to the country after 1991 by Turkish and Arab religious authorities.

In 2005, the Emir of Qatar gifted the resplendent Nur-Astana Mosque to Kazakhstan, which accommodates five thousand worshippers (Fig. 17), and in 2012, the exquisite Khazret Sultan was opened to commemorate the city's foundation (Figs. 18–19).[75] Both mosques represent the epitome of lavish Islamic architecture in the twenty-first century and have assisted in galvanizing contemporary Muslim identity by aligning the new Republic with its pre-Soviet Islamic ancestry. The revival of Tengrianism supplements this Islamic patrimony by reappropriating the golden age of Kazakhstan's "indigenous" religious traditions and ethnic past. Characterized by toleration and communion with nature—in contradistinction to Islamic tendencies of centralization and conformity—Tengrianism infuses the foundation myth of Astana with an ancient spiritual core devoid of doctrinal orthodoxy or control.

## Mythic Ancestors

Dubbed the "Golden Cradle of the Turkic World," the memorial complex at Berel in the Altai region consists of twenty-four burial tombs, called *kurgans*.[76] Constructed by ancient Scythians (or *Saka* in Persian and Sanskrit sources), as well as other inhabitants of the steppes, kurgans showcase an extremely high level of technological advancement. The grave goods they contain provide dazzling evidence of a prosperous culture with networks of exchange stretching from Judea to China.[77] Similar burial mounds (or *tumuli*) are found throughout Europe, Scandinavia, the Aegean, the Near East, Asia, and even among the ancient cultures of the Americas, such as at Cahokia near Collinsville, Illinois. Scythians were a large group of Eurasian nomads who

**FIG 18** Exterior of Khazret Sultan Mosque, Astana. Architects: Shefik Eskendiruly and Sagyndyk Zhanbolatov, 2012.

Like the threads that make up a Persian rug, the cultural achievements of many nations are interwoven into Kazakhstani history, forming a rich tapestry of crafts, traditions, technologies, and values.

**FIG 19** Interior of the hypostyle prayer hall of the Khazret Sultan Mosque, Astana.

mastered horse-riding and metallurgy, and stand out for their invention of microsoldering, using a process that can only be replicated today through advanced electrolysis (Fig. 20).[78]

Of all epochs in Central Asian history, this period forged an indelible impression on both Kazakhstani and Soviet identity. For early twentieth-century Russian intellectuals such as Aleksandr Blok (1880–1921), Andrey Bely (1880–1934), Yevgeny Zamyatin (1884–1937), and R.V. Ivanov-Razumnik (1878–1946), "Scythianism" served as the bedrock of a revolutionary social movement representing an Asiatic strain of Russia's national consciousness.[79] The idealization of Scythian culture provided Russian artists and intelligentsia with a romantic image of the dynamic and creative "eternal nomad," a figure in perpetual revolt against bourgeois rationalism, materialism, and the stolid constraints of contemporary civilization.[80] Known for developing its distinctive style of animalistic art, Scythian culture is present in nearly all aspects of Astana's built environment, from reconstructions of Scythian jewellery lining its main boulevards to being incorporated into the design of bridges, railings, parks, and monuments.

Kurgans were vital elements of Scythian heritage and a fiercely protected ancestral focal point. Herodotus tells us that the Scythian queen Tomyris (reigned ca. 530 BCE) beheaded Cyrus the Great (ca. 600–530 BCE) for attempting to invade her homeland in a failed ruse (Fig. 21).[81] A monument to Tomyris stands in a public square in Astana, ennobled in bronze as a potent symbol of Kazakhstani

independence. One kurgan dated to the fourth century BCE contained thirteen buried horses dressed in richly decorated head masks adorned with wooden horns. The equine symbolism at Berel has been assimilated in modern Kazakhstani heraldry and monuments in the capital, which embody the spiritual heritage of the ancient nomads and the diversity of nations living in the country (Fig. 22).

But it was the exceptional discovery of the burial site of a Scythian prince (or princess) in the foothills of Mount Talgar that provided the most enduring record of Kazakhstani statehood and imagination. Dated to the fifth century BCE, it was uncovered in 1969 by archaeologist Kemal Akishev, who found an extraordinary figure in full parade attire, comprised of over four thousand individual gold plates.[82] The level of workmanship, completeness, and remarkable state of preservation are comparable to the scintillating death mask of Tutankhamun (reigned 1332–23 BCE). Despite the question of its gender being unanswered, the figure was affectionately dubbed the "Golden Man." Decades after its discovery, this figure was quickly adopted as one of the primary symbols of the modern Kazakhstani state and its likeness has been thoroughly integrated into Kazakhstani visual culture, from the national monument in Independence Square in Almaty to being featured on the front lawn of the Embassy of Kazakhstan in Washington, D.C. In the political rhetoric of Kazakhstan, the Golden Man is extolled as an icon of independence, prosperity, and heritage, being Kazakhstan's very own Statue of Liberty (Fig. 23).

**FIG 21** *Head of Cyrus Brought to Queen Tomyris* by Peter Paul Rubens (1577–1640), ca. 1622–23.

**FIG 22** Berel Monument Fountain, with Khazret Sultan Mosque and Palace of Independence in the background.

For Kazakhstan's Ambassador to Russia, Imangali Tasmagambetov, the collection of images found on the Golden Man serves as a type of decorative magico-ritualistic code in which symbolism, colours, shapes, and animals express the mythical worldview of the Scythians.[83] An avid collector and enthusiast of ancient Kazakh art, Tasmagambetov rearticulates Nietzsche's notion of myth in that "every scene, plot, form and manner of their expression is a concentrated conception of the world."[84] Extending this unity of aesthetic, social, and religious principles to the architecture of Astana, we discover several variations of the Golden Man's attire incorporated into the city's Master Plan, as seen most notably in the cone-shaped golden towers of the House of Ministries (Fig. 24). Appealing to this distinctive feature of Scythian regalia, the House of Ministries achieves symmetrical balance along the central esplanade, while at the same time marrying the prosperity of Scythian jewellery with the mythology of Scythian art.

## Mythic Ethnogenesis

Scythians were the earliest people to master mounted warfare and they ruled most of Northern Eurasia from the ninth to the first century BCE. However, the precise origins of these nomadic peoples remain uncertain due to a lack of written documents from the ancient Scythians themselves.[85] From their emergence on the world stage, these formidable warriors pastured their flocks over a vast territory stretching from modern-day Ukraine north of the Black Sea to the borders of Mongolia.[86] Scythians contributed to the development of many ancient cultures, from Greece to China, and they participated in some of the greatest nation-building campaigns of the age, defeating such mighty adversaries as Assyria, Urartu, Babylonia, Media, and even Persia. Their distinctive headwear is featured on a relief at the southern end of the Apadana staircase at Persepolis, which depicts a delegation of Scythian tribesmen bearing tribute to the Achaemenid king, Xerxes (518–465 BCE). United by a loose cultural coalition with an elite social stratum, Scythians established the first political entity within the territory of Kazakhstan known to history. Herodotus offered a detailed account of their diet, customs, and achievements, while their territories have been documented in the Zoroastrian book of *Avesta*.[87] Their descendants, the Indo-Scythians who fled the Xiongnu in the second century CE into South Asia, appear in the ancient Chinese historical chronicle, the *Book of Han*.[88]

Sometime after the second century BCE, a confederation of pastoral nomads known as the Wusun (or Usun) became the new power in the area, occupying southeastern Kazakhstan and northern Kyrgyzstan.[89] They were the predecessors of the Huns, who under the leadership of Attila (434–53 CE), moved their base in the Pontic steppe to the hinterlands of the Eastern Roman Empire, where they exacted tribute from Rome and Persia and successfully forced their payment through border wars.[90] Though chiefly remembered as the "Scourge of God," Attila was also a brilliant political

**FIG 23**  Golden Man in parade armour, Issyk burial mound, east of Almaty.

**FIG 24** Golden tower of the House of Ministries and its main plaza. Architects: Shokhan Mataibekov, Zhexen Aynabekov, and Rafik Musabayev, 2007.

**FIG 25** *The Feast of Attila* by Mór Than (1828–99), 1870.

strategist who united the isolated nomadic tribes of the steppe into a single, extraordinarily effective army (Fig. 25).[91] In the area of statecraft, the Huns established complex bureaucracy, introduced fair taxation, advanced literacy, codified laws, and were the first to develop a feudal system in which land-holding was exchanged for labour.[92] Attila's exploits have inspired British novels, American films, French Romantic art, and even the Renaissance master, Raphael (1483–1520), who painted a fresco of the great conqueror's meeting with Pope Leo I (ca. 400–61) in Vatican City's Apostolic Palace. Kazakhstan is also well acquainted with the mythologization of this fearless warrior, and in 2009, the country's National Bank issued a commemorative coin in honour of Attila, even though his lands never stretched beyond the Ural River.

Attila's death in 453 CE plunged the Hunnic state into chaos and the already scant historical record about the nomadic peoples of the near steppe fell completely silent until the rise of the Turkic Khanate (552–744 CE). This new Turkic feudal dominion established its own history and language, instituted the office of Khan (Qaghan), and developed extensive political and economic relations with the neighbouring empires of Byzantium, Iran, and China.[93] The Turks were the first truly Eurasian empire, and they created a distinctive culture and an alphabetic runic script, known as *Orkhon*, that displays rhythmic and parallelistic passages resembling that of epic literature.[94] But with its cultural epicentre in the Altai, the Turkic Khanate was isolated, and

a series of political conflicts and civil wars led to the empire's division into eastern and western factions.

The eighth century saw the arrival of Islam as well as Turco-Mongol invasions, which gradually supplanted the remaining Iranian character of the region. This period also marked the rise of Pontic Steppe nomads (the Kimek, Cuman, Kipchak, and Polovtsy peoples), and the Jewish Khazars, who were neighbours to the Kievan Rus' and Byzantium. In the late twelfth century, Genghis Khan (1162–1227 CE) transformed the entire political map of the area and marshalled in a period of unprecedented miscegenation. Although branded as a ruthless despot by contemporary accounts, in Central Asia Genghis Khan is hailed as a tolerant liberator who granted universal religious freedom, destroyed feudal systems of aristocratic privilege, and brought about the blossoming of civilization (Fig. 26).[95] After his death in 1227, his empire was partitioned among his sons and according to the fifteenth-century historical chronicle, *Tarikhi Rashidi* (1541–46), the Kazakh Khanate was formed and later divided into three broad territorial and tribal divisions, or *Jüz/Zhüz* ("hundreds"), in 1465.[96] The Senior Zhüz (*Uly Zhüz*) occupied south-eastern Kazakhstan, the Middle Zhüz (*Orta Zhüz*) settled north and west, and the Junior Zhüz (*Kishi Zhüz*) straddled the borders of the nascent Russian Empire.[97]

By the late 1600s, the Kazakhs faced their greatest struggle for survival from advancing Jungars (*Oirat*) tribesmen from the Altai region competing for increasingly crowded pasturelands. Reciprocated raids and sieges raged between the Kazakh Khanate and Oirat tribes for an entire century until the annihilation of the Jungars by the Qing Empire in the 1750s. As early as the 1730s, several Junior and Middle Horde rulers swore an allegiance to the Tsar in exchange for protection against Russian subjects—the Kalmyks, Cossacks, and Bashkirs. Incursions and conquest over the next 150 years put the whole Kazakh territory under the yoke of the Russian Empire, which had a strong centralized government located in Tashkent, Uzbekistan. Aided by the Cossack fortress town of Almaty (the capital of Soviet Kazakhstan and the Republic of Kazakhstan until December 10, 1997), Russian and Soviet imperial leaders controlled regional politics, undermined clan and family loyalties, and disrupted the social autonomy of the Kazakh population.

## Mythic Nationalism

In *Myths and Memories of the Nation* (1999), Anthony Smith explores the enduring power of myth and "ethnosymbolism" to mobilize, define, and shape the destiny of nations. For Smith, the roots of nationalism are inseparable from the rediscovery of myths, memories, traditions, and symbols, which he refers to as the "inner world" of ethnic communities. In line with Smith, historian Keith Cameron went so far as to claim that "myth is inextricably linked with the concept of national identity," while the political scientist, Stuart Kaufman, declared a "myth-symbol complex" to be at the very core of ethnic identity. [98] As fictionalized narratives elevated to a position of "truth," national myths overdramatize real events, omit important historical details, and imbue the past with symbolic meanings for which evidence is either lacking or contrived. But more than just state-sponsored propaganda, national mythologies have even resulted in the mystical exaltation of the state, as in the case of the Kosovo Myth of the Serbs or the ideological occultism of the Third Reich. [99] In Astana, mythic nationalism not only reinforces the power and durability of the state, but it also endows the entire country with a providential character distinguished by a beneficent global destiny.

The Kazakhstani government proposed numerous logistical and economic rationalizations for the relocation of the capital, but as Richard Wolfel and Shonin Anacker have observed, the renewal of a modern Kazakhstani identity connected with Almaty was inconceivable, for the former capital carried many deep-rooted associations with Soviet Communism. [100] A cosmopolitan centre of creativity and culture, Almaty could not provide a "blank canvas" upon which to imprint a new national consciousness. [101] When the Japanese architect, Kisho Kurokawa, drew up the Master Plan of Astana, he astutely noted: "the best hieroglyph is produced when it is drawn on a clean sheet of paper." [102] This statement underscores one of the most remarkable aspects of the new capital—the wholesale utilization of monumental architecture on a nearly barren *tabula rasa*. Kurokawa's Master Plan complemented Nazarbayev's credo of Eurasianism—the view that Kazakhstan is a bridge between Europe and Asia and a vital member of a broad civilizational state. [103] The President's policy was rooted in the theories of ethnogenesis advocated by the Soviet Orien-

**FIG 26** Grand council during which Temūjin proclaimed himself Genghis Khan. *History of the World* by Rashid-al-Din Hamadani (1247–1318), f.44v.

**FIG 27**   Underground chamber of Sultan-Epe Mosque (ca. ninth–twelfth century), Mangystau Region, southwestern Kazakhstan.

talist, Lev Gumilyov (1912–92), who presented ancient steppe nomads as peace-loving civil pastoralists. Gumilyov's notion of "enlightened nationalism" derived from his socio-biological theory of *superethnos* in which Russian, Slavic, Turkic, and Eurasian peoples are like-minded members of the same ethnic superfamily.[104]

Since Kazakhstan's independence in 1991, Nazarbayev has insisted on conceptualizing Kazakhstan's rebirth within the context of a unified historical territory and fate. His romanticization of early Kazakh culture has become a new paradigm for Kazakhstani virtues of political liberty, social responsibility, and multicultural peace. The government's sponsorship of several high-profile archaeological expeditions has overturned the widely assumed view of the region as being exanimate and uninhabited. The President's mission nationalizes Jaan Puhvel's investigations into the shared mythic, religious, and cultural heritage of Central Asia, India, Iran, Greece, Rome, the Baltic and Slavic states, and Celtic Europe.[105] By placing Kazakhstan at the crossroads of the globalized world community, Eurasianism has become the foundation of an entirely new vision of civil society.[106]

Eurasianism is visibly expressed in the storybook fantasy buildings of Astana, which embody the rational mentality of the West and the sacred qualities of the East. Some examples of this global eclecticism include the acutely Islamic Ministry of Agriculture; the pagoda-shaped Beijing Palace Soluxe Hotel Astana; and the row of large, themed restaurants along Turan Avenue designed in turn to mimic a Russian townhouse; a Roman villa; and a Ukrainian windmill.[107] The exaggerat-edly modern built forms in Astana are more than just the pretentious whims of a political elite striving for legitimization.[108] The appearance of the capital employs mythic nationalism and a universalizing aesthetic language intended to appeal to a broad compass of world cultures, mythologies, and beliefs.

## Mythic Urbanism

The history of the early architectural development of Kazakhstan is long and complex. It ranges from the elementary constructions of antiquity to the impressive monuments of the Middle Ages, such as the large cult complexes at Baba Ata in the Suzak, Kazygurt, and Baydibek districts. Since the first millennium BCE, the southern regions of Kazakhstan were populated with towns, fortresses, and cities of interregional trade and agricultural settlement.[109] The city-states of Bukhara, Khwarezm, Samarkand, and Tashkent of modern-day Uzbekistan were influenced by a panoply of faiths, that commingled with indigenous rituals, Islam, Nestorian Christianity, Manichaeism, and Buddhism. The further confluence of Zoroastrianism, Sufism, and ancestor worship is epitomized by the extraordinary underground mosques and necropoles in the Mangystau Region of Kazakhstan, which attract pilgrims from all parts of the country (Fig. 27).

The symbolism and aesthetics of Astana derive in large part from this golden age of medieval Islamic culture, a period exemplified by the figure of Abū Naṣr Muḥammad Al Fārābī (872–950 CE), a renowned jurist and philosopher. Although he lived and died in Syria, we know from his *nisba* (attributive surname), "Al Fārābī," that he originally hailed from Farab (Otrar) in southern Kazakhstan. Al Fārābī sought to reconcile Greek philosophy and Islamic piety, thus providing a synthesis of Classical thought with the Qur'an. According to Rafis Abazov, the current government administration in Kazakhstan has given considerable attention to Al Fārābī's concept of an "ideal state," which stressed the importance of a virtuous society ruled by an Islamic philosopher-king. [110] For Leo Strauss, Al Fārābī was the master of an ancient art of esoteric writing and for Christopher Colmo, he was a patriarch of modernity and the first philosopher to offer a holistic analysis of metaphysics, cosmology, human nature, ethics, and logic.[111] His systematic and practical approach to philosophy unified both knowledge and action, to better serve humanity and to aid us in the pursuit of happiness. That Al Fārābī's portraits are found on seven denominations of Kazakhstani currency, with his name prefixing the Kazakh National University in Almaty, testifies to his importance as a guiding light to the cultural development of Kazakhstan.

Al Fārābī's Central Asia played a key role in the flowering of Islamic science, which laid the foundations of the European Renaissance.[112] The urban hubs of the Central Asian Middle Ages were not, as is so frequently depicted, the home of rapacious barbarians, but rather economic, cultural, and intellectual centres of great importance and renown. In the preface to his book on Astana, Nazarbayev expressly invokes Al Fārābī's *The Principles of the Opinions of the Citizens of the Virtuous City*—"a city where people unite to help one another in the quest for true happiness is a virtuous city."[113] The city planners of Astana devised a capital that sought to reflect Kazakhstan's rich cultural heritage, while evoking the state sovereignty of Washington, D.C., the metropolitan poise of London, the monumental scale of Moscow, the bling of Dubai, and the decorative arts of the Far East (Fig. 28). For thousands of years, architecture has efficiently triggered emotional responses that lead to renewed ethnopolitical aspirations. In Astana, this architectural programme is expressed through ultra-sleek administrative, corporate, and civic buildings that project the themes of environmental sustainability, religious tolerance, and peace among all the nations of the world.[114]

As Kofi Annan, the former Secretary-General of the United Nations once declared, "Kazakhstan may serve as [an] example of a peaceful multi-ethnic country where ethnic diversity is a blessing, not a curse."[115] Like the threads that make up a Persian rug, the cultural achievements of many nations are interwoven into Kazakhstani history, forming a rich tapestry of crafts, traditions, technologies, and values. Kazakhstan blends the contrasts between the East and the West, and the diversity of its landscape contains every type of conceivable topography—from soaring mountain heights to the limitless Kazakh Steppe. This endless variety and cultural heterogeneity have been aestheticized in Astana, providing a fitting backdrop for the ethnic harmony of the world in a complete architectural setting.

**FIG 28** Astana cityscape showing a medley of architectural styles.

Interior of a nomadic yurt in Turkistan, Kazakhstan.

# CHAPTER TWO

# Architectural Mythmaking

*We shape our buildings and afterward our buildings shape us.*[116]
Winston Churchill

## *Foundation Myths*

Foundation myths have been at the heart of Western culture since the first urban settlements appeared in the Fertile Crescent nearly 5000 years ago. It seems that every nation required its own foundation myth, whether it was the Magna Carta's precocious championing of civil rights in England, or the Puritan pilgrims' providential invocation of the Exodus in America.[117] In the Classical world, *The Iliad* solidified Greek national pride, and the fable of Romulus and Remus consecrated the sacrality of Rome, while in tenth-century Iran, the *Shahnameh* fused the totality of Persian culture into a poetic masterpiece encom-

passing the creation of the world to the dawn of the Arab invasion.[118] The story of Houji, the founder of the enduring Zhou Dynasty (1046–256 BCE), and the myth of Wusun and Buyeo-Goguryeo attest to the importance of foundation myths to Asian culture as well. As Yessenova has shown, Kazakhstan's nationalist mythic history is inseparable from the leaders of the three Kazakh Hordes, themselves sons of the Great Alash—the first Kazakh patriarch and the forefather of Genghis Khan.[119] Like his counterparts in Rome, Alash was reared by a she-wolf, raised by shepherds, and successfully established the world's "first" Turkic empire.[120]

For Jarich Oosten, myths are a kind of sociopolitical reality for the cultures of the ancient steppe, where fantastic sagas and heroic epics such as the "war of the gods," the "mead of immortality," and the "magic cauldron" related to a consistent "social code."[121] In *Myth, Cosmos, and Society* (1986), Bruce Lincoln distinguishes a similar grand pattern in ancient Indo-European culture, which repeatedly depicts the homologies between cosmic creation and the human body.[122] These mythic elements, which allude to a set of fundamental ideas shared by Eurasian people, correspondingly underlie the monumental art and architecture of Astana.

According to Robert Jewett and John Shelton, an archetypical narrative also permeates the whole of American culture, informing everything from the millennial hopes for the Colony of Virginia to the epic blockbuster, *Star Wars*. The authors identify an "American Monomyth" as the emergence of a selfless hero who restores a community to its paradisiacal state, ensures victory over evil, and then recedes into obscurity.[123] This primordial meta-narrative persists in American nationalism, patriotism, and foreign policy. Christopher Beckwith explores this same theme in *Empires of the Silk Road* (2011), where he isolates a recurring "Central Eurasian Cultural Complex" expressed in foundation myths stretching from ancient times to the formation of the modern Kazakhstani state.[124] As with Jewett and Shelton, the crucial element of Beckwith's complex is the rise of a formidable leader who overthrows an old regime and secures the freedom and independence of an oppressed community. Today, this golden thread is epitomized in the figure of Nursultan Nazarbayev, the first President, hero, and lifelong "leader of the nation."[125]

## Epic Literature

Every great civilization has produced epic literature, from Vyasa's *Mahabharata* (ca. 400 BCE) to John Milton's *Paradise Lost* (1667). Epics embody a culture's entire conceptual world-view and are one of the oldest forms of literary expression.[126] They touch upon perennial aspects of the human condition, from identity, law, ethics, and justice, to the stark demarcations between good and evil. The epic tradition condenses all knowledge into an easily transferable story, which is conserved, redacted, and written down. But more than mere literary exercises—as some might consider Virgil's *Aeneid* (29–19 BCE) or Dante's *Divine Comedy* (1320) epics have also been conceived on a grand urban scale, such as Frank Lloyd Wright's scheme for Broadacre or Hitler's plans for "World Capital Germania" (Fig. 29).

In Central Asia, epics are traditionally sung by *bakhshi*—a Turkic word that is used to describe both shamans and bards—who act as spiritual interlocutors with the supernatural world (Fig. 30).[127] Bakhshi, or *zhyraus* in Kazakh, play a decisive role in forging Kazakhstani

**FIG 29** Dante Alighieri (1265–1321) holding the *Divine Comedy* between Florence and the heavenly spheres. Fresco by Domenico di Michelino (1417–91), 1465.

**FIG 30** Zhyrau singing folk songs at a wedding, ca. 1950. RAS No. 2035-213.

nationhood, a notion well at home within the philosophy of Johann Gottfried Herder (1744–1803).[128] Indeed, this father of Romantic nationalism once wrote that "a poet is the creator of the nation around him, he gives them a world to see and has their souls in his hand to lead them to that world."[129] In Kazakhstan, folklore is more than poetic commemorations of liberation, heroism, and bravery—it also comprises a complete set of values safeguarded for millennia.[130] The pioneering culture critic, Walter Benjamin (1892–1940), believed folktales to be "the first tutor of mankind" and for the father of modern Kazakhstani historiography, Chokan Valikhanov, they were a reflection of our highest aspirations.[131] In the nineteenth century, Valikhanov compiled early accounts of oral epics sung by nomadic peoples of Central Asia, including the massive *Epic of Manas*, a fundamental expression of Kyrgyz notions of freedom, goodness, and moral order.[132]

Familial bonds and values are at the centre of traditional Kazakh lifestyle and prevail under a banner of trust and hierarchy rooted in the wisdom of the elders. Kazakh identity for many begins and ends with one's ability to name their seven paternal ancestors, known collectively as *jetiata* (seven forefathers)—a genealogical list of relatives and exogamic barriers that link back through the kinship structures of nomadic pastoralism.[133] The even broader Kazakh phenomenon relating to notions of identity is called *shejýre* (literally "lineage tree")—a set of oral narratives that articulate

ancestral ties and offer a historical succession of individuals who shaped communities and events.[134] Dina Zhansagimova reminds us that detailed knowledge of one's ancestors is an instrument of social cohesion that typifies "the essence of Kazakhness."[135] Kinship terminology among Kazakhs is among the most detailed anywhere in the world. Genealogies include hundreds of names, geographies, and dates along with foundational stories characterizing the virtues, vices, triumphs, and setbacks of their ancestors. Every contemporary Kazakh person can be aptly described as a living folk epic, a messenger of the past, and a carrier of the future.

In 1928, the Russian folklorist, Vladimir Propp (1895–1970), published his astonishing discovery that there was a structural universality to folktales.[136] He broke down one hundred Russian folktales into analyzable elements (*morphemes*) and identified thirty-one narrative units (*narratemes*), which comprised the structural basis of mythical stories. By probing into these irreducible narrative components, Propp delineated recurring plot patterns and provided an overarching theory of fairy tales. Propp's revelation had an enormous influence on the pioneering cultural anthropologist, Claude Lévi-Strauss (1908–2009), who founded an entire intellectual movement known as *structuralism*. Lévi-Strauss scrutinized thousands of myths into essential constituent units called *mythemes*, showing how Australian Aboriginal oral stories have the same structural blueprint as Amerindian mythology.[137] Influenced by the structural linguistics of Jakobson and de Saussure, Lévi-Strauss explored the underlying patterns of thought in all forms of human activity.[138]

In Astana, Propp's morphology and Lévi-Strauss's structuralism assume the medium of monumental architecture, which transmits the narratemes and mythemes of world peace, ethnic harmony, and environmental renewal. The architecture of Astana provides a glimpse into the cultural soul of Kazakhstan, the aspirations of the world community, and the actions of historical and mythical figures. This synthesis of mythemes is characterized by the recently opened National Museum in Astana, an enormous giant blue iceberg encased in ornamented white stone (Fig. 31). Occupying 74 000 square metres of exhibition space, including a Hall of Ethnography, the Museum's unusual structure symbolizes the past, present, and future, and provides an enchanting history of Kazakhstan in a dynamic layout of holograms, LED technology, touch-sensitive kiosks, and interactive multimedia.

## Inventing Tradition and Identity

In weaving together themes of pilgrimage, paradise, fantasy, and urbanism, the architecture of Astana illustrates the distinct combination of domestic politics and epic storytelling. Since the dawn of civilization, architecture and urban planning have been manipulated in the service of political agendas, and behind every twisting street or eccentric skyscraper in any city lies a repository of hidden cultural meaning. In Astana,

architecture sets the stage for the invention of a new national identity Nazarbayev has defined as "The Kazakhstan Way," an aphorism embodying four fundamental values—"Freedom, Unity, Stability, and Prosperity."[139]

For the British historian Eric Hobsbawm, nations emerge by "inventing tradition" through public rituals and by creating ideological symbols that inculcate values and normative behaviour.[140] Romantic fascination with national origins in the nineteenth century prompted many northern Europeans to investigate the Celtic past in an attempt to construct a common national identity. Today, we assume as fact that Scottish Highland culture is synonymous with kilts, tartan plaids, and bagpipes, but as Hugh Trevor-Roper has shown, these ostensibly age-old traditions are mostly the product of Victorian fabrication.[141] For David Cannadine, the same applies to the ceremonial pomp of British royal pageantry, which was invented in the nineteenth century to institutionalize the monarch as the head of the nation.[142]

Britain, in particular, became a battleground for competing national identities with spokesmen for Welsh, Scottish, or Irish nationalism all appealing to a Celtic pedigree in order to assert their freedom from ascendant Anglo-Saxon culture. Stephanie Barczewski showed how the construction of images of national heroes Robin Hood and King Arthur played a critical role in the formation of a uniquely British ethnic character.[143] As patriotic icons, Robin Hood and King Arthur were employed in forging a national identity that reinforced notions of a mythical past while encouraging

**FIG 31** National Museum in Astana. Architects: Vladimir Laptev, Anton Maximov, and Michael Svetashov, 2014.

**FIG 32** · *The Last Sleep of Arthur in Avalon* (detail) by Edward Burne-Jones, 1881–98.

the support of tradition and ancient institutions. While Robin Hood concerned himself with working-class issues and liberal reform, King Arthur promoted British imperial interests and the idea of England as the civilizer of the modern world. Just as mythic literature galvanizes national sentiment in Britain, mythic architecture concretizes national identity in Kazakhstan.

Despite being intrinsic to British self-identification, the myth of King Arthur may remarkably have its origins in Kazakhstan. C. Scott Littleton and Linda Malcor showed how the core Arthurian legends—from the Sword in the Stone to the quest for the Holy Grail—descend from folktales that had been told by Eurasian horsemen nearly 1000 years before the first stories of Arthur were written down in the early twelfth century. The exploits of Arthur appear to derive from the triumphs of Lucius Artorius Castus, a Sarmatian nomad conscripted by the Roman cavalry to serve in Britain during the second century CE. Over time, Scythian folklore blended with the historical character of Artorius (the Welsh name for Arthur), and by the fifth century, a new myth emerged in Britain lionizing the victories of a great king. The Knights of the Round Table—Gawain, Bedevere, and Kay—were not real people, but the anglicized names of Sarmatian gods anthropomorphized into noble warriors.[144] So quintessentially British was the Arthurian legend that it helped spawn an entire period of Victorian chivalry and Romanticism shaped by such figures as Lord Tennyson (1809–92), William Morris (1834–96), and the Pre-Raphaelite artist, Edward Burne-Jones (1833–98) (Fig. 32).

A close examination of post-Soviet Kazakhstani cinema reveals yet another dimension of this merger between invented tradition and national identity. Rico Isaacs has identified persistent themes in a recent collection of image-enhancing Kazakhstani films, such as *Nomad: The Warrior* (2005) and *Myn Bala: Warriors of the Steppe* (2012).[145] These government-funded epics assist in inventing tradition through the story of Kazakhstan's eighteenth-century struggle for independence. Set against the magical backdrop of the Kazakh Steppe, the films imbue a collective sense of unity, resistance, patriotism, and heroism among the Kazakhstani population. As Satybaldy Narymbetov, the Kazakh director of *Myn Bala: Warriors of the Steppe,* proudly admitted: "we make historical movies, not for entertainment, like they do in Hollywood; instead our goal is to introduce history to the younger generation so we can learn more about ourselves."[146]

The themes of identity and nationhood are also central to the biopic *The Sky of My Childhood* (2011), which depicts the coming of age of Nazarbayev. The film is both a eulogy to the life-term President of Kazakhstan and a revisionist account of modern history, highlighting the ruthless Soviet attitudes toward the traditional life of free-spirited Kazakh nomads. National unity is presented through a mélange of ethnic markers including apples, horses, yurts, mountain vistas, as well as themes that are derived from filial piety, folklore, the primal steppe, and the mythic fable of the Bayterek and the Simurgh. This cinematic campaign in the direction of modern nation-building is far more dramatized in the skyline and monuments of the capital.

The architecture of Astana seeks to inspire a common sense of belonging and nationhood through symbolic reinterpretations of ancient myths, fables, and invented traditions about nomadism and ethnocultural unity. In an act of Promethean audacity, President Nazarbayev has authored a grand urban epic — a megamyth, which Leon Yacher has poignantly described as a "Megadream, Megacity, Megadestiny."[147] Astana provided Nazarbayev with the perfect *mise en scène* for a new pan-national epic that uses heroic architecture to chronicle Kazakhstan's triumph over Soviet despotism in fulfilment of its global destiny.

## Capital Myths

Capital cities are like totems that embody their communities, project the identity of their nation, and establish their political legitimation. However, they are often a mere artifice of statecraft and an imposed symbol of governmental power, and for this reason, they are frequently viewed with suspicion and cynicism. In Astana, however, we find something more revealing than the typical agencies of political fabrication. Take for instance the close visual parities between Astana and Washington, D.C. Both capitals impart ideological messages through grand buildings, spacious avenues, and a tripartite approach. Astana's city planning clearly emulates Washington's National Mall, but the Kazakhstani capital includes mythical elements that both promote the national identity of its citizenry and embrace the multiculturalism of the world family.

Washington's principal nodes of state power are the Capitol Building, the White House, and the Washington Monument, which are mirrored by Astana's Pyramid, Presidential Palace, and Bayterek Tower (Figs. 33–34). In Washington, D.C., the powers of the Executive (White House) and Legislative (Capitol Building) branches of government are mediated through the memory of its founding father (Washington Monument). In Astana, Nazarbayev's commitment to nuclear disarmament (Akorda, pages 119–23) and his plea for religious accord (Pyramid, pages 226–41) intercede through the memory of the mythic Tree of Life (Bayterek, pages 130–43). In Washington, D.C., the chief monuments demonstrate the firm rule of presidential authority, congressional law, and military prowess, whereas in Astana, their corresponding monuments illustrate the tolerant aspirations of myth, peace, and amity.

National heroes are portrayed as pillars of virtue in Washington, D.C., while symbols of allegorical patriotism are employed to foster the uncritical veneration of the founding fathers. President Lincoln's colossal statue is withdrawn and set inside a Classical temple. In Astana, Lincoln's counterparts — the celebrated eighteenth-century judges, Tole Bi, Kazybek Bi, and Aiteke Bi — sit humbly on a plinth in an open public square (Figs. 35–36). Whereas Lincoln epitomizes the high-minded ideals of nobility and prudence, the three judges embody modest Kazakh values of

**FIG 33**  Skyline of the central axis of Astana, featuring Bayterek Tower, the Akorda Palace, and the Pyramid of Peace.

**FIG 34**  Aerial view of Washington, D.C. showing the U.S. Capitol and the Washington Monument along the National Mall.

**FIG 35**  Lincoln Memorial in Washington, D.C.

**FIG 36**  Monument to the three great Kazakh judges, Tole Bi, Kazybek Bi, and Aiteke Bi, Astana.

КАЗЫБЕК БИ       ТОЛЕ БИ       ӘЙТЕКЕ БИ

honest justice and the wisdom of the elders. In Washington, D.C., monuments are haughty and aloof; in Astana they are inviting and inclusive. The bronze relief of Nazarbayev set at the base of the Kazakh Eli Monument starkly contrasts *The Apotheosis of Washington* fresco painted on the oculus of the Capitol Building's dome. In the former, Kazakhstani common folk surround Nazarbayev; in the latter, Washington sits exalted in the heavens surrounded by the gods of the Olympian pantheon.

Monumentality has emerged as an art of government in Kazakhstan, and is a powerful tool for what Anna Tsing refers to as the "Ethnography of Global Connection," where "image is everything" and "perception is reality."[148] Whether it is a monument to Bogenbay Batyr (1680–1778), the renowned Kazakh warrior who struggled against the Jungars, or a sculpture of Kenesary Khan (1802–47), who led a bloody resistance against Russian colonization in the nineteenth century, Astana is carefully composed of monuments that serve as mnemonic devices for Kazakhstan's providence and independence. These monuments celebrate mythic heroism, while also communicating "collective memories" that not only connect the past with the present, but provide a new framework for a shared global community.[149]

In this regard, Astana's monuments function as a type of memory theatre in which history, imagination, myth, and reality occupy the same stage. This paradigmatic city acts as a beacon of adaptability and inclusion, borrowing the designs of other great capital cities, from Christopher Wren's plan for London to Pope Sixtus V's monumental programme for Rome. The aesthetic contours of the city provide a social experiment in national unity inherited from the Baroque absolutism of cities like Dresden, Kraków, and Karlsruhe, the former capital of Baden. Like Astana, Karlsruhe features theatrical visual spectacles in a fan-like distribution of streets and a geometrical arrangement of public space, crowned with a sleek Egyptian pyramid that memorializes the vision of the city's founder (Fig. 37). But Astana does not appropriate blindly from the historical precedent at Karlsruhe; it instead unites the urban heritage of the Baroque with the aesthetic language of Central Asia.

In *Architecture, Power, and National Identity* (1992), Lawrence Vale makes a convincing case of how political regimes build capital complexes to serve "supranational interests rather than to advance national identity."[150] In Astana, however, the opposite is true as its building programmes catalyze national identity through the promotion of a supranational agenda. Far too often the quest for ethnic identity has resulted in tragic confrontations, such as those in the former Yugoslavia, the Soviet Union, Mexico, Sri Lanka, and Northern Ireland. In an age dominated by the fear of religious violence, nuclear destruction, and environmental catastrophe, Astana offers a prescriptive urban salve in which architecture and city planning are not ancillary to the state, but rather the instruments of a global message that seeks to fundamentally change our world.

In recent decades, a new frontier in the study of architecture has emerged, which explores the links between neuroscience and the human responses to what we build.[151] Our neural systems and pathways are the Rosetta Stone to understanding the ways in which architecture governs our interactions with the world. Whether it is the heavenly grandeur of the Selimiye Mosque in Turkey or the sensual curves of the Guggenheim Museum in Bilbao, architecture influences our thoughts, feelings, behaviours, and well-being. The mute monoliths of Stonehenge continue to ignite speculation, awe, and wonder, and inspire us with a palpable sense of extraordinary human achievement. In Astana, architecture operates in a similar manner by engendering a new paradigm of thinking that presents the heart of Eurasia as both the nursemaid of civilization and the peaceful forebear of a new world order.

## Semiotic Urbanism

The discipline of semiotics is the study of signs, symbols, and their meaningful communication. Urban semiotics focuses more directly on how the formal characteristics of designed forms contain coded messages that constitute a transmittable language.[152] The Swiss semiotician, Ferdinand de Saussure (1857–1913), provided a framework for reading cities as texts, and also documented the remarkable analogies between urban centres and the sign system of language.[153] Donald Preziosi extends this further by positing that an "architectonic

code" is latent within our built environment. On the basis that every aspect of human culture is a system of signs, symbols, and signification, Preziosi argues that architecture contains something analogous to a vocabulary that is rivalled only by language in terms of its power and flexibility.[154]

Astana's signs and symbols constitute exactly this kind of architectonic system, in which the buildings signify and evoke meanings in the mind of the beholder. The built environment in Astana is more than just a mere product of glitzy Post-Modernist buildings—it is a type of architectural text with subliminal semantic meanings.[155] In official discourse, the capital is referred to as the beating "heart of the motherland" and the place where Kazakhstan defines its own history and destiny. On the surface, Astana's aesthetic programme is a stylistic mix of Islamic details and Kazakh historicism, but on a semiotic level, it weaves together the cultures of the world in a grand narrative that touches upon the importance of religious tolerance, environmental sustainability, and global peacekeeping.

Victor Buchli explores the materiality of built forms and explains how architecture gives meaning to our lives while also shaping and untangling social relations.[156] For millennia, architecture has played this fundamental role in the formation of cultures and societies, providing new vistas of understanding that reflect who we are and what we would like to project about ourselves to others. The most successful urban designs link tradition and innovation, and integrate disparate components into a unity that addresses emotional needs,

**FIG 37** Plan of Karlsruhe with building views and ground plan, ca. 1720.

ethical aspirations, and material resources. For Christopher Day, architecture should be a "place of the soul," where physical shapes, spaces, and appearances provide a picture of reality that nourishes human emotions and improves the human condition.[157] This is similiary picked up by Christopher Alexander, who presents architecture and environmental design as a "healing art" in careful balance with the harmony of nature.[158] Astana fuses Day's architectural humanism with Alexander's ecological design patterns to produce a unique language of architecture that is poly-ethnic in nature, sustainable in scope, and united in aspiration.

## Decoding the Astana Aesthetic

The architecture of Astana allows us to peer into the politics of modern mythmaking. If we examine the capital's urban design, we can see how architectural symbolism operates as a critical agent in the formation of national identity. But it is also much more, for to decipher the real language of a city, as philosopher Roland Barthes (1915–80) famously suggested, one "needs to be at the same time semiologist (specialist in signs), geographer, historian, planner, architect, and probably psychoanalyst."[159] In his provocative essay, "The Death of the Author" (1967), Barthes questions the entire notion of authorship, arguing that no author can claim any absolute authority over their own text. As any creative work is merely a compilation of pre-existing ideas interwoven into something that only

appears to be original, all interpretive power is thereby transferred over to the reader. For Barthes, there is no ultimate meaning in a text, since everything is a veiled sign waiting to be deciphered.[160] Turning a Barthian gaze to the architecture of Astana, we see on one level that it appears to have a single political author (Nazarbayev), yet on another, it imparts semiotic messages open to a wide variety of interpreters (including conspiracy theorists).

The celebrated Italian polymath and semiotician, Umberto Eco, provided the framework for precisely this type of architectural decipherment. Eco saw architecture as offering a primary utilitarian function and a secondary symbolic function. He divided these modes of communication into "denotative" and "connotative" markers of meaning.[161] For Eco, a Gothic window's denotative use of light serves to illuminate a dark cathedral nave. But when the light passes through the images on the stained glass, the same light becomes connotative of the symbolic qualities of divine illumination.[162] Similarly, the symbolism employed in Astana features a cross-pollination of denotative and connotative bearers of meaning. The intentional messages chosen by the state are denotative of independent nationhood and suggest economic openness, but the connotative messages point to collective global security, greening the environment, and open covenants of world peace. The architecture of Astana thus creates a symbolic link between the past and the present and employs symbols that resonate with utopian themes. As the distinguished American architect and professor, Robert A.M. Stern, perceptively noted: "as an art, architecture is not only a mediation of the present on the past but also a speculation of the present on the future."[163]

No monument, however, expresses a tidy or independently agreed upon meaning; rather, like Barthes's text, each is fundamentally multivalent and susceptible to many elucidations depending on its audience. This is particularly evident in the several unexpected sobriquets that have been applied to Astana's most iconic buildings: the Astana Tower is also known as "the Banana Building"; the Ministry of Agriculture has been nicknamed "the Syringe"; the Ministry of Finance is better known as "the Dollar Sign"; the Northern Lights mixed office and residential building is called the "the Dancing Drunkard"; the Transport Tower has been dubbed "the Cigarette Lighter" and is positioned appropriately near "the Ashtray," or the KazMunaiGas building. Furthermore, the National Archives building is known as "the Egg," the Central Concert Hall has been christened "the Cabbage," and the most prominent landmark—Bayterek Tower—goes by the alias of "the Big Chupa Chups," in reference to a popular brand of Spanish lollipops (Figs. 38–41). These references show that, while national symbols can be built and imposed, their meanings are not necessarily bound to a single authoritative interpretation.

A close examination of the built environment offers a captivating view into a nation's psyche. Architecture not only shapes the urban landscape, but also provides the framework for constructing social identity. In Astana, the *shangïraq*—the circular opening at the top of a yurt—serves as a metonym of Kazakhstani independence into which the support staves are inserted (Fig. 42).[164] One of the fathers of semiotics, Charles Sanders Peirce (1839–1914), provides an important key to unlocking the coded language inherent in the shangïraq. Within the framework of Peirce's tripartite typology of signs—namely, *icon*, *index*, and *symbol*—the shangïraq represents an index, as there is a direct causal link between a sign and the object. Peirce illustrates this relationship using the analogy of a weathervane as an index for the direction of the wind.[165]

The shangïraq symbolizes values shared by the entire community of Kazakh peoples, but it also functions as an index of homeland, generational reproduction, and the unity of different ethnicities under one roof. It assures continuity of life, time, and kinship.[166] The circular tents we know as *yurts* were never called so by the nomads themselves, but rather by their Russian observers. To Kazakhs, they were merely "houses" or, more precisely, "felt houses." The Russian word *yurta* likely derived from the Turkic word *zhurt*, meaning variously "population, territory, community, or family."[167] In a yurt, the shangïraq frames the blue sky, itself an index of the realm of the ancestors and the heavens.

The intersection of support beams within the circumference of a shangïraq represents the four cardinal directions of the world, a motif ascribed to an almost identical ritualistic symbol in ancient Rome—the *templum*—which was composed of a circle dissected by two perpendicular lines. Used during the foundation of settlements, the circle of a templum represented the sky, while the crossing lines

**FIG 38**   Astana Tower, known as "the Banana Building." Architects: Ahsel Group, 2001.

In an age dominated by the fear of religious violence, nuclear destruction, and environmental catastrophe, Astana offers a prescriptive urban salve in which architecture and city planning are not ancillary to the state, but rather the instruments of a global message that seeks to fundamentally change our world.

**FIG 39**   Northern Lights building, known as "the Dancing Drunkard." Architects: A. Saumenov, Y. Ezau, and S. Mataibekov, 2009.

**FIG 40** Central Concert Hall, known as "the Cabbage." Architects: Studio Nicoletti Associati.

**FIG 41**  Bayterek Tower, known as "the Big Chupa Chups," as seen from Nurzhol Boulevard, 2002. Architect: Akmurza Rustembekov.

symbolized the axis of the sky's rotation. Roman surveyors would plough a sacred furrow along the boundary of the templum and divide the site into perpendicular main roads known as the *cardo* and the *decumanus maximus*, often placing at their centre an *umbilicus* stone, representing the point that unites Heaven and Earth. The templum was linked to surveying, divination, and incantations that represented a divine cosmologic boundary.[168]

Similarly, the entire circular roof-hole of the shangïraq is a symbol of the firmament, the "gate of the sky," and the complete image of the world.[169] As a decorative motif, the shangïraq is an important national symbol, appearing on everything from banknotes and the national flag, to the official state seal and in street art. The shangïraq is a sacred family heirloom passed on from youngest son to youngest son. Raising a shangïraq into place is the duty of the head of the household; thus, from a traditional perspective, the collapse of a shangïraq indicates a family line dying without progeny. Given these profound generational associations emblemized by the shangïraq, what better form could serve as the basis for a children's school?

Built by the celebrated St Petersburg architect, Nikita Yaveyn, the Palace of Schoolchildren exhibits an ecumenical set of references ranging from European Revivalism to universal symbols of kin relations and family. The design of the School is double-coded, alluding to both Russian Suprematist art and Kazakh traditions of dwelling and national ornamentation.[170] However, the signature element of the building is its giant disc roof

designed to represent a shangïraq (Fig. 43). This sacred emblem of traditional Kazakh life and identity is reinterpreted as a cylindrical frame 156 metres in diameter. The metal mesh along the sides of the cylinder alludes to the folding wooden frame of the yurt, while carefully placed openings and skylights allow natural light to stream into the central atrium.

The building is comprised of stepped arrangements of rectangular "boxes," with each containing a functional element: skating rink, shooting gallery, swimming pool, museum, multipurpose hall, canteen, media library, and theatre. The exterior façades of the boxes are embellished with national ornaments, and they are placed on top of each other as reminders of *shabadan*, traditional felt suitcases emblematic of nomadic life. The layout of the disc further alludes to Kazakh yurt décor, as its interior is highly functional and decorated with ornate furnishings. The plan of the disc accommodates a variety of departments and offers a sweeping panoramic view of the steppe landscape.

## Yurt Myths – Khan Shatyr

The visual magnetism of Khan Shatyr Entertainment Centre lifts our eyes to the blue sky of the steppe. Doubling as both a retail mall and an ideological space for reimagining Kazakh ethnicity, Khan Shatyr (Kazakh for "Tent of the Khan") is the world's tallest tensile structure (Fig. 44). This expansive, self-contained leisure complex is a modern reconstruction of the massive kurgans found at Besshatyr

**FIG 42** Kazakh men hold up the shangiraq of a yurt in Saty Village, southern Kazakhstan.

**FIG 43**   Palace of Schoolchildren, Astana. Architect: Nikita Yaveyn, Studio 44 Architects, 2011.

**FIG 44**   Entrance to Khan Shatyr Entertainment Centre in blue luminous glow at night.

(Five Tents), dated between the fourth and fifth centuries BCE.[171] Designed by the prominent British architect, Norman Foster, Khan Shatyr is held together by a mast comprised of three 2000-ton beams and coated with a polymer material that maintains summer temperatures inside throughout the year (Fig. 45). Foster's biographer, Deyan Sudjic, opines that Khan Shatyr was inspired by Buckminster Fuller's utopian vision of bubbled urbanity.[172] Both the materials and the ingenuity employed in the creation of this Xanaduesque "pleasure dome" evoke an international assembly, from its use of German technology, its Maldivian sand and Spanish tropical plants, to its construction by a Turkish company. Spanning ten football stadiums and rising to a height of 150 metres, Khan Shatyr houses a tropical water park, wave pools, a river, a waterfall, and green spaces that surround retail shops and a multipurpose central hub (Fig. 46).

The triumphal yurt is meant to rouse national memory and instil a sense of traditional heritage alongside shared concepts of community and modernity. Up until the devastating famines that accompanied the Soviet Union's "collectivization" project of the early 1930s, the traditional life of most Kazakhs was spent in a yurt, and it is only through experiencing the variety of seasons on the steppe that one can appreciate the life-giving value of this universal nomadic dwelling. But more than merely evoking a traditional sanctuary against the elements, Khan Shatyr also emblemizes sacred nomadic knowledge. Yurts may appear to look crude and elementary, but each step in their construction has practical purpose and is endowed with profound symbolic meaning.

Assembling a yurt constitutes "a magic act of the First Creation," as it embodies the universe in microcosm and encompasses the entirety of nomadic culture in a single form.[173] In this manner, the yurt approximates the notion of the "Primitive Hut" described by the foremost Enlightenment architectural theorist, Abbé Marc-Antoine Laugier (1713–69), as the origin of architecture and a symbolization of humanity in congruence with nature.[174] Laugier's idealized structure, like the yurt, represents primal ethnicity and underscores the relationship between genealogy, nature, and the cosmos.[175] The mobile tent served a similar purpose in the biblical tradition, where the Tabernacle of Moses represented both the spiritual identity of the Hebrew nation and a portable dwelling place for God.[176] The same is true in the Islamic tradition. According to the hadith of the fifth Imam, the angel Gabriel gave Adam a celestial tent to set up in Mecca, where it served as the precursor to the cubical Kaaba.[177] In Sufi commentaries of the twelfth century, the Kaaba symbolized the cubic form of man, with its four corners corresponding to "human nature, its six faces to the human figure, and its three dimensions of length, breadth, and depth to the human body."[178]

The yurt is an anthropomorphic reconstruction of an analogous sacred enclosure. Every aspect of its design is named after parts of the human body: the hearth is the *kindik*, or "navel"; the lattice frame is the *qarïn*, or "womb"; the walls are "thighs," or *bökse*; the roof is the "shoulder," or *ïyïq*; the wooden frame is the *qanqa*, which means "skeleton"; the felt covering is the *zhabu*, or "clothing";

**FIG 45**  Interior tripod mast supporting the three-layer ETFE envelope cladding of Khan Shatyr Entertainment Centre.

and the opening in the centre is the shangïraq, also called the *köz*, or "eye."[179] Each yurt is believed to have its own indwelling spirit that should be formally acknowledged by visitors, who must bow their heads and express their greetings. More than just a shrine to consumerism, Khan Shatyr mall offers a reminder of the psychological and philosophical truths that find symbolic expression in the architectural mythography of Astana.

Nomadic dwellings are ubiquitous around the globe, from the Lapps of northern Scandinavia to the Inuit of Labrador. Like the Kazakh yurt, the conical, skin-covered tipi used by the peoples of the North American Great Plains was a repository of myth, history, and cosmology. For Peter Nabokov and Robert Easton, every aspect of Blackfoot tipis of the northern Plains is a lesson in supernatural knowledge and a convergence with spiritual powers.[180] The floor of a medicine tipi represents Mother Earth; the lodge cover represents Father Sky; the interlocking poles link humankind with the heavens, and the central hearth symbolizes spiritual communion with the Great Mystery.[181] Khan Shatyr mall provides a spectacular urban reminder of this shared indigenous heritage, alongside abiding notions of ethnic attachment and nomadic purity, which are immensely important to the self-image of Kazakhstan.

**FIG 46** Sky Beach Club water park, with wave pools and slides on the upper terrace of Khan Shatyr Entertainment Centre.

President Nazarbayev in the Akorda presidential residence.

CHAPTER THREE

# The Hero

*The hero draws inspiration from the virtue of his ancestors.*[182]
Goethe

## Nursultan Nazarbayev

The life of President Nazarbayev is the stuff of storybook legend. From his humble beginnings in a shepherd's hut on the steppes of Ushkonyr, he rose to become the leader of one of most strategically important countries in the world. As a direct descendant of the fifteenth-century Khanates and the legendary warrior, Karasay Batyr (1703–53), Nazarbayev's life and achievements fit all the criteria of Joseph Campbell's "hero's journey," which lays out an archetypal plot pattern echoed in religion, folklore, world mythology, literature, and the feats of rulers, from King Gilgamesh of Uruk to Lee Kuan Yew of Singapore.[183] Accounts of Nazarbayev have either been "wondrous hagiographies" or plagued by inordinate criticisms, but here we depart from both antipodes and situate the President within folklorist terms as the requisite hero of a national epic.[184] Without any need for embellishment, Nazarbayev is the guardian spirit of Astana and the perpetual benefactor of the state. Even his birthday coincides with the day Astana acquired its status as the official seat of government. In no uncertain terms, Astana is Nazarbayev and Nazarbayev is Astana.

Nazarbayev's decision to move the capital from Almaty to Astana in 1997 marked the most ambitious building project undertaken on the steppes since Darius I (550–486 BCE) laid the foundations for Persepolis nearly 2500 years ago. Persepolis was, like Astana, intended to be the centre of a vibrant multicultural state in which diversity, tolerance, and the dignity of humanity took precedence over racism, tyranny, and oppression.[185] Guarded by a pair of colossal bulls, or *lamassu*, the Gate of All Nations at Persepolis welcomed delegations of different peoples in the spirit of international cooperation and the participatory governance of the world (Fig. 47).[186]

Following in Darius's footsteps, Nazarbayev summoned artisans from every corner of the globe to work with local architects in devising a Master Plan with monumental buildings, which would celebrate cultural unity and panethnic expression.[187] The President's efforts to consolidate a new Kazakhstani identity on fresh soil are also comparable to the endeavours of Peter the Great (1672–1725) at St Petersburg, which was designed as Russia's "window to the West."[188] The Kazakhstani President also takes a page from the Brothers Grimm in using fables to cement a unified sense of nationhood and inherited notions of cultural patrimony.[189] In marrying Kazakh folklore to a utopian metropolis, Nazarbayev continues the legacy of the traditional Kazakh oral epics of Koblandy Batyr, Alpamys Batyr, Kambar Batyr, and Er Targyn. From his earliest age, Nazarbayev was fascinated with Kazakh folklore. He attended Kazakh plays, recited Kazakh poems, and held Kazakh art, painting, and traditional craftsmanship in the highest esteem.[190] He is also fond of quoting ancestral heroes, including the Sufi master, Khoja Akhmet Yassawi (1093–1166 CE), a

paragon of compassion who brought together Qu'ranic mysticism and nomadic acceptance and adaptability.[191]

In envisioning the birth of a nation, Nazarbayev constructed an ideal city that would serve as a microcosm of the entire country. While urban planning heroes from John Nash to Jane Jacobs have influenced the future of city design, no one seems to have devised a more wholesale mythography of architecture as successfully as Nazarbayev. He may be the first modern leader to have used architecture and fantasy to crystallize the dreams of a nation, while also conveying broader objectives committed to world peace, global ecology, and interfaith harmony. It is not so much that Nazarbayev is trying to create a universalist Shangri-La as he is striving to elevate Kazakhstan as an indispensable participant in global affairs. The President recognized that the lure of legends rested in their ability to reify abstract concepts and that more than any other medium, architecture was the most effective public instrument for turning ambiguous feelings into concrete ideals.

No other founding father seems to have been more committed to architecture as a vehicle for civic solidarity and national identity formation. Not even Thomas Jefferson—a great architect and champion of architectural principles—had written a work of architectural theory. But Nazarbayev did. In his book, *The Heart of Eurasia* (2010), he explored the philosophy and aesthetics of city planning and offered insights on such disparate capitals as Ankara, Brasília, Canberra, Oslo, Karachi, New Delhi, Yamoussoukro, Lagos, Madrid,

**FIG 47** Gate of All Nations amid the ruins of the ancient city of Persepolis, Iran, ca. 486–65 BCE.

**FIG 48**  Promenade and gazebos along the embankment of the Ishim River, Astana.

St Petersburg, Alexandria, and the ancient Assyrian city of Nineveh.[192] Like Jefferson before him, Nazarbayev was directly involved in devising the plan of his capital, and, also like Jefferson, he envisioned his efforts as a commemoration of national sovereignty. For both men, architecture was a preserver of historical legacy and an emblem of liberty and independence.[193]

## Nazarbayev the Architect

Nazarbayev developed his own brand of providentialism by contriving a cityscape that apotheosizes themes of unity, peacebuilding, and sustainable progress. As Natalie Koch informs us, his vision of the capital can be traced to two distinct sources: Alexandre Le Maître, whose *La Métropolitée* (1682) offers a pioneering examination of the circulation of power in an ideal capital city; and Michel Foucault, who observes that a capital should be a wayshower of moral order.[194] Although he had no formal training, Nazarbayev was directly involved in the design of many of the built works in Astana, applying his deft hand to concept drawings, diagrams, and drafts, as well as working closely with "starchitects" Kisho Kurokawa, Norman Foster, Manfredi Nicoletti, and Adrian Smith, the latter having designed the awe-inspiring Burj Khalifa Tower in Dubai.[195] Nazarbayev provided the ideal platform for the emergence of a vanguard of local architects, such as Tolegen Abilda, to develop a body of work on the international stage.[196] Providing clear statements on the appearance and symbolic content of Astana, Nazarbayev believed in purely Le Maîtrean terms that his capital would consolidate state sovereignty and nationalism, while opening up opportunities for international commerce and exchange.

The President's contributions to reinventing the city as a monument of national autonomy revealed him to be highly skilled at urban planning. During a tour along the banks of the Ishim River early in 1998, Nazarbayev was struck by an epiphany and directed his lead architects to construct an embankment with wide promenades interspersed with beautiful rotundas (Fig. 48). Within three months, 2000 heavy vehicles and 15 000 workers laboured round the clock on nearly one hundred major construction projects. The magnitude of the task was almost inconceivable, hampered by insufficient access to materials and the most extreme weather conditions on Earth. Astana became a massive, frenetic construction zone operating twenty-four hours a day. In a single year, from 2007 to 2008, over 140 construction cranes were working in Astana. For hundreds of kilometres, the steppe was illuminated by the glow of the "white nights of Astana" produced by the swarm of labour squads and thousands of halogen lights that transformed the night sky into *aurora borealis*.[197] The development of Astana amounted to an extensive process of de-Sovietization through urban design. The aim was more than just the creation of a national capital; it was the creation of a new national identity, which was devised, crafted, and brought into being by Nazarbayev.

# Peacebuilding and Nuclear Disarmament

For all the misgivings levelled against his policies or his character, Nazarbayev has single-handedly altered the destiny of his nation. Aided by perspicacious judgment and Kazakhstan's enormous petroleum reserves, he has masterminded one of the most improbable success stories of modern times.[198] As a shrewd political tactician, the President was pivotal in the break-up of the Soviet Union and his promotion of limited privatization, economic reform, and the free market has transformed Kazakhstan from teetering on the brink of financial ruin to becoming the wealthiest country in Central Asia. For a number of Kazakhstani parliamentarians, Nazarbayev emulates the lives of Washington, Atatürk, and Gandhi, not only in having given birth to a new nation, but also by ushering in modernity through his steadfast commitment to the communion of all faiths.[199]

During the Cold War nuclear arms race, Kazakhstan was a weapons laboratory for the Soviet Union, and from 1949 to 1989, 456 secret nuclear tests were conducted within its borders.[200] Within the first decade of declaring independence, Nazarbayev closed the Semipalatinsk Test Site, dismantled all Soviet weapons facilities, signed major international non-proliferation treaties, and voluntarily surrendered the fourth-largest nuclear arsenal in the world (Fig. 49). In 2009, the United Nations General Assembly unanimously adopted Kazakhstan's Resolution 64/35, declaring August 29 (the day Nazarbayev closed the test site in 1991) as the International Day against Nuclear Tests.[201]

With over 1200 thermonuclear warheads and 600 kilograms of uranium, the munitions at Semipalatinsk were equivalent to 2500 times the payload unleashed on Hiroshima.[202] Known by the ominous sobriquet, "the Polygon," the site was once home to 40 000 scientists and military personnel. Semipalatinsk had weighed heavily on Nazarbayev since his youth, for the tests conducted there had decimated the natural environment and subjected the local Kazakhstani population to terminal radiation exposure, resulting in high rates of cancer, mental illness, and premature births (Fig. 50). The pernicious history of this site was all the more personal for Nazarbayev, as the district around Semipalatinsk was also the birthplace of the beloved social reformer and poet, Abai Qunanbayuli (1845–1904), who promoted literacy, ecumenism, and the purity of nature as a remedy against enslavement, war, and corruption.

In 1994, Nazarbayev became the key figure in Project Sapphire, a top-secret operation conducted in partnership with the United States that sought to reduce the threat of nuclear proliferation, and to transport the 600 kilograms of highly enriched uranium from Kazakhstan to Oak Ridge National Laboratory in Tennessee.[203] Nazarbayev offered his expertise and provided detailed plans and diplomatic approaches to forming nuclear-weapon-free zones around the world. In 2012 the President launched a global campaign against nuclear testing through the online platform "Abolish Testing. Our Mission." (ATOM) Project. This was followed by an agreement in 2015 with the International Atomic Energy

**FIG 49** *Stronger than Death*, monument to victims of nuclear testing by Shota Valikhanov. Semipalatinsk, northern Kazakhstan, 2001.

**FIG 50** *Polygon I* (detail) by Julian Charrière, 2014.

Agency (IAEA) to establish a low-enriched uranium bank in Kazakhstan. In December of that same year, the United Nations General Assembly approved the Universal Declaration for the Achievement of a Nuclear-Weapons-Free World that was initiated by the Republic of Kazakhstan and cosponsored by thirty-five countries.[204] Nazarbayev may very well be regarded as the face of international consensus on the constructive uses of nuclear technology. His vision of voluntary denuclearization is unmatched by any other global leader, and since the early 1990s, no other nation has been more dedicated to the principled choice of a world freed from weapons of mass destruction.

At the 2016 Nuclear Security Summit in Washington, D.C., Nazarbayev announced that the highest priority of the modern era must be "to free humanity from the threat of deadly wars forever."[205] His manifesto, *21st Century: A World Without Wars*, urged heads of state to take decisive steps toward global demilitarization, citing that in any modern war, "everyone is on the losing side." For the President, war is a "virus" driven by the military-industrial complex and he pleaded for "peaceful dialogue and constructive negotiations on the basis of equal responsibility for peace and security."[206] He also advocated the dissolution of military blocs, which he claimed have only impeded international cooperation and consensus. Nazarbayev's entire political life has been marked by far-reaching global initiatives. These include the formation of the Eurasian Economic Union, the Conference on Interaction and Confidence-Building Measures in Asia, the Global Coalition Against Terrorism, and the Congress of Leaders of World and Traditional Religions.

## To Elevate the Steppe

It is often misunderstood that July 6 was selected for Astana Day as it falls on Nazarbayev's birthday, but the date has a much deeper historical context. On this day in 1994, Nazarbayev persuaded Parliament (then the Supreme Council) to transfer the capital from Almaty to Astana (then Akmola). His arguments were based on a comprehensive analysis of socioeconomic, political and geographic considerations, as a technical assessment of urban development potential. The President found inspiration in two unlikely sources. One was from the distinguished Kazakh academic, Kanysh Satpayev (1899–1964), who proposed relocating the former capital of the Kazakh SSR to the geographical centre of the country, and the other was a single line of prose from the influential Kazakh poet-scholar, Olzhas Suleimenov (b. 1936). The line, "to elevate the steppe without abasing the mountains," impressed Nazarbayev with the challenge of constructing Astana in the middle of the arid steppe while preserving an appreciation of the former capital of Almaty set in the lush foothills of the Trans-Ili Alatau Mountains (Fig. 51).[207]

The punishing climate of the region would be a deterrent for most planners, but for Nazarbayev, it was the ideal place to construct a "green oasis." One of the trademarks of

Nazarbayev's "The Kazakhstan Way" is turning an apparent deficiency into an alluring asset. It is not surprising that one of the first symbols chosen to embody independent Kazakhstan was the snow leopard, a recurring image in the animalistic art of the stalwart Scythian nomads. As Nazarbayev himself explains, the snow leopard "will neither be frightened by the severe cold of threats nor made soft in the intolerable heat of opportunities."[208] It is for this reason that a winged leopard adorns both the Standard of the President and the flag of Astana.[209]

Building a modern civic utopia in the most inhospitable terrain carries with it the ancient memories of the first nomads who prevailed over the harshest conditions in the last glacial age. Astana is the second-coldest capital city in the world, with temperature ranging from winter lows of -48 °C and summer highs of +40 °C (Fig. 52). The capital contains all the ingredients of mythic wonder—it is barren, windswept, indomitable, and remote. From Tenochtitlán to St Petersburg, Astana rivals every other courageous effort to build an urban paradise from scratch on virgin soil. Following a decade of political and economic turmoil that began in 1989, Kazakhstan has emerged from uncertainty and hardship to experience a new era of unprecedented growth, renewal, and sociopolitical stability.

To advance his goal of constructing a capital that would consolidate national identity, Nazarbayev appealed to symbolic tales of nomadic life and parables of Kazakh independence. Even the name of the national currency, the *tenge*, was itself a throwback to Kazakhstan's medieval heritage, when clan groups used *tanga* coins for barter and interregional trade. As inheritors of the Great Steppe, the Kazakh citizenry helped nativize new power structures in Astana. Nazarbayev introduced laws that required public servants to pass a Kazakh-language exam and established other unifying discourses to solidify the ongoing "Kazakhification" of society. This speaks to the utter uniqueness of Astana, as the city's ultra-modern outlook hinges upon an indigenous reawakening of ancient Kazakh values and mores. At the same time, the President has repeatedly stressed multilingual equality as one of the guiding principles of modern multi-ethnic Kazakhstan.[210]

Despite these admirable reforms, Nazarbayev's decision to move the capital was tantamount to political suicide, for Kazakhstan was then languishing from rising unemployment, crumbling education, industrial inefficiency, and a beleaguered healthcare system. As he recalled in 2006: "I put everything at stake, including my career and my name. I knew if I had [*sic*] failed it would be a fatal failure, but the success would also be the real success. It was a huge risk, and I took it intuitively."[211] Although Nazarbayev cited several practical and logistical reasons for moving the capital, the *Kommersant* newspaper accused him of hysterical hubris, while some of his colleagues claimed he was suffering from delusions of grandeur.[212] They could not have been more wrong, and after thorough review and consultations, government leaders ulti-

**FIG 51**   Aerial view of Almaty with the Trans-Ili Alatau Mountains in the background.

**FIG 52** Khan Shatyr Entertainment Centre at Christmastime.

mately voted in favour of this historic undertaking. Today, Astana is the best-known symbol of the emerging Central Asian market, the centrepiece of Kazakhstan's official nation-building revolution, and the prime geographical location for global intercommunication.

Nazarbayev reached back to the remotest ages of antiquity, finding precedence and inspiration in great, ambitious leaders of old to justify relocating the capital to Astana. From Pharaoh Amenemhat I (reigned 1991–62 BCE), he learned that relocating the official seat of government could serve as a symbol of national unity. From the Neo-Assyrian king, Sennacherib (705–681 BCE), he came to learn the importance of centralized state power; and from Alexander the Great, he realized how a synthesized form of cultural expression could guide community cohesion, permanence, and stability among multi-ethnic populations stretched over a vast terrain.[213] In magnitude and revolutionary verve, Nazarbayev's Astana parallels with Pharaoh Akhenaten's Amarna (ca. 1346–32 BCE). Not only were they both controversial capitals constructed at breakneck speed and away from the traditional centres of power, but they also brought together groundbreaking innovations in art, architecture, and city planning within the context of a new national mythology. Mythic ancestry, historical continuity, and ethnic perennialism are essential elements of Kazakhstan's post-1991 national imagination. It is no surprise that in 2015, Astana hosted the 550th anniversary of the Kazakh Khanate, which is believed to have played a crucial role in the emergence of the modern Kazakh nation state.

## Akorda Presidential Palace

The Akorda Palace is the official residence and workplace of President Nazarbayev. Located along the central boulevard of the new half of the capital city, it is one of the most potent symbols of Kazakhstan's independence, restructured solidarity, and ethnic renewal. Perched on the left bank of the Ishim River, this spectacular showpiece of the new Kazakhstan combines Beaux-Arts architecture and Eurasian aesthetics with exceptional achievements in modern engineering, construction, and craftsmanship (Fig. 53). The Presidential Palace is the city's conceptual centre and is situated along Astana's design axis, along with Khan Shatyr Entertainment Centre, Bayterek Tower, the Pyramid of Peace and Reconciliation, and the Kazakh Eli Monument. The total area of the building encompasses over 36 000 square metres spaced out over seven floors, including two below ground. Burnished gold is used extensively throughout the presidential complex, both as a reflection of the national flag and in recognition of the Scythian medium of choice, which reaches back to the cultural bedrock of Central Asia.

The azure sky, blazing sun, and outstretched wings of a golden eagle form a vital part of the design language of this architectural gem. This symbolism is echoed in the massive blue and gold striped dome that rises to a height of 86 metres and incorporates elements of the Pantheon in Rome, St Paul's Cathedral in London, and the Bibi-Khanym Mosque in Samarkand. The building is a lesson in architectural pluralism and in its capacity to amalgamate

**FIG 53** Front elevation of the Akorda Presidential Palace at night. Architects: Arapbay and Baygutty Tortayev, 2003.

the cultures of the world community, it is a reflection of Kazakhstan's motto of adaptability: "To Unity—Through Diversity." In embodying the artistic heritage of the East and the West, the Akorda Palace represents the permanence of presidential authority and the vitality of a nation committed to architectural excellence and societal regeneration.

The main entrance is clearly inspired by the Château de Rastignac near Bordeaux and the bow-fronted south portico of the White House in Washington, D.C. (Figs. 54–55). Even the name "Akorda," which translates as "the White Camp of the Khan" (or Camp of the White Khan), suggests a deeper semantic meaning that is echoed in the white colours and light tones of its façades and interiors.[214] The Presidential Palace, distinctly an exaggerated copy of Washington's White House, is influenced by the architecture of the Renaissance master, Andrea Palladio (1508–80). Emulating Palladio's timeless proportions, crisp lines, and integrated geometries, the Akorda Palace also draws upon the visionary buildings of Étienne-Louis Boullée (1728–99) and his epic use of Platonic shapes, exemplified in his plan for a Metropolitan Basilica (1781–82).

## From Earth to Heaven

In one of the greatest studies of the city ever undertaken, *The City in History* (1961), the scholar-urbanist, Lewis Mumford, proposes that the first conception of the city took expression "as a place where eternal values were represented and divine possibilities revealed."[215]

Nazarbayev invoked this sentiment when he inaugurated the capital of Kazakhstan on November 8, 1997, declaring that the city would "become the focus for our national spiritual richness, sanctity, and tradition."[216] Following his decree, the President performed an *Alastau*, a Mongolian fire-purification ritual mentioned in histories of Genghis Khan, which culminated in a processional walk along a white carpet—the same kind used to elevate Khans to their positions of power. A theatrical reenactment of this ritual is performed during the opening ceremony of the Astana Day celebrations, where the President receives the authority to move the capital from a characterization of Ablai Khan (1711–81), the visionary leader who sought to maintain the independence of the Kazakh Khanate against encroachments from the Russian Empire, the Qing Empire, and the Kokand Khanate.[217]

Nazarbayev has poetically compared the relocation of the capital to the fateful "flight of the stars," and he has linked Astana to the celestial motions of the heavens. Beyond its practical function, Astana always had "an important sacred and even mystical dimension" for Nazarbayev.[218] The relocation of the capital to the middle of the Eurasian steppe underscored a central truism of myth as articulated by the influential historian of religions, Mircea Eliade. In his landmark study, *The Myth of Eternal Return* (1954), Eliade notes that the concept of eternity is linked with primeval time and what he calls "a return to the centre," a point of spiritual connection between Heaven and Earth.

**FIG 54**  South portico of the White House, Washington, D.C.

**FIG 55**  Detail, bow-fronted porch, Akorda Presidential Palace, Astana

**FIG 56** *Jacob's Ladder* by William Blake (1757–1827), ca. 1805.

In his follow-up work, *The Sacred and the Profane* (1957), Eliade argues that every sacred space is characterized by two governing principles: *hierophany* and *axis mundi*. A hierophany was Eliade's term for the commemoration of a mythic act and the manner by which something becomes a receptacle of supernatural power. Ascribed to sites where a revelation has occurred, hierophanies are impregnated with hypostatic properties and memorialized by a vertical structure, such as a mountain, staircase, obelisk, lighthouse, or tree. Eliade explains that hierophanies are differentiated from their milieu. By this prescription, the place would then become an axis mundi, or "world centre," and thereby function as a primordial umbilical cord through which the numinous would penetrate, and then be diffused throughout the phenomenal world.[219] Cities, temples, and sacred places became real by their assimilation to this cosmic centre, a tradition that can be found the world over from Mount Meru to Delphi, and from Golgotha to Jacob's Ladder (Fig. 56).

This communion with the cosmos is a very real element of Kazakhstan's historical record, in which those who first travelled the Earth also journeyed to the stars. It is a little known fact in the West that the space age was born in Kazakhstan, tucked away in one of the most secretive and isolated corners on the planet. On the right bank of the Syr Darya River, about 200 kilometres east of the Aral Sea, rests Baikonur Cosmodrome, the world's first and largest operational space facility (Fig. 57). *Sputnik*, the first satellite to orbit Earth, was launched at Baikonur in 1957, and it was from here that Yuri Gagarin became the first cosmonaut to venture beyond the terrestrial world. Since that time, Kazakhstan has produced three additional cosmonauts— Toktar Aubakirov, Talgat Musabayev, and Aidyn Aimbetov—who were dispatched from Baikonur in 1991, 1994, and 2015 respectively. Nazarbayev noted the extraordinary case of historical symbolism that "Kazakhstan's sovereignty was first begun in space" before being officially established on Earth.[220] Under the auspices of the Commonwealth of Independent States, Baikonur Cosmodrome was declared Kazakhstani Republican property three months before Kazakhstan's official independence on December 16, 1991.

The area of Baikonur also coincides with one of the presumed burial places of Korkyt Ata, the legendary Turkic lyricist and composer of the ninth century, who spent his life in search of eternal life and Earth's axis mundi, or *zher tangiri kindigi* (the umbilical cord linking Heaven and Earth). Everywhere he went, Korkyt was struck by the inevitability of death. Driven by his forlorn quest, he travelled throughout the world before eventually returning home in defeat to settle down on the banks of the Syr Darya River. It was there that he carved out the first *kobyz* (a two-stringed bowed instrument) and in solitary anguish, poured out his soulful heart in song. Korkyt died of a snakebite, and a monument was later erected in his honour, very close to the Baikonur launch facility (Fig. 58).[221] But it is in Astana that hierophany and axis mundi are brought even closer together by Nazarbayev, who was intent on erecting a cosmic tree in an earthly paradise.

**FIG 57** Soyuz TMA-10M rocket launches from the Baikonur Cosmodrome in Kazakhstan, 2013.

## The Tree in Paradise

*They planned a city*
*The gods laid its foundations*
*They planned the city*
*"Let Etana be the architect,"*
*… He had built a tower, the shrine …*
*In the shade of that shrine*
*a poplar was growing,*
*In its crown an eagle settled …* [222]

These lines are from the first two tablets of one of the oldest myths in recorded history. The Sumerian *Tale of Etana* (ca. 2100 BCE) begins with the construction of a great city with a monumental central tower and concludes with the quest for eternal youth with the help of an eagle (Fig. 59). Isidor Levin documented 274 variations of the Etana legend in Ireland, Brittany, Russia, Finland, North Africa, South Arabia, the Arctic Circle, and among the Turkic nomads of Eurasia.[223] This may account for the eagle (or related bird of prey) playing such a prominent role in the rise of civilizations from ancient Susa in the fourth millennium BCE to the creation of the modern Republic of Kazakhstan. As Nazarbayev recalled, "one night the perfect name for the capital came to me—Astana."[224] Although seemingly banal and unimaginative, the Kazakh word is multilayered and nuanced. On the surface it means "capital," but it also implies the flight of an eagle or a winged journey.[225]

The President was likely unaware that Astana is phonetically similar to Etana, the Sumerian tale's eponymous hero who is immortalized for overpowering a snake and being lifted up to heaven on the back of a mythical eagle. The notion of an ascent on the back of an eagle persists in the stories of Ganymede, Roman apotheosis, the Alexander Romance, and Garuda, and takes on a modern architectural form in Astana's Bayterek ("Great Poplar Tree") Tower (Fig. 60). This unforgettable monument embodies an ancient myth about the Tree of Life that grows on the summit of a mountain. According to Iranian legends, every year, the Simurgh (*Samruk* in Kazakh) griffin (or eagle) lays a golden egg (the sun) in the crown of a poplar tree, which is then devoured by a malevolent serpent. One day, a warrior intercedes and kills the snake, saving the Simurgh's sacred egg, who in return rescues the valiant hero from his relegation to the Underworld.[226]

The white base of Bayterek represents the tree, the golden orb represents the egg, and the steel latticework represents the branches that reach up to the sky, reflecting the bright future of the country (Fig. 61). The tower is a compulsory destination for all visitors to Astana. Just as the Statue of Liberty symbolizes the universal message of freedom and the Reichstag showcases the unified image of Germany, Bayterek emblemizes modern Kazakhstan, mixing the engineering prowess of the Eiffel Tower with a Kazakh folktale about the unity of humankind. Barthes once observed that urban symbols attract meaning in the same way "a lightning rod attracts thunderbolts."[227] True to this observation, Bayterek serves as a lightning rod for Nazarbayev's mythologization of the urban steppe.

**FIG 59** *Etana's Flight to Heaven*, cylinder seal, ca. 2250 BCE.

**FIG 60** Garuda in flight bearing Vishnu and Lakshmi, watercolour, ca. 1780–90. Bundi, India.

FIG 61 · Bayterek Tower at dusk as the centrepiece of the national boulevard of Kazakhstan

FIG 62   Luxor Obelisk and Assemblée Nationale at the Place de la Concorde, with Les Invalides in the background, Paris.

The President drew up the first designs of Bayterek, which was faithfully copied by the Kazakhstani architect, Akmurza Rustembekov. Bayterek shares several striking similarities with the Atakule tower in Ankara, the dome of which harkens back to the solar disc of the ancient Hittites, analogous to Kazakhstan's Scythians as the supposed progenitors of early civilization. As the centrepiece of Astana, Bayterek compares closely to Jacques Ignace Hittorff's plan of the Place de la Concorde in Paris (1833–46), not only in being a focal point in the capital but also in celebrating the national unification of France.[228] The axis from Bayterek Tower in relation to the Kazakh Eli Monument in Astana echoes the link between the Place de la Concorde and the Place de l'Étoile in Paris. Here, Hittorff punctuated his ceremonial urban vision of the City of Light with a 240-ton Egyptian obelisk selected to symbolize a politically neutral stance of national unity (Fig. 62).[229] This Parisian display of civic grandeur extols the 1848 Revolution in France and is emulated in Astana by Bayterek, which memorializes a myth of ethnic permanence and common ancestry.

Bayterek Tower also echoes the aspirations of Ernst Neizvestny's unrealized sculptural project, the "Tree of Life" (1956), a spiralling architectural monument composed of seven Möbius strips shaped like a human heart. The immense size of Neizvestny's proposed abstract design, 150 metres in height and diameter, would allow visitors to enter through one of four passageways and participate in the spiral ascent of the piece. At the centre of the structure stood the figure of The Prophet, which was directly inspired by the moralizing lyrical work of the same name by the Russian national poet (and Freemason) Alexandr Pushkin (1799–1837), one of Nazarbayev's favourite authors.[230] The Tree of Life was Neizvestny's visionary solution to the conflict between the individual and the community, so central to the purpose of Bayterek Tower (Fig. 63), yet so elusive to Russian society for much of the nineteenth and twentieth centuries.

## Hieroglyph of the Nation

For the Soviet-Kazakh poet and diplomat, Olzhas Suleimenov, the people of Kazakhstan are direct heirs to the culture of ancient Sumer.[231] Eliade and George Rawlinson (1812–1902) have both suggested that Tengrianism derived from the religion of Sumer. Their conclusion rested on the similarity between *tengri* and *dingir*, the Sumerian ideogram for "sky/heaven."[232] As Suleimenov surmised, this affinity between Sumerian and Turkic languages not only points to a single cultural federation, but also one that appears to be "conditioned by the same religion" and cultivated by the same values.[233] A variation of the Bayterek myth is found in yet another Sumerian epic called *Lugalbanda and the Anzu Bird*, where the mythological Anzu (Simurgh) nests within a tree, whose roots penetrate into the river of the solar deity, Utu (golden egg).[234]

In Astana, the symbolism of the Simurgh forms the centrepiece of the Presidential Park situated along the main urban axis between the Akorda Palace and Independence Square (Fig. 64). Nazarbayev requested that the

**FIG 63** Observational deck inside the "golden egg" (sun), Bayterek Tower.

Nazarbayev may be the first modern leader to have used architecture and fantasy to crystallize the dreams of a nation, while also conveying broader objectives committed to world peace, global ecology, and interfaith harmony.

**FIG 65** Shohan, the eagle hunter, with his golden eagle. Altai Mountains, Mongolia.

Simurgh frame the entire park, thus creating an ideological link between Kazakh mythopoesis and Kazakhstani identity formation. In Astana, this universal myth has been elevated to the status of a national archetype that reflects the ideals of a regenerated republic. With its obvious association with the beginning of life, the motif of the egg is further reflected in the design of the National Archives building, which is located within the visible range of Bayterek.

The mythic drama of Bayterek reflects the binary cycles of life: day and night; summer and winter; good and evil; and light and dark. The annual contest between the sun and serpent (or dragon) represents the cycle of the seasons inherently central to nomadic life on the steppes. Parallels recur in the Egyptian *Book of the Dead*, where the sun-god Ra battles the serpent-demon, Apophis, who is the nemesis of cosmic order.[235] Similarly, the Aztec capital of Tenochtitlán was founded on the site where the leader of the Mexica people, Tenoch, came upon an eagle (sun-god) perched upon a cactus eating a snake.[236] The Aztec hieroglyph depicting this event has remarkably survived the Spanish conquest of the sixteenth century, the reign of the Emperor Maximilian I (1864–67), and remains in use today in Mexico's Coat of Arms. The eminent art historian, Rudolf Wittkower, identified numerous variants of the eagle and serpent myth over 5000 years and across cultures of the ancient Near East, the Mediterranean, Europe, Central Asia, Siberia, the Indus Valley, China, Japan, Indonesia, the Philippines, Sumatra, Borneo, Java, Oceania, and the Americas.[237] Even today, amid the high-altitude crags of the Altai Mountains, tradi-tional Kazakh nomads maintain a millennia-old practice of falconry, reflecting the primal relationship between the eagle and humankind (Fig. 65).

The "Cosmic Tree" has been present in the mythological art of the steppe nomads since the fourth century BCE. Both an emblem of their ceremonial practices and an extension of their social hierarchy, Gamkrelidze and Vjačeslav posit that it was "a basic symbol around which the Indo-European model of the world was built."[238] It "comprised of the totality of all living beings" and encapsulated the three-part vertical structure of the universe, consisting of Upper, Middle, and Lower Worlds. Each of the three realms is marked by a particular "zoomorphic code": birds symbolize the Upper World; hoofed animals, the Middle World; while fish, snakes, and predators occupy the Lower World.[239] This tripartite schema likely derived from Proto-Indo-European culture, which French mythographer, Georges Dumézil, claimed reflected the three class divisions—priest-kings, warriors, and commoners—that corresponded to the sacred, martial, and economic aspects of society.[240]

A multitude of cultures have formed enduring bonds with trees, often believing them to be repositories of knowledge that symbolize vitality, nourishment, self-regeneration, and the cosmos. Trees are among the most prevalent religious symbols: the Bodhi Tree of Gautama Buddha, the spirit-dwelling sycamores of Egypt, the Sun Dance rituals of the Indigenous peoples of the Plains, and the evergreen Yggdrasil Tree, a giant ash that supports the universe in Norse cosmology.[241] Since the earliest prehistory of Central Asia, trees have been ennobled in the collective memory of the ancient nomads. One of the most profound living metaphors of human experience and the primeval axis mundi of the universe, the Tree of Life is firmly rooted in mythologies of creation and the rites of passage of our most remote ancestors.[242] Inspiring architecture, art, history, and lore from the bedrock of the Earth to the summit of the sky, the Tree of Life is an essential element of the foundation myth of Astana.

The observation deck of Bayterek provides a breathtaking view of the young metropolis and the surrounding steppe, and features a mold of Nazarbayev's right handprint that is set within a triangular gold ingot (Fig. 66). The tradition of placing one's hand in it and making a wish places the spectator in the role of participant in the rebirth of the new nation. This association led Paul Starobin to impetuously describe Bayterek as "right out of the Architecture for Dictators 101."[243] But following Peirce's trichotomy of signs (icons, indices, and symbols), the handprint more directly functions as a type of index or sign that is interrelated to an object through a causal connection.[244] By uniting our hands with the President's, we tacitly engage in Nazarbayev's governance of the state. Both as a symbol of Kazakhstani identity and the chief emblem of the capital, Bayterek translates Kazakh folklore into an index for the entire country. It also bestows a sense of collective patronage in consort with a long Central Asian tradition of recognizing that the destiny of the leader is the destiny of the nation.

**FIG 66** Visitors match palms with President Nazarbayev's handprint, Bayterek Tower.

Birds-eye view from the Kazakh Eli Monument to the Pyramid of Peace and Reconciliation.

# CHAPTER FOUR

# Genius Loci

*Like people, cities have destinies, and each has a name and an individual biography of its own,
a character, which cannot be confused with that of any other place on Earth.*[245]
Nursultan Nazarbayev

## *Rebirth of Sary Arqa*

In 1998, the same year Nazarbayev issued a tender for the development of a Master Plan for Astana, the archaeologist who uncovered the Golden Man, Kemal Akishev, made a second startling discovery. He stumbled upon ruins at Bozok Lake, a mere five kilometres from the new capital, which showed settlement habitation stretching back to the eighth century.[246] Kemal's extraordinary archaeological find was a revelation, as he had uncovered what appeared to be the political centre of Sary Arqa, a site of enduring national pride that played a significant role in the development of nomadic civilization and culture in Kazakhstan. Long associated with Kazakh heroism, ancestry,

and independence, Sary Arqa has a modern political dimension synonymous with the birth of Kazakhstani statehood and identity.[247]

The relocation of the capital to a region noted for its correlation with the primordial qualities of tradition, nature, and place appealed to Nazarbayev's poetic imagination.[248] For the President, the discovery of this promised land of national heritage was not arbitrary, but connected to the fundamental existence, identity, and destiny of Kazakhstan.[249] Classical Romans referred to this notion of place as its guardian spirit or *genius loci*. This very animist idea of the world was also integral to traditional Central Asian notions about the natural environment, in which every locale, tract, and corner of the Earth was endowed with its own unique supernatural reality. It is through this lens that we must view the history and architecture of Astana.

Astana is foremost a steppe city set against the magical backdrop of the eternal blue sky, a place of ever-shifting identities, uses, and names. In its first incarnation under Russian colonization, the Kazakhstani capital was a Cossack trading post called Akmolinsk; its name changed to Tselinograd in 1961, when it became the principal city in Khrushchev's mass grain cultivation experiment (Fig. 67). It remained this way until 1992 when it returned to its original name Akmola, or "white tomb," which in Kazakh culture carries a deeper meaning as a shrine—a place of worship.[250] Finally, in 1998, the city became Astana, marking the rebirth of Sary Arqa in the form of an ultra-modernist utopia.[251] This chronology also marks three historical stages that shaped the urbanization of Astana—Russian colonization, Soviet exploitation, and post-Soviet re-emergence—with each leaving its distinct mark on the architecture of the Kazakhstani capital.

## Legacy of Soviet Urbanization

Akmolinsk emerged at a main intersection on the northern branch of the ancient Silk Roads, linking the Urals and Western Siberia with Central and Middle Asia in the East. When Ivan Shangin, a Russian mining engineer, wrote his first expeditionary reports in 1816, he described the area in summer as a pristine land where "flowers are planted by a lover of nature's beauty,

and you appear to forget entirely that you are travelling in a country untouched by the labour of man."[252] Siberian Cossacks established a post at Akmolinsk in 1830 as a military garrison to attempt Kazakh sedentarization on the frontier— a social experiment that faced a century of failures and a colossal loss of life in the early 1930s. Akmolinsk soon became a minor trading centre and a crucible of Russian expansionist policies, culture, and institutions, while Kazakh pastoralists were pushed to the less fertile peripheries. When the first official Master Plan of the city was drawn up in 1881, the fledgling city was enriched with a grand imperial project: a cathedral dedicated to St Aleksandr Nevskiy, the thirteenth-century Tsarist saint, who rose to legendary status for repelling the Golden Horde. The urban message was clear: Akmolinsk was a linchpin in the Kazakhstani vassal state.

In 1961, a General Plan for Tselinograd predicated on the four areas of housing, jobs, recreation, and transportation was implemented following Nikolai Miliutin's linear socialist model and Le Corbusier's concept of a "Functional City" (ca. 1933) (Fig. 68).[253] The massive 57-acre Pruitt–Igoe housing project in St Louis, Missouri (1954), adopted Le Corbusier's principles, but proved to be an iconic failure and became infamous for its abject poverty, crime, and racial segregation. Khrushchev's intention, however, was to expand the city as part of his agricultural production scheme, a project that was later revived with a different utopian aim by Nazarbayev. At the time, the city was confined to the right bank of the Ishim River, but it has since experienced a major construction boom (Fig. 69). Along wide tree-lined boulevards and

**FIG 67**　Nikita Khrushchev visits the Moskovsky State Farm in Kazakhstan, 1964.

**FIG 68**　Mira Street in Tselinograd, 1979.

FIG 69   Astana's administrative centre at night, as seen from the Left Bank.

**FIG 70** Palace of the Soviets competition project (unexecuted), 1934. Architect: Boris Iofan (1891–1976).

squares was an ensemble of new majestic civic buildings, which included the Virgin Lands Palace, the Palace of Youth, and the Palace of the Soviets—all designed to reflect socialist grandeur.[254] The prefix, "Palace" (*Dvorets*), is attached to many of the civic institutions in Astana today, and as Michaela Pohl has pointed out, "more than any other factor, [it] laid the foundation for Tselinograd's transformation into President Nazarbayev's Astana."[255]

The dissolution of the Soviet Union and the independence of Kazakhstan in 1991 marked a period of tremendous uncertainty, during which Tselinograd was restored and renamed in the modified form as Akmola. As a remote regional centre, Akmola lacked the necessary transportation, public utilities, and infrastructure to fulfil its future role as the capital of Kazakhstan. In the late 1990s, efforts were made to repurpose the older Soviet buildings and replace the vestiges of Tsarist hegemony with the aspirations of a new Kazakhstani identity—the current Office of the Ministry of Foreign Affairs, for instance, was formerly the Hotel Moscow. In less than twenty years, Astana has been transformed from an assemblage of slums and outdated housing into a city of skyscrapers and opportunity.

Although outwardly divorced from its urban Soviet parentage, Astana has inherited the philosophy of Soviet city planning and Marx and Engels's notion of the city as an instrument for rescuing citizens from the idiocy of rural life.[256] With the Bolshevik rise to power, cities were imagined as the cradle of progress and tasked with producing new urban citizens. Stalin's plan for the reconstruction of Moscow intended to transform the capital into the model city of the world's first socialist country. The revamped state capital was declared the ideal archetype for urban development and an embodiment of Stalinism. Moscow functioned as a geopolitical shopwindow for worldwide Communism, and Stalin's ideologies were manifested in projects that cast the image of Moscow as the central site for the articulation of Soviet supremacy.[257]

In Astana, we see reverberations of Moscow's General Plan of 1935. The cohesive development of both capitals featured a system of grand public spaces, embankments, and buildings showcasing the high-minded ideals of a unified national awakening. As in Nazarbayev's Astana, Stalin's Moscow was conceived as a striking parade of monumentalism combined with patriotic art, traditional symbolism, cultural motifs, and Piranesian grandeur.[258] On the site of the demolished Cathedral of Christ the Saviour, Stalin scheduled the construction of the massive Palace of the Soviets, the most significant example of proletarian architecture ever conceived (Fig. 70). The doyens of International Modernism—Gropius, Mendelsohn, Perret, Poelzig, and Le Corbusier—were all invited to submit designs in 1931, but by the following year the rubrics of the competition favoured the merger of new experimental forms with the timeless character of Roman Classicism.[259] The plan of Moscow, like many of the elements in Astana, borrowed urban ensembles from the Italian Renaissance, the French monarchic *ancien régime*, and the architectural fantasies of the visionary American draftsman, Hugh Ferriss (1889–1962).

Stalinist architecture offered an eclectic adaptation of Russian Baroque, Art Deco, and Gothic Revivalism on an epic scale that was intended to express Soviet strength, power, and triumphalism.[260] This pastiche of architectural styles is exemplified in the colossal Seven Sisters complex—seven huge tiered skyscrapers built around Moscow, which include the Ministry of Foreign Affairs and the main building of the Moscow State University. Its Kazakhstani equivalent takes the form of the Triumph of Astana, a luxury hotel and apartment complex that borrows the proportions and skyline of the Seven Sisters, while offering a graphic reminder of the grey days of Stalinist imperial design (Fig. 71). As one commentator noted, "the Triumph of Astana may be interpreted as a (subconscious) post-colonial attempt to come to terms with Soviet trauma."[261] Yet it is because of the painful legacy of colonialism and conquest that the Triumph of Astana shines its own light as an *aide-mémoire* for the rise of Kazakhstan from the ashes of Soviet authoritarianism. This impetus to accept all parts of the past and to find an adaptable solution for the future resides at the very core of Kazakhstani identity.

## Kazakh Eli Monument

No other structure in Astana more clearly signifies Kazakhstan's liberation from its colonial past than the Kazakh Eli Monument (Fig. 72). The ensemble of the Monument comprises a triumphal arch flanked by a curved colonnade that encircles a central column crowned by a golden Simurgh. Emblemizing the freedom, pride, and future of the Kazakhstani nation, the Monument's column stands 91 metres in height in reference to the year of Kazakhstan's independence—1991. The base of the central column features four bronze bas-reliefs situated in arched doorways along the pedestal. The carving in the western side depicts the diversity of the Kazakhstani nation and features Nazarbayev surrounded by people of different ethnicities. The southern relief represents the courage of the Kazakh warlords and freedom fighters. The north side portrays an allegorical depiction of the epochal stages of Kazakhstani development from nomadism to spaceflight, and the eastern carving symbolizes the future of the nation, emblemized by family. The Monument rekindles a collective memory long impaired by Soviet policies that suppressed the history of Kazakh heroism and obliterated the traditions of the Kazakh people, who had become minorities within their own nation.

The Monument finds inspiration in the memory of Kül-Tegin, the eighth-century ruler of the Turkic Khanate, whose marble head features the relief of a Simurgh with outstretched wings. Commemorating self-determination and home rule, the Monument appropriates the Classical canon and endows it with numerical symbolism, national rhetoric, and influences from Siberian shamanism.[262] The arch is 20 metres high to reflect Kazakhstan's twenty years of independence, and the central column parallels the tall pole erected by Yakut shamans (the Yakut speak a Turkic language not too distant from Kazakh) to signify the "Tree of the World," on top of which perches an eagle symbolizing the creator of

**FIG 71** Triumph of Astana. Architects: Nikolay Boriskin and Anatoly Zuyev, BAZIS-A, 2006.

**FIG 72**  Kazakh Eli Monument. Architects: Samatbek Bokebay and Sembigali Smagulov, 2009.

While the technological development of Astana reflects its broader themes of modernity, national politics, and invented traditions, the city is also a commentary on utopianism, mythmaking, and the creation of a new social psychology.

the universe.[263] The Monument is also laden with authentic Kazakhstani symbolism, ornamentation, and sculpture in order to reflect the President's National Unity Doctrine, which is based on the values of stability, tolerance, and equality for all people, irrespective of religious and ethnic differences. The composition is completed by a multisculptural ensemble featuring Mother Umay, an ancient Turkic goddess of fertility and prolificacy, who watches over the diverse citizenry of Kazakhstan (Fig. 73).

The tradition of erecting stone monuments in memory of noble deeds goes back to the golden age of Kazakh prehistory as reflected in the Kurgan stelae, which have been interpreted as cosmic pillars, or axis mundi that connect Heaven and Earth.[264] These anthropomorphic stone sculptures implanted in the ground served a variety of purposes, including memorials for the honoured dead, the deification of ancestors, tribal boundary markers, or representations of the enemies killed by a hero.[265] Known as "stone grandfathers" (*kamennye baby* in Russian or *balbal* in Kazakh), some have been dated to the sixth and fifth centuries BCE. There is more than a passing resemblance to the practice of making stone *menhirs* among Neolithic Europeans as far west as France. These stone figures typically face east to venerate the blue sky and life-giving water, and are found from Switzerland to Mongolia, dating from prehistory up until the first century CE. Several of them sit with crossed legs in the "Kazakh style," while others stand holding a ritual bowl with sacred water, as imitated in the Otan-Ana (Motherland) Monument in Astana. After the Turks and their descendants arrived, the tradi-

tional balbals were replaced in the Mangystau Region in western Kazakhstan by more traditional headstones, called *kulpytas*, with highly stylized geometric patterns and Arabic inscriptions to reflect the Islamic influence of the ninth to fourteenth centuries.

## Constructivism – Herald of Astana's Monumentality

The architecture of Astana is largely indebted to Russian Constructivism, an avant-garde architectural philosophy linked to industry and manufacturing that blossomed in the Soviet Union in the 1920s and early 1930s.[266] The Constructivist artists Konstantin Melnikov, Moisei Ginzburg, and the Vesnin brothers (Leonid, Viktor, and Aleksandr) ignited a radical new language of Russian art dedicated to complete abstraction and a devotion to modernity.[267] The spirit of the Russian Revolution and the messianic aspirations of the Vesnin brothers resulted in a series of extraordinarily novel buildings that combined advanced engineering, warped geometries, and technology with Communist principles. The pioneering projects produced by these Constructivist architects were geometric, minimalist, and experimental forms that extolled the universal virtues of unity and peace. Indeed, the Constructivist themes of societal betterment and change permeate the optimistic architecture of Astana.

Underlying Astana's enormous KazMunai-Gas state petroleum administration complex (Fig. 74), is the legacy of the Vesnin brothers

**FIG 73** Mother goddess Umay surrounded by the citizens of Kazakhstan.

**FIG 74** KazMunaiGas building. Architects S. Mataibekov, Z. Aytnabekov, and R. Musabayev, 2007.

**FIG 75** People's Commissariat of Heavy Industry in Red Square, Moscow, 1934. Artist: Aleksandr Aleksandrovich Vesnin.

**FIG 76** Ground plan, Theatre of the Russian Army, Moscow, 1934–40. Architects: Karo Alabyan and Vasily Simbirtsev.

and Ivan Leonidov's plan for the unbuilt Stalinist project, Narkomtyazhprom (People's Commissariat of Heavy Industry) in Red Square (Fig. 75). Through the work of the Russian architect and painter, Vladimir Tatlin (1885–1953), traces of Constructivism can also be found in the House of Ministries in Astana, which stretches across the main axis of the capital for nearly a kilometre. Tatlin unveiled his plans for the gigantic Monument to the Third International (the Comintern) in 1920. A synthesis of architecture, painting, and sculpture, Tatlin's monument was a towering "symbol of the modern spirit of the age."[268] This unrealized precursor to Bayterek consisted of an iron framework that contained internal revolving glass blocks that housed congress facilities, lecture halls, conference rooms, media centre, and the very latest in technical prowess. Designed to reach a height of 300 metres—100 metres higher than the Eiffel Tower—Tatlin's monument emblemized the dream of a new society and faith in the promise of industrialized technology, and remains one of the most famous unbuilt projects in architectural history.

The Constructivists sought to build an ideal egalitarian world within the parameters of socialism through the harmonious marriage of art and technology. Rejecting notions of taste as obsolete bourgeois ideals and subverting aesthetic trends in favour of method, they believed that an art of organization and real construction was necessary for the new technological age.[269] Tatlin's famous motto, "Art into Life," is a precursor to Kurokawa's architecture for the "Age of Life." Following

the October Revolution of 1917, Constructivist architects produced a plethora of imaginative designs that are echoed throughout the architecture of modern Astana. The vast classicizing state building programmes of the Stalinist era supplanted Constructivism through socialist realism, which is exemplified by the Theatre of the Russian Army, a dominating building in the shape of a red Soviet star reminiscent of the so-called Devil Pentagram of Kazakhstan (Fig. 76).

## Emerging from Stalin's Shadow

Between 1929 and 1932, the Soviet Communist Party imposed a policy of forced collectivization which consolidated individual landholdings and labour into party-controlled farms. The tyranny of the Stalin era eradicated whole communities and shattered a cultural way of life that had flourished for over two millennia.[270] It was one of the most horrific human tragedies of the last century, resulting in the deaths of approximately 4.5 million people, including 6 million Kazakhstanis—nearly 40 percent of the population (Fig. 77). To this day, the Soviet displacement of millions of Kazakhstanis is almost completely unknown in Western historiography. By 1935, 91 percent of agricultural land in Kazakhstan had been "collectivized," prompting the migration of entire ethnic populations, many of whom survived in yurts and refugee camps built by empathetic Kazakhs. This long tradition of Kazakh hospitality is beautifully inscribed on the walls of Yassawi's twelfth-

stranger, do not do him wrong. God does not love people with cruel hearts…"[271]

Perhaps the darkest chapter in Kazakhstan's recent past was the construction of Stalin's gulags, a vast array of ghastly labour camps in the remote regions of the USSR, including northern Kazakhstan. The gulags were known as "Stalin's dumping ground" and millions of political prisoners, including the great writer and dissident, Aleksandr Solzhenitsyn (1918–2008), ultimately found themselves exiled to these camps where they were forced to live under appalling conditions of human suffering.[272] In his masterwork, *The Gulag Archipelago* (1974–78), Solzhenitsyn provides a harrowing portrait of the endless brutality and mindless drudgery inflicted on prisoners in the camps (Fig. 78). One of the most wretched camps was located just outside modern-day Astana in a place called ALZHIR, which is a Russian acronym for the Akmolinski Camp for the Wives of the Betrayers of the Motherland.

Nazarbayev was well aware of the grim history of the site and sought to banish its memory as part of an extreme makeover that expunged all traces of Stalinist despotism and inhumanity. He replaced all the Soviet-era street names and monuments, and renamed, repurposed, and remodelled various Soviet institutions by using a variety of abstractly historicized postmodern façades. By blending Neo-Classicism and gold-tinted modern materials, this vitiated skeleton of Soviet authority was transformed into an exemplar of Kazakhstani state architecture and a perfect microcosm of Kazakhstan's complete departure from its colonial heritage.

Nikita Khrushchev's overreaching, optimistic Virgin Lands Campaign of 1954 triggered an additional wave of radical transformation. The traditional grazing lands in the Akmola Region were appropriated for crop cultivation, while significant portions of northern Kazakhstan underwent extensive industrialization. Far from transforming Kazakhstan into the "granary of the Soviet empire," Khrushchev's initiative ushered in a period of tremendous adversity for the ethnic makeup of Kazakhstan, resulting in Kazakhs becoming a minority in their homeland, outnumbered by Slavic peoples—mostly Russians and Ukrainians. The massive irrigation works and water diversion projects in neighbouring Uzbekistan initiated one of the planet's most atrocious environmental catastrophes—the drying out of the Aral Sea (Fig. 79).[273] This ecological calamity was compounded by an equally woeful human tragedy, where over a period of forty-two years the Semipalatinsk Test Site detonated 116 air and surface nuclear blasts (Fig. 80). These horrible events were witnessed by thousands of Kazakh villagers who were unaware that their communities, children, and livestock were being enveloped in a radioactive cloud that would have noxious long-term effects.

From this bleak history of devastation and near destruction, Kazakhstan has emerged as a paragon of intercultural exchange (Fig. 81). In 1998–99, Astana received an honourable mention for the UNESCO Cities for Peace Prize for "strengthening social cohesion,

**FIG 77** Coffins carried on stretchers during the famine in the Volga region of Russia, October 1921.

**FIG 78** Inside a barrack in the Panyshevsky work camp, 1940.

**FIG 79**   Abandoned fishing boats litter the dry landscape of the former Aral Sea near Dzhambul, Kazakhstan.

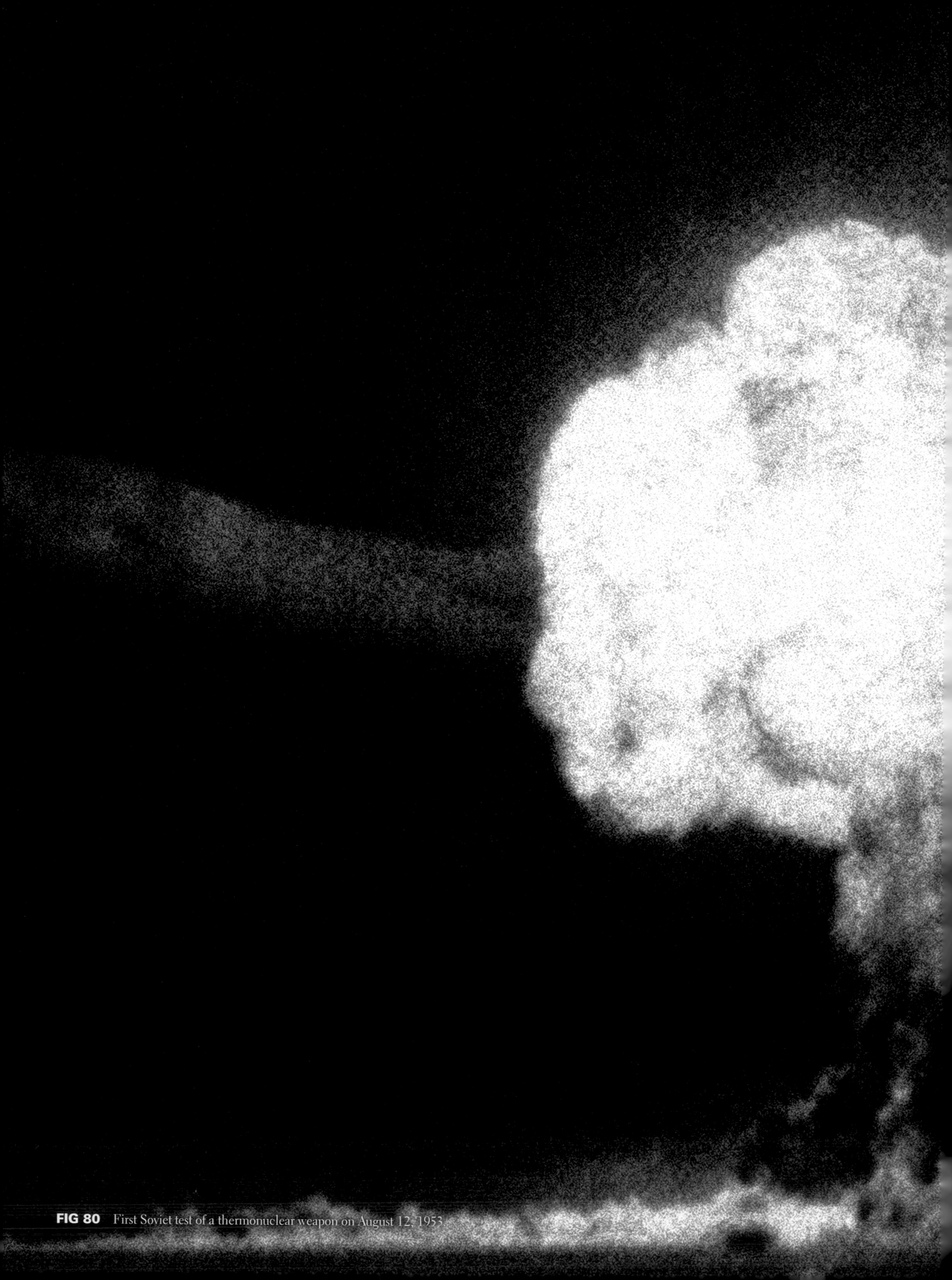

**FIG 80** First Soviet test of a thermonuclear weapon on August 12, 1953.

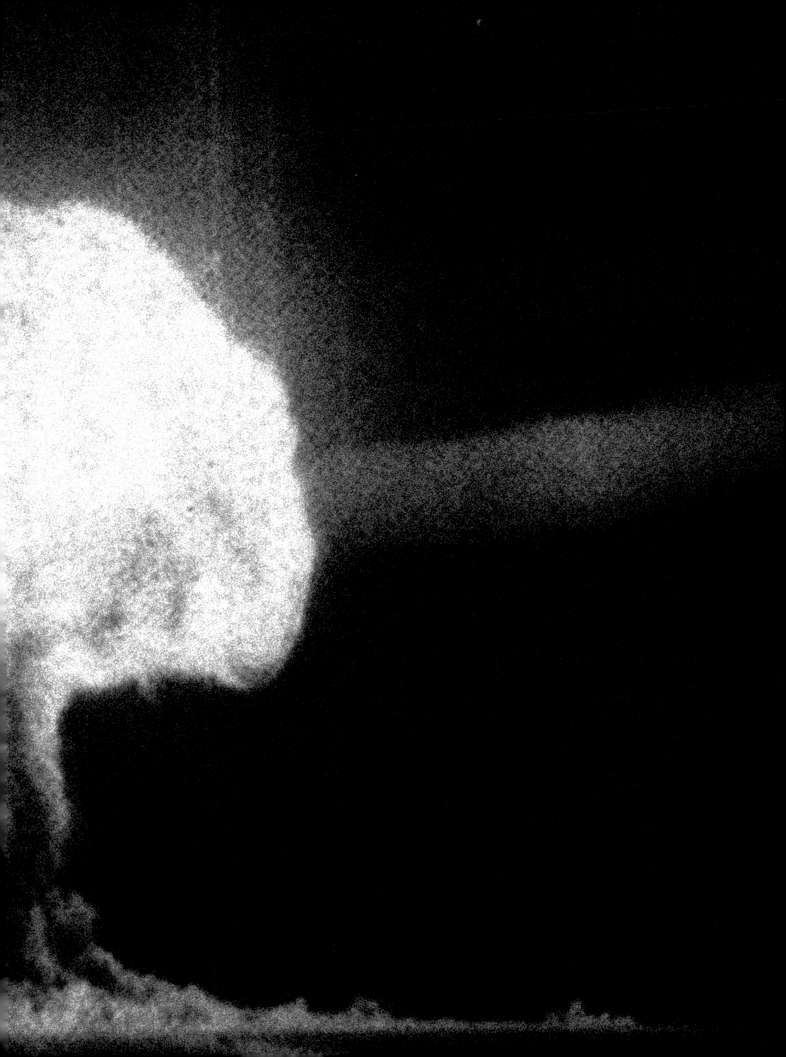

**FIG 81** Astana cityscape with fireworks above Bayterek Tower.

**FIG 82** *The Ideal City,* attributed to Luciano Laurana (ca. 1420–79), ca. 1470.

**FIG 83** *The Ideal City,* attributed to Fra Carnevale (ca. 1420–84), ca. 1480.

**FIG 84** Aerial view of the Master Plan for the "Green City." Designed by KANNFINCH, 2008.

during the tumult of the French Revolution. Robert Owen's ideal communities were in response to the harsh conditions of the Industrial Revolution in England. The German Expressionists sought to remedy the consequences of the First World War, and Kisho Kurokawa's Metabolism emerged within the chaotic societal conditions of Japan's postwar Economic Miracle.[284]

A reaction to centuries of imperial rule and the atrocities of the twentieth century, the utopian capital of Astana provides the perfect platform to showcase Kazakhstan's legacy of triumph over hardship. The Kazakhstani capital is the most recent addition to a vast continuum of utopian cities dedicated to achieving maximum collective happiness through social restructuring, rational progress, and technocratic architecture. What makes Astana *sui generis* in its historical context is that it may be the first utopian city with both global and mythic aspirations constructed entirely from the ground up. While the technological development of Astana reflects its broader themes of modernity, national politics, and invented traditions, the city is also a commentary on utopianism, mythmaking, and the creation of a new social psychology.

Order, efficiency, and optimal functionality are central to the urban philosophy of Kazakhstan. This utopian agenda is attested in the development of four satellite cities, which cover 70 000 hectares and have been designed as cutting-edge sustainable urban settlements. Each town-within-a-city bears a name that reflects its respective function, and each has been developed to house a full range of specific services for self-sufficiency. The "Green City" (21 000 inhabitants) is a hub for hotels, resort islands, and a theme park; the "Growing City" (50 000 inhabitants) is a hi-tech intermodal logistics-free port; the "Golden City" (82 000 inhabitants) is a university, medical, and sports precinct; and the "Gate City" (153 000 inhabitants) is an urban centre with retail and commercial uses (Fig. 84).

Within its Central Asian context, Astana harkens back to the first utopia ever constructed on the steppe—Pasargadae, built by Cyrus the Great (ca. 580–30 BCE). When completed in 546 BCE, Pasargadae was the most extraordinary capital in the ancient world. Even the name *Pasargadae*—like the English word "paradise"—derives from an Old Iranian term *paradaida*, and refers to an enclosed area within a city surrounding a lush garden. The famous "Royal Garden" at Pasargadae became the key innovation of the imperial capital and the symbolic heart of an empire.[285] At Pasargadae, the formal design of the garden was characterized by its geometric designs—squares, rectangles, and floral patterns carefully arranged among trees, wild grass, roses, and lilies—and these constituent parts re-emerge in the urban landscape of Astana. Both in physical form and emblematic of a conceptual message, Pasargadae, as with Astana, was conceived to exemplify religious tolerance and multiculturalism.

The notion of modernity has given rise to understanding progress and tradition as contrasting antipodes. In the context of Astana, however, it is intrinsically married with the myth of an emerging Kazakhstani superethnos. This utopian impulse is manifested on an unprecedented scale in the unfinished megaproject, Astana City Vision, a sustainable indoor city capable of housing 30 000 residents. This ambitious project advances an entirely new model of intelligent urban development beneath a perfectly climatized domed area spanning nearly 2 million square metres. Astana City Vision unites concepts from Buckminster Fuller's *Geodesic Dome Over Manhattan* (1950) with H.G. Wells's science fiction novel, *The Sleeper Awakes* (1910), in which a comatose man wakes up to a futuristic London covered by an enormous glass vault (Fig. 85).[286] Fuller's revolutionary credo of architecture emphasized the conservation of the Earth and the promotion of high-efficiency, environmentally responsible design. Astana's superdome would make Fuller's "Spaceship Earth" a reality.

Astana also fulfils the utopian promise of the City Beautiful Movement, a late nineteenth-century urban design philosophy that used beautification and monumental architecture to inspire civic pride. The Movement was launched at the World's Columbian Exposition in Chicago in 1893 with the goal of creating rational, scientific, disciplined cities to ameliorate the problems of uncontrolled growth, congestion, and anomie. City planning was then perceived to have a didactic role in the betterment of society, and architecture provided innovative solutions to social cohesion and the quality of life. Influencing the design of North American cities from San Francisco to New York, the Movement advocated city planning that favoured broad, tree-lined boulevards and monu-

mental civic buildings inspired by the Classical vernacular.[287] Astana offers its own solution to the dense and decaying cities of the world by combining the principles of the City Beautiful Movement with Eurasian mythology and urban utopianism. Today this marriage is best exemplified by Disneyland's Main Street, U.S.A., which embodies an idealized reflection of American values, hopes, and dreams in the form of an idyllic early twentieth-century American town.

## *Disneyland of Eurasia*

Astana has often been likened to Disneyland as being a wholesale "Magic Kingdom" centred upon nationalistic fairy tales and utopian aspirations of a Master-Planned community. The appeal of both urban plans derives from their thematic designs, which distill a complex physical and cultural reality into alluring images of vibrancy and charm. Astana has produced a new generation of attractions and urban space that navigate between authenticity and illusion, creating a condition of *hyperreality*, in which everything is brighter, larger, and more entertaining than in everyday life (Fig. 86). Coined by the French sociologist, Jean Baudrillard, hyperreality is an extension of his notion of simulacra and the ways in which postmodern society simulates "reality" through symbolic signs and relationships. For Baudrillard, hyperreality is a hallmark of the postmodern age, wherein the lines between what is "real" and what is "imagined" are blurred and seamlessly blended.[288]

ᛉᛒᛘᛁᚺᛊᛁᛃᛞᚨᚦᛉᛁᛈ

**FIG 85** Astana City Vision, conceptual design for an efficient new urban community. Designed by DRA&U, 2014.

**FIG 86** City centre and central administrative district of Astana with serpentine Ishim River in the foreground.

For more than sixty years, Disneyland has been a pilgrimage site of children's fantasies, which are played out in an urbanistic Garden of Eden that celebrates the imaginal world. In some respects, Astana is a nationalist version of Disneyland that hovers on the edge of visionary grandeur and architectural folly. Under the banner of "Future Energy," the World Expo reiterates the dream of Walt Disney, who dedicated his life to seeking out solutions to the problems of the modern city. Like Nazarbayev, he began by not merely devising cures for the ills of chaotic urban settings, but by building an entirely new community rooted in myth, imagination, and the latest advancements in design. Disney proclaimed that his theme park was an antidote to urban malaise, discontentment, and poverty, and his enduring dedication to the regeneration of cities spurred him to develop his most ambitious project—EPCOT, an Experimental Prototype Community of Tomorrow (1966).[289] EPCOT is not to be mistaken in toto with Epcot, the theme park in Florida that opened in 1982 as a celebration of human achievement, technological innovation, and international culture.[290] In its original form, EPCOT (code-named Project X) was designed as a model utopian community for 20 000 residents, complete with a 50-acre, glass-domed town centre, visitor attractions, manufacturing sites, cultural districts, and satellite housing, all interlinked by a state-of-the-art monorail and flanked by a "green belt" (Fig. 87).[291]

Disneyland was similarly conceived as a modern city in miniature—a village utopia, built upon the ideas of Clarence Perry (1874–1944),

Henry Wright (1878–1936), Clarence Stein (1882–1975), Le Corbusier (1887–1965), Victor Gruen (1903–80), and Ebenezer Howard (1850–1928), the English founder of the Garden City Movement.[292] Howard's solution to overpopulation and squalor in urban centres was to construct constellations of optimally-sized "Garden Cities," an idea that would spark a revolution in twentieth-century urbanism. His landmark work, *To-Morrow: A Peaceful Path to Real Reform* (1898), was introduced to Astana through Vladimir Semenov (1874–1960), the principal architect of Moscow from 1930 to 1934. The Master Plan of Tselinograd was directly influenced by Semenov's designs, and it was through Semenov that the Garden City became the indisputable model for ideal Soviet town planning.[293]

Astana inherits from Semenov the notion that the built environment can shape political subjects, but goes beyond pure state-driven objectives to reflect global aspirations of peace, unity, and sustainability. It is the latest example of an enduring human desire to recreate paradise on the most uninhabitable of terrains. Drawing upon Garden City idealism and monumental architecture, we find in the capital the echoes of a long list of city planners who endeavoured to create a green-based peaceful path to real urban reform. As Lewis Mumford extolled, Garden Cities are mere drops in the bucket, and what is really needed is "to change the shape of the bucket itself."[294] Astana offers this kind of complete systematic urban transformation.

**FIG 87** Conceptual artwork for Walt Disney's EPCOT (Project X) by George Rester and Herb Ryman, ca. 1966.

Satellite view of Astana

# CHAPTER FIVE

# The Master Plan

*This other Eden, demi-paradise, this fortress built by nature*
*for herself against infection and the hand of war.*[295]
William Shakespeare

## *Architectural Eden*

John O'Gaunt's eulogy of England in Shakespeare's *Richard III* (ca. 1592) provides a fitting introduction to Kisho Kurokawa's nature-inspired Master Plan for Astana, which unites the clean air of the steppe with the architectural glories of a great capital city. In 1998, one of Japan's leading architects won the international competition to design Astana. His plan's fluid adaptability allowed every foreign visitor to see "his own native city" in the urban design of the capital.[296] Kurokawa's Master Plan produced a new kind of built environment that reflected the plurality of life, and his refrain from imposing an artificial form on the capital resonated with

Nazarbayev's advocacy of national heritage and local history. His designs became a key platform of Kazakhstan's 2030 Development Plan, which served as the blueprint for the nation's future security, stability, prosperity, and well-being. Nazarbayev stipulated that the capital should embody a future dedicated to the gradual termination of fossil fuels and the massive expansion of renewable resources. Kurokawa did not disappoint, and his urban philosophy proved well-matched with the President's ideological vision for the capital.

Kurokawa amalgamated the existing old Soviet town of Akmola on the right bank of the Ishim River into a completely new administrative capital. Dubbed "the Left Bank" in homage to the historic Rive Gauche of Paris, Astana's centre of gravity serpentines along the Ishim's artificially widened banks—a Kazakhstani equivalent to the Thames in London and the Neva in St Petersburg (Fig. 88).[297] Astana scenically meanders and merges the old (Russian) and new (Kazakhstani) sectors into a single unity, and provides a symbiosis between tradition and modernity, the fabricated and the natural. Kurokawa did not replace the existing infrastructure. Instead, he integrated Soviet industrial heritage into the aspirations of a newly independent nation—a synergic construct of water, history, growth, and urbanity.

Kurokawa was a leading proponent of Metabolism, a Japanese architectural movement that proposed urban utopias modelled after the biological, reproductive, and transformative aspects of nature.[298] He believed that this radical transformation of city space would engender an equally radical transformation of society. Metabolism appealed to the cultural roots of Kazakhstan insofar as nomadic pastoralism was determined by the dictates of nature and was therefore in a constant state of flux. The movement was launched in 1960 with the publication of the manifesto, *Metabolism 1960: Proposals for a New Urbanism*. Metabolists were the progeny of a long utopian tradition of city planning that stemmed from Robert Owen (1771–1858), who combined architecture with ideals of social progress, and Frederick Law Olmsted (1822–1903), whose concept of shared community is expressed in the most beloved

public spaces in the United States, including Boston's Emerald Necklace and Central Park in New York.

Inspired by Watson and Crick's discovery of DNA, Kurokawa proposed his first Metabolist project, Helix City, envisioned as a series of helical structures coupled with an organic city plan. Helix City offered a solution to the severe shortage of dwelling space in Japan by distributing residential buildings (like chromosomes) through an infrastructure of bridges spanning land and sea. Although many of the Metabolist urban fantasies were never realized, Kurokawa found great patronage in Nursultan Nazarbayev. As Bernhard Köppen reminds us, Kurokawa wanted the new capital to "be a symbol of Kazakhstan's resurrection and the rebirth of an authentic Kazakh spirituality."[299] This was to be achieved through his concept of symbiosis, which he described as "living together" and forging relationships that are "not only advantageous, but necessary."[300]

Symbiosis emerged from traditional Japanese philosophy and Edo architecture, which is typified by hybridity, abstraction, and synthesis. Drawing on symbiosis, Kurokawa promoted an intercultural aesthetic theory that was perfectly adaptable to, and reflective of, Kazakhstani cultural identity. Kurokawa described symbiosis as "the philosophy of the nomads of the new age," referring to the society of the contemporary world, which is characterized by movement, exchange, discovery, pluralism, and heterogeneity.[301] The Supreme Court, Parliament, and Presidential Palace, for instance, imbue the architecture of symbiosis through simplified geometric forms that evoke

**FIG 88** Ishim River embankment, developed by Akmurza Rustembekov.

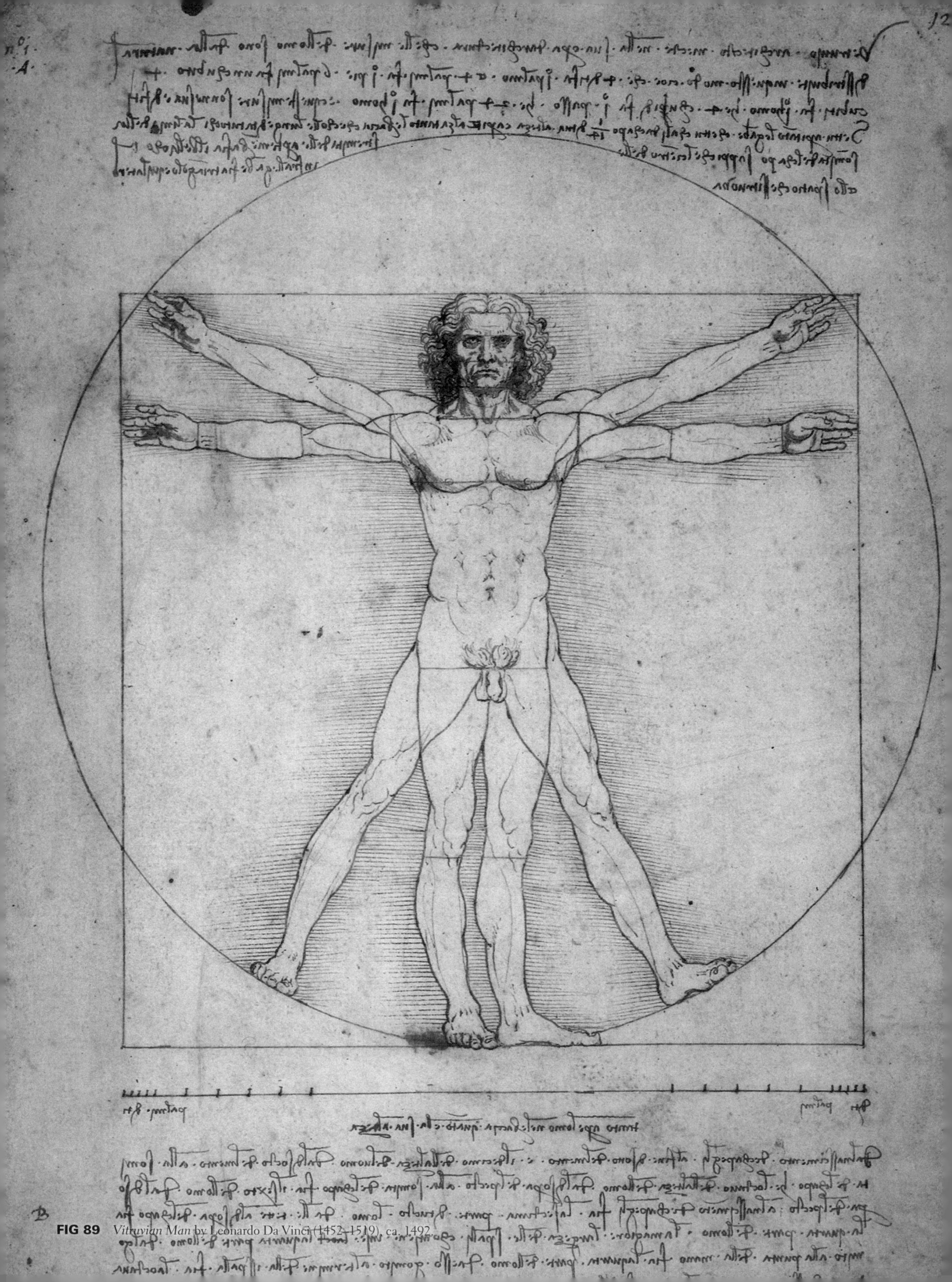

**FIG 89** *Vitruvian Man* by Leonardo Da Vinci (1452–1519), ca. 1492

the historical significance of Kazakhstan's native symbols. For Kurokawa, this constituted "the symbiosis of the Local and the Universal within the city and its architecture."[302]

Metabolists saw modern cities as being enveloped in "a cancerous and harmful tissue" and they proposed a solution to this chaotic development that was inspired by the flexibility of biological organisms.[303] Their vision of the future city was analogous to the human body: it should be composed of a circulatory system and cellular elements that develop, mutate, decay, and regenerate. The Roman architect and engineer, Vitruvius (ca. 80–15 BCE), introduced anthropomorphism in architecture 2000 years earlier. In his *Ten Books on Architecture* (ca. 30–15 BCE), the oldest and most influential treatise on architecture ever composed, the human body becomes the ideal of harmony and proportion (Fig. 89).[304] Kurokawa repudiated the Swiss architect Le Corbusier's maxim that city planning should reflect "the age of the machine," but he adopted the architectural pioneer's anthropomorphic model of linear urban designs, based upon the abstract shape of the human body, complete with head, spine, arms, and legs.[305]

## Ecological Urbanity

Many of Astana's features derive from Le Corbusier's pure forms and his grandiose "rational" schemes for transforming the social face of the world. However, as we now know, Le Corbusier's city planning revolution was closely tied to total-itarian principles of social engineering, moral progress, and hygienic cleanliness.[306] Kurokawa went far beyond Le Corbusier's puritanical doctrines by providing an urban model that interfaces two organically developed systems: the city and nature. His approach to architecture heralded the "Age of Life," in which the city was a living organism in cohabitation with the natural environment. City plans should, therefore, be integrated with the surrounding ecosystem and complement every existing element and diverse community of organisms, from fauna and sources of water to forests, street life, and cohesion of neighbourhoods.

Kurokawa's urban blueprint is greatly indebted to Patrick Geddes (1854–1932), the Scottish biologist and forefather of modern urban planning, who was the first to recognize the city as an organic entity.[307] Geddes's description of the city as a biopolis and his tripartite model of urban theory based on geography, history, and spirituality underpins Kurokawa's own manifesto, which calls for a return to nature through urban metabolism and symbiosis. In adopting Kurokawa's symbiotic prescriptions, Astana formulates a new doctrine of city planning that actively promotes the ecological preservation of the natural environment.

At present, the greatest factor affecting the environmental footprint of modern cities is sustainable transportation. Astana aims to address this issue by implementing large-capacity car parks, rapid transit, and high-speed light rail transit within the city.[308] Kurokawa's strategy for decreasing our dependence on cars has influenced the ideas of Stephen M. Wheeler, Rem Koolhaas, Mitchell Joachim, and others, who have endeavoured to create eco-cities that support sustainability and human ecology.[309] Astana provides an ideal model of a city that acknowledges the environmental limits of urban growth, while promoting greener livelihoods, cultural diversity, and a vibrant civic life directed toward happiness, health, and the fulfilment of human needs.

Kurokawa's holistic model has further ensured the harmonious and sustainable development of the city through an ecological waste management system, strict water protection zones, and eco-corridors, including a 55 000-hectare "greenbelt" forest perimeter around the city. Along with 15 000 hectares of afforestation within the city limits, the total area of local woodlands is planned to reach 100 000 hectares by 2020, leaving a living legacy inscribed on verdant land for future generations.[310] Designed to insulate Astana from the harsh climate of the steppe, the parkland along the banks of the Ishim River and the encircling greenbelt provide a microclimate and rich biodiversity that carry out the invaluable duty of cleaning the air for the entire community (Fig. 90). This lush forest around Astana has become a distinctive feature of the capital, thematically intermingling paradaida with notions of homeland, sustainability, and global religious communion. The closest American effort in this regard is Joseph Smith's revelatory Plat of the City of Zion (1833), a green-spaced and grid-patterned spiritual utopia, which he envisioned as the axis mundi for the Church of Jesus Christ of Latter-day Saints.

## A Viable Urban Model

Astana deviated from other planned federal capitals, which, due to their rigid designs, did not allow for unpredictable development. By Kurokawa's account, Lúcio Costa and Oscar Niemeyer's Master Plan of Brasília imposed a top-down formalism unable to adapt to the necessities of dynamic growth. While Astana drew from ancient archetypes, flexibility, and symbiosis, Brasília celebrated functional rationalism, autocracy, and architectural uniformity. The new capital was meant to transform Brazilian society, but as James Holston has shown, it instead produced social segregation, increased poverty, and embodied a series of paradoxes that rejected the country's traditional past.[311] In Brasília, the regeneration of the present required an invented future in which the past was seen as an impediment to a new social order. In Astana, deference was instead given to the past as an essential element of an entirely new society in symbiosis with ancestral values and traditional identity.

Brasília's grand axial boulevards, pedestrian-barren plazas, and dated "iconic" monuments contrast the lively and integrated urban squares in Astana. Streamlined monumentality and physical separation are the trademarks of modern Brasília, which cloak culturally relevant symbolism with International Style clichés (Figs. 91–92). Holston's anthropological critique exposes the failures of Brazil's "blueprint utopia," revealing how its political class imposed grandiose dreams and ideologies on a blank canvas and how its architectural heroes, Costa and Niemeyer, created

**FIG 90** Section of the parkland that meanders around Astana and the banks of the Ishim River.

**FIG 91** Congress Building, Brasília. Architect: Oscar Niemeyer, 1960.

**FIG 92** Lone man walks past the National Museum of the Republic, Brasília. Architect: Oscar Niemeyer, 2006.

superstructures devoid of cultural sensitivity and an intimate sense of place. Astana stands as a viable alternative to the model of Brasília in that it is mythic yet adaptable, practical yet symbolic, and monumental yet not divorced from its ethnic cultural heritage.

Astana evokes clear signs of John Hannigan's notion of the "Fantasy City," where "theme-o-centric" and "branded" "urban entertainment developments" assemble around technologies of simulation and spectacle.[312] While Hannigan criticizes this type of post-industrialist city as glorifying consumption through "solipsistic" theme parks, megamalls, and megaplexes, Eric Rabkin insists that above all other human drives, it is fantasy that compels us forward and allows us to dream about what we may accomplish and become. The skyline of Astana at night has an unmistakable Las Vegas appeal—indeed, the entire cityscape glows in an ethereal display of coloured light (Fig. 93). Surface comparisons are also often drawn with Dubai, but unlike the mecca of architectural ostentation in the United Arab Emirates, Astana offers a triumphal urban space set within the context of real historical legitimacy. With its glittering medley of architectural wonders, Dubai's presentation of contrived multiculturalism lacks a genuine sense of settled identity and social cohesion.[313]

Though it appears that Astana and Dubai have developed along similar lines—incentivizing foreign investment and exhibiting the work of starchitects—these urban parities are merely superficial. Astana taps into an authentic epic past and its architecture represents a culture that has long celebrated adaptability while acknowledging the dark reminders of Soviet hegemony and ethnic oppression. These aspects are an indispensable part of Astana's unique genius loci. The cynical view that Astana provides an architectural lesson in state-sponsored propaganda belies the deeper message of the capital's role as a global leader in sustainable urbanism, smart growth, and livability.

## Multicultural Urbanism

The urban design institute, AstanaGenPlan, significantly modified Kurokawa's plan into a new, original, and more locally meaningful form. The most significant revision was to supplement Kurokawa's symbiosis with nature with a radial layout that closely reflected the Kazakh tradition of nomadic encampment. The harsh climatic conditions of Astana made it necessary to concentrate offices, residences, schools, and entertainment centres within walking distance of one another. Also, the livability scales of other major cities were examined along with other indices, such as per capita living space, the number of trees planted annually, the square metre of greenery per person, and snow-clearing procedures in reference to curb height.[314]

By incorporating the "best standards" of the "best cities" in the developed world, AstanaGenPlan was determined to construct a sustainable Eurasian city *par excellence* and usher in a new paradigm of urban planning. Expertise was gathered from the municipal plans of Ottawa, Minneapolis, and Toronto. The latter's Emerald Park Condos inspired

**FIG 93** Cultural centre of Astana, featuring Khazret Sultan Mosque, Pyramid of Peace, Shabyt Palace of Arts, and Kazakh Eli Monument.

Astana's gracefully curved Emerald Towers that punctuate the capital skyline and bolster the image of international business prowess (Fig. 94). The Northern Lights building in Astana embodies a similar capitalist aesthetic, as do the sustainable and elegant Talan Towers, designed by the hugely influential architectural firm of Skidmore, Owings & Merrill LLP. Located along Astana's main artery, the Talan Towers provide a dialogue between exclusive luxury and the mythic nationalism of Bayterek Tower, with distinct elements comprising a strong underlying order of opulent materials and elegant proportions (Fig. 95). Unlike the stylistic admixture of Beijing and Hong Kong, which have accreted over decades, the aesthetics of Astana are the result of a singular and securely managed "Eurasian Style" and approach to city planning.

For Sarsembek Zhunusov, the former Chief Architect of the Master Plan, Eurasian Style constitutes an openness to different styles and ideas, providing "a synthesis of the best, which has been accumulated in contemporary urban planning and architecture."[315] This fusion of modern innovation and collective heritage is indicative of Kazakhstan's innate multiculturalism and its spirit of creativity and inclusion. AstanaGenPlan pointed out the dichotomy between postmodern architectural theory and the methodology of urban planning expertise on the ground, noting that abstract philosophical principles do not necessarily provide a coherent methodology leading to declared goals. By distilling Kurokawa's design language, AstanaGenPlan addressed specific local concerns that were tied directly to Nazarbayev's Neo-Eurasianism and Kazakhstan's role as a multicultural conduit between Europe and Asia.

## Eurasian Aesthetics

The term "Eurasian" was first introduced during the Russian Empire era and was later used by the Soviet Union to bridge the divisions between nationalities and ease transcultural relations. In Astana, Eurasian identity is aestheticized as a uniquely identifiable style, which blends Post-Modernism, Central Asian art, Islamic decoration, and the architectural revivalism of Classicism, Orientalism, and Russian Baroque (Fig. 96). Historically, revivalist architecture was a tool of national unification. In the Italian Renaissance, Classical revivalism conveyed the symmetrical proportions of absolute beauty and the perfect state. In nineteenth-century France, Germany, and England, Gothic revivalism was an expression of national sentiment and religious primacy. In twentieth-century America, the Beaux-Arts style was a reflection of the authority and permanence of the ideal Republic. Astana's revivalist architecture has an altogether different complexion, and acts as a transmitter of a pan-Eurasian identity nourished by the cultural wealth of the world community.

Kurokawa had the difficult task of incorporating Eurasian features into the design of the Astana International Airport. Here, the recurring motifs of the yurt and of national unity are expressed using two unique types of blue tile in the decoration of the central dome (Fig. 97).

**FIG 94** Emerald Towers, with Temir Zholy National Railway Company building (at left). Astana. Architect: Roy Varacalli, 2011; Tolegan Abilda, 2009.

**FIG 95** Talan Towers, Astana. Architects: Skidmore, Owings & Merrill LLP, 2017.

Astana provides an ideal model of a city that acknowledges the environmental limits of urban growth, while promoting greener livelihoods, cultural diversity, and a vibrant civic life directed toward happiness, health, and the fulfilment of human needs.

**FIG 96** Classical colonnade with the Khazret Sultan Mosque and the Shabyt Palace of Arts in the background.

This binary tile pattern reflects both ancient Tengrianism, in which azure blue symbolizes grace and Sufi mysticism, and turquoise (the colour of the Turks) represents true assurance and faith.[316] Elements of Sufi mysticism continue to play a profound role in the spiritual life of Kazakhstani Muslims who place an emphasis on personal revelation — the illuminationist dimension of Sufism — which is revealed in dreams and visionary experiences.[317] The inspiration for Kurokawa's dome comes from one of the wonders of the Islamic (Sufi) world — Khoja Akhmet Yassawi's mausoleum in the historic city of Turkistan, commissioned in 1390 by the conqueror Tamerlane (1336–1405) (Fig. 98).

Revered as a pilgrimage site and "Second Mecca" by Kazakhstani Muslims, Yassawi's tomb is noted for its two monumental, majolica-tiled blue domes, which are among the largest in Central Asia.[318] The mausoleum marks the zenith of Timurid architecture, the pinnacle of Islamic art in Central Asia, and a major contributor to the vibrant hybridity of seventeenth-century Mughal art. During his conquests, Tamerlane assembled craftsmen from all over the region and initiated a Eurasian renaissance — a period of brilliance in the history of Islamic art and architecture. This Renaissance was not localized, and proved to be an inspiration to distant Indo-European cultures from Turkey to India. Timur's descendants produced a spectacular style of architectural fusion that was often characterized by axial symmetry, monumental scale, and polychromic tilework — all of which were appropriated in Kurokawa's designs.

Eurasian Style is further exemplified in the enormous semicircular state-owned oil and gas complex, KazMunaiGas, which soars high above the steppe as a bold symbol of Kazakhstan's petrowealth and a focal point of Astana's central axis (Fig. 99). The KazMunaiGas facility combines the stunning façade of the Bellagio in Las Vegas with the mythically-inspired Atlantis resort in the United Arab Emirates. A more subdued statement of Eurasianism is the House of Government building, which closely resembles the marble monument at Ordabasy commemorating the legendary 1726 unification of the three Kazakh Hordes to repel the Jungars. The stand against the Jungars has become one of the brightest and most memorable chapters in Kazakh history, and this optimistic zeal is reconstituted symbolically by the House of Government's stone façade and reflecting blue glass surfaces. The defeat of the Jungars in southern Kazakhstan signalled the crystallization of Kazakhstani independence, and the House of Government stands as a marker of the nation's socioeconomic advancement through partnerships with its global neighbours.

In Astana, Eurasian architecture is the most visible reflection of Kazakhstan's cultural inclusivity and global progressivity. The Eurasian medley of architectural motifs produces a transnational aesthetic that finds its chief expression in the colossal Astana Opera, the third-largest of its kind in the world (Fig. 100). The Astana Opera house commingles the Parthenon with Imperial décor, and Kazakh ornamentation with the interior of the Teatro alla Scala in Milan (Fig. 101). At first

**FIG 97** Astana International Airport. Architect: Kisho Kurokawa, 2005.

**FIG 98** Mausoleum of Khoja Akhmet Yassawi, Turkistan, Kazakhstan.

**FIG 99** City centre at night with the semicircular KazMunaiGas building towering above the steppe.

**FIG 100** Astana Opera. Architects: Mabetex Group, 2012.

**FIG 101**  Concert hall of Astana Opera.

**FIG 102** Bayterek Tower plaza, with interlocking squares at the base in the manner of Filarete's scheme for Sforzinda.

glance, the quadriga crowning the façade's pinnacle appears to be an unoriginal clone of the Bolshoi Theatre in Moscow. However, the quadriga is a genuine expression of an ancient Eurasian innovation. Evidence that Bronze Age Central Asian nomads first invented the chariot is attested by imprints of wheels with spokes found at the burial sites of Ulubay, Berlik-2 in northern Kazakhstan, and at Satan in the Karaganda Region, both of which date back to ca. 2100–1900 BCE. Reconstructions of these spoked wheels have been incorporated in the design of the central column of the Kazakh Eli Monument as a distinctive reminder of the marriage of ancient innovation and modern independence.[319]

The urbanism of Astana is more than just a straightforward adoption of European Classicism. It is an amalgam of global belief systems, which touches upon Kazakh folklore and mythology just as readily as it expresses the urban aesthetics of Warsaw, Vienna, Rome, Moscow, and Washington, D.C. As an expression of the city's destiny, the architecture of Astana offers a simultaneous understanding of the entire country, and by extension, the entire world. Due in large part to its nomadic past, Astana embodies thousands of years of adaptability and openness, which makes it an ideal model of global ethnic harmony, multiculturalism, and peaceful accord. These ideals are magnified in the urban planning of Astana, making it a crystal city that not only reflects the unity of an entire nation, but one that also blurs the stark divisions between East and West.

## Metabolist Geometry

A cornerstone of Kurokawa's design philosophy was his principle of "abstract symbolism" in the form of "discernable geometric figures, which were intended to express traditional cultural symbols of Kazakhstan."[320] This universalizing Platonic concept enabled formal geometry to be applied to the visual expression of the city and to be infused into all aspects of its civic design. Kurokawa believed that forms such as triangles, cones, and crescents symbolize fundamental constituents of creation and the traditional aesthetics of nomadic people. His reification of geometry echoes the Florentine architect, Antonio Averlino (1400–69), who referred to himself as Filarete ("lover of virtue") and whose design for the ideal city of Sforzinda (1464) was inspired by the idea that cities should reflect unchanging principles of geometry and symbolic correspondences, as conduits for the enhancement of virtue and the mitigation of vice. Filarete outlines these principles in his *Treatise on Architecture* (ca. 1462–64) in which he synthesizes anthropomorphism, functionality, and humanism with the mysticoreligious geometry of medieval Masonic theory and practice.[321] The evidence of Kurokawa's use of this geometric coding can be found in the circular footprint of Bayterek, which is circumscribed by two interlocking squares in a manner that echoes Filarete's scheme for Sforzinda. Its radial layout was created by the superimposition of two squares within a circle on the very spot Filarete planned to construct a symbolic central tower (Fig. 102).

Utopian cities are almost exclusively laid out upon strict geometric lines to show dominion over the chaotic forces of the natural world. Embedded in the architecture of Astana are a potpourri of geometric elements (circles, triangles, and diamonds) that are wedded to zoomorphic figurations (rams, camels, and birds) and a wide variety of botanical symbols and representations. Kurokawa intended these elements to connect in configurations endowed with spiritual principles, much in the same way that Buddhist mandalas represent a microcosm of the universe. Kurokawa's design language incorporates Buddhist ideas on a grand urban scale and draws upon the musings of the ancient Indian sage, Nagarjuna (150–250 CE), who "inspires us to rethink architecture along the lines of semiology or semantics."[322]

Kurokawa adapted his notion of "flux and mutation" from the *I Ching*, a foundational text of Taoist divination and philosophy, which profoundly impacted Japanese urbanism and the periodic reconstruction of the Ise Grand Shrine. The symbolic rebuilding that celebrates the fundamental idea of regeneration in Shintoism became an essential source of inspiration for Kurokawa's Master Plan for Astana. In Shinto architecture, each decorative scheme acts as a microcosm of the universe, a commentary on tribal affiliations, the Circle of Life, the Five Elements (Earth, Air, Water, Fire, and Ether), and the union of male and female opposites.[323] Circles, in particular, permeate the design of Astana as the representation of perfection, the course of time, natural cycles, the shape of the sun, and infinity.

## The Order of Nature

The rhythmic linear patterns of scrolling and interlacing foliage, tendrils, lines, formal symmetry, and fire symbolism in Kazakh ornamentation indicate a rich inheritance from the cultures of the ancient Silk Roads, as well as Islamic and Zoroastrian sources. Originating in the northern steppe of Kazakhstan approximately 3500 years ago, Zoroastrianism was the state religion of the Persian Empire before the rise of Islam in the seventh century CE.[324] Combining monotheism with the cosmogonic struggle between good and evil, the legacy of Zoroastrianism has influenced the mystery cults of the Roman Empire, the Cathars of medieval France, and provided a system of moral precepts that inspired Voltaire, Mozart, and Nietzsche.

For ancient Platonists, the universal order was mathematical and inherent in the Greek word *kosmos*, which expressed the notion of an ordered perfection that conformed to a series of forms, proportions, relationships, and dimensions. The five Platonic Solids (tetrahedron, cube, octahedron, dodecahedron, and icosahedron) were archetypal forms of the five elements that governed the structure of the universe. These polygons regularly inform the aesthetics of Astana and serve as the basis of the city's entire urban design (Fig. 103). This geometric idealism is so well-entrenched that the government launched an educational project called "Geometry of Astana," which uses the buildings of the capital to solve practical geometric problems (Fig. 104). Khan Shatyr mall, for instance, contains a solution for integrated isosceles trapezoids, while

**FIG 103**   Formal geometry is infused in the aesthetics of Astana's main axis.

**FIG 104** Aerial view of the geometric formalism incorporated into the Shabyt Palace of Arts. Architect: Shokhan Mataibekov, 2009.

**FIG 105** Otan-Ana war memorial, Astana.

Astana's Temir Zholy building holds the key to problems of trigonometry, and the Shabyt Palace of Arts proves the degrees of a right-angled triangle.[325]

Such a programme goes far beyond the geometrical truisms propounded by fifteenth-century architects who believed the ideal city should be adapted to the same mathematical rules that governed the harmony of the cosmos. The heretical Catholic rebel, Tommaso Campanella (1568–1639), examined the radial configuration, the unbroken streets, and the cosmological nature of the city in his utopian masterpiece, *City of Sun* (1602). Campanella's work was the inspiration behind Vladimir Lenin's Plan of Monumental Propaganda—his strategical exploitation of monumental art to propagate revolutionary communist ideals.[326] Although decidedly different in context and plan, aesthetic elements of this socialist influence are present in the Otan-Ana Monument in Astana, which is a cross between Moscow's Constitution Monument and the Monument to the Conquerors of Space in the former Soviet Square (Fig. 105).

The Otan-Ana Monument's central feature is an eternal flame, burning steadily to memorialize the heroes that fell during the Jungar invasions and the Great Patriotic War. It is a reminder of the peace and unity of Kazakh nations and an homage to ancient Persia's religious tradition of Zoroastrianism, which is deeply embedded in the cultural territory of Kazakhstan. At the heart of Zoroastrian belief is the worship of Ahura Mazda, who is venerated by sacred flames and eternal fires,

which represent order, beneficence, fairness, piety, and justice.[327] The spontaneous bursts of natural gas along the borders of the Caspian Sea may have served as the main inspiration for the sacred status of fire, according to Reshad Karimov.[328] Like many of the great treasures in Astana, we find in the Otan-Ana Monument the astonishing fusion of world cultures and beliefs, from sixteenth-century utopian literature to Leninist reforms and Zoroastrian ritual. We also see the unexpected imprint of Johannes Itten (1888–1967), the mystic *Bauhaus* teacher whose Expressionist designs were inspired by the neo-Zoroastrian fire cult of Mazdaznan, which flourished in Germany during the formative period of architectural Modernism.[329]

The inceptive aim of city planning was to promote the building of a harmonious world endowed with divine mathematics and rational purpose, and, in doing so, to uphold the highest expression of virtue, dignity, and glory. As the kernel of all advancement, truth, and mystery, geometry was considered to be a kind of touchstone of sacred power that held within it the possibility to recreate the Divine in physical form—a veritable blueprint for the mind of God. Renaissance luminaries Leon Battista Alberti and Andrea Palladio presented the alluring idea that everything in nature was determined by inviolable geometric rules.[330] Le Corbusier, for whom "Geometry was the language of man," developed a system of mathematical order and harmony bound to the proportional mysticism of the Golden Section and the Fibonacci series. He described these as rhythms "at the very root of human activities ... [and which] resound in man by an organic inevitability."[331] According to J.K. Birkstead, these ideas, along with Pythagoreanism, Freemasonry, and the occult, were a vital part of Le Corbusier's design philosophy and the spiritual rebirth he imagined his buildings would engender.[332]

The very notion of universal harmony found in nature also informs the designs of Manfredi Nicoletti's bright aquamarine Central Concert Hall in Astana, which is distinguished by a corolla-shaped shell that unfolds like an origami flower. The Italian architect's "Flower of the Steppes" is a marvel of technical geometry constructed around a configuration of overlapping veils made of concrete with glass-panel cladding. The petal-shaped structure epitomizes Nicoletti's brand of "sustainable bioclimatic architecture," as it provides geometric protection from the extreme weather of the steppe. Nicoletti's theory of design rests on the creation of energy-efficient buildings inspired by expressive morphologic articulations. He draws on the interrelated connections between the environment and cultural values, through the lenses of a diverse range of disciplines, such as psychology, anthropology, biology, engineering, botany, urban history, acoustics, and the economy.[333]

A bird's-eye view of his Concert Hall reveals the distinct shape of the *vesica piscis*, a pointed elliptical figure produced by the intersection of two equal circles passing through each other at their midpoints (Fig. 106). For medieval Freemasons, formulations of the vesica piscis constituted an advanced system of architectural knowledge, and they functioned as a master key to unlocking the geometric secrets encoded into ecclesiastical buildings. This mysterious motif was employed in the plans and elevations of dozens of medieval abbeys and Gothic cathedrals, including at Carlisle, Worcester, Cologne, and Chartres in France. For Cesare Cesariano (1476–1543), the first commentator on Vitruvius, the vesica piscis and complex system of circles, triangles, squares, and hexagons informed the design of Milan Cathedral. Gothic proportions can be conceived as a type of Masonic code formulated by mystical laws of geometry, the vesica piscis, and rules of triangulation.[334] Numerous pseudotheories have been advanced on the origins and meaning of the vesica piscis. Though it first appears in Proposition One of Euclid's *Elements* (ca. 300 BCE), some have posited a secret historical genealogy descending from a long line of Gnostic adepts who transmitted it to the Masonic fraternity, where it was incorporated into the brotherhood's signs, symbols, and degrees.[335] By grounding their lore in an idealized image of order and geometry, Freemasons made use of a universal language of harmony and conceived a utopian society based on the same principles by which master-builders constructed ancient temples. Hence, it is fitting that the most enduring of all Masonic symbols—the pyramid—should make such a conspicuously bold statement in the cityscape of Astana.

**FIG 106** Aerial view of the Central Concert Hall, "The Flower of the Steppes," featuring the *mandorla* of a vesica piscis.

Front entrance of the Pyramid of Peace. Architects: Foster + Partners, 2006.

CHAPTER SIX

# Demythologizing Astana

*Many people are deceived by the façade of a structure; it is the unusual mind that perceives
what the artist took great pains to tuck away in some inner nook.* [336]
Phaedrus

## *The Masonic Myth*

Remarkably, Astana has gained more Internet acclaim for its reputation as an alleged command centre of global Freemasonry than it has for being a modern civic utopia built from scratch on the unremitting steppe. Its futuristic architecture and extraordinary feats of engineering—including its giant glass pyramid, the world's largest tent, and an enormous aluminum spaceship—have led misinformed pundits to reach the same ominous conclusion: Freemasonry must be behind it (Fig. 107). The only merit to these claims is that many of the daring buildings in Astana carry on the legacy of Étienne-Louis Boullée and Claude-Nicolas Ledoux, two visionary architects who were at the heart of Freemasonry's engagement with public architecture two centuries earlier.[337] Amid the revolutionary fervour of Enlightenment France, Ledoux and Boullée appealed to the mysticism of Freemasonry and the Masonic promise that architecture could lead to social harmony and the amelioration of the world.[338]

Dedicated to self-improvement and charity, Freemasonry underwent a transformation in the 1640s, when it shifted from being a guild of "operative" stonemasons to becoming "a peculiar system of morality, veiled in allegory and illustrated by symbols."[339] Within a century membership rocketed, and soon included such luminaries as Voltaire (1694–1778), Frederick

**FIG 107** Astana Circus building at night. Architect: Tolegen Abilda, 2005.

the Great (1712–86), Benjamin Franklin (1705–90), George Washington (1732–99), Mozart (1756–91), Count Stroganov of Russia (1733–1811), as well as the most illustrious Russian writers and social critics of the period, such as Mikhail Shcherbatov (1733–90), the leading exponent of the Russian Enlightenment (Fig. 108).[340] For Stephen Baehr, this proliferation of Freemasonry in Russian society was a critical aspect of a propagandistic "Paradise Myth" in Russian literature and culture.[341] He further argues that this megamyth served as a powerful ideological tool for portraying Russia as a paradisiacal Eden and extolling the Tsar as a divine mediator in the restoration of the world. This golden age of utopian social order has ostensibly striking parallels to Nazarbayev and Astana.[342] While the brotherhood influenced the intellectual, cultural, and social climate of eighteenth-century Russia and introduced Western cosmopolitan ideas about nature, social order, and science, Freemasonry as an institution has had no direct impact on the architectural advancement of Astana.[343]

The Renaissance historian, Frances Yates, astutely notes that "the origins of Freemasonry is one of the most debated, and debatable, subjects in the whole realm of historical enquiry."[344] To the layman, the brotherhood evokes fears of world domination by an elite coterie who enjoys privileged access to wealth and power. The rigid secrecy of its rites has spawned countless conspiracy theories and condemnations, including sixteen papal pronouncements denouncing the fraternity as an agent of political sedition in league with the Devil.[345] Infernal agendas aside, the brotherhood's greatest threat to Rome was that it potently disseminated Enlightenment ideas and that Masonic lodges were places where individuals of diverse backgrounds and distinctions of rank dissolved into an egalitarian credo of sociability.[346] For Margaret Jacob, Freemasonry was a force of social change and a vehicle for political reform, which anticipated modern civil society and played a pivotal role in the formation of democratic ideology and constitutional rhetoric.[347]

The history of Freemasonry has been treated at length elsewhere, but a few essential details warrant mentioning, bearing in mind that there is no reliable consensus on the formation of the institution either as a benevolent social club or as a medieval brotherhood of builders.[348] The first recorded use of the term "Freemason" is found in the 1325 London Coroners' Rolls, as an abbreviation of a "free-stone" mason, a highly-skilled artisan who could "freely" sculpt stone in any direction.[349] The earliest surviving testimonies of Freemasonry are the so-called Regius and Cooke Manuscripts, composed in the second quarter of the fifteenth century, which provide legendary histories of architecture and the stonemasons' craft.[350] According to David Stevenson, the origins of Freemasonry reside in Scotland, where at the close of the sixteenth century, masons met in "lodges" in order to discuss an initiatory system of "degrees" that combined the geometric secrets of the medieval master-builders with Hermetic philosophy and Renaissance mysticism (Fig. 109).[351] The Scottish genesis led the lodges to organize on a territorial basis, and to hold regular meetings

**FIG 108**  *George Washington Laying the Cornerstone of the National Capitol by Allyn Cox (1896–1982), 1952.*

FIG 109   *Building the Temple Within* by Peter Waddell, 2005.

**FIG 110**  *King Solomon and the Iron Worker* by Christian Schussele (1824–79), 1863.

**FIG 111**  *The Pyramid at the Château de Maupertuis* by Claude-Louis Châtelet (1753–95), ca. 1785.

through which "non-operative" or "speculative" stonemasons could become members of the fraternity.

The principles of Freemasonry are more than 800 years old, and its members infused the art of building with a sense of mystery, meaning, and mythical symbolism unprecedented in the history of architecture. Freemasons ascribed esoteric meanings to the working tools of medieval craftsmanship—the gauge, chisel, gavel, plumb rule, level, and square became symbolic guides for spiritual illumination and ethical probity. According to Masonic legend, the legendary hero and architect, Hiram Abiff, established the brotherhood during the construction of King Solomon's Temple in Jerusalem (Fig. 110). The Temple of Solomon is the central leitmotif of Freemasonry—an emblematic reminder of what has been lost, and hopefulness for what may be recovered in a Mason's personal development. Masonic rituals imbue the construction of the Temple with spiritual significance and illustrate how the candidate metaphorically transforms "rough stone" (man, in an ignorant, unpolished state) into "perfect ashlar," which represents "expanded intellect, controlled passions, and purified life."[352] Within the confines of a lodge (itself a facsimile of the original Temple in Jerusalem), Freemasons provide an allegorical path to virtue interwoven with moral philosophy, secret passwords, and Masonic signs.[353]

Much of the architecture of the eighteenth century was inspired by the utopian tenets of Freemasonry. In Paris alone, between the years 1774 and 1789, more than 120 architects were listed as members of Masonic lodges, many of whom were prominent in the development of Neo-Classicism, either as authors of influential texts or by executing important designs.[354] The important architect and Freemason, Nicolas Le Camus de Mézières (1721–93), defined the role of architecture as an "expressive language" that could evoke human sensations, arouse the intellect, as well as "speak to the mind and move the soul."[355] Even Marc-Antoine Laugier, who first formulated the Primitive Hut theory in an essential work of Neo-Classicism, *Essai sur l'Architecture* (1753), had links to the Masonic brotherhood.[356] During this period, the symbolic and allegorical aspects of antiquity were seen as embodiments of the most august truths, and Masonic ceremonies were mined as repositories of ancient wisdom, lost antiquity, and human understanding.[357]

Freemasonry was thought to represent a hidden stream of architectural mysticism inherited from ancient Egypt, and this idea played a profound role in the design of several picturesque gardens in Enlightenment France. Racine de Monville's Le Désert de Retz and Montesquieu's Elysée at Maupertuis were designed as moral lessons, motivated by the Masonic idea of a "journey of initiation," and reconstructed ideas derived from the Egyptian practice of passing through an open court (Fig. 111).[358] It was believed that the exemplars of ritual initiation were Egyptian in origin, and that the ruins of their great temples were the remains of ancient ritual structures and prototypes that informed the development of higher Masonic degrees. The Martinist mystic, Jean-Baptiste Willermoz (1730–1824), posited that Egyptian architecture had been deliberately constructed to affect the state of mind of the initiate:

*Thus the Triangular form of the pyramids, which in Egypt cover the underground vaults destined for initiations, the form and number of the Routes that lead there, all the ceremonies that were there observed, offered to the aspirants a sense of mystery, relating to the principal object of initiation.*[359]

Collectively, the notions of a "Paradise Myth" linked to social utopianism, expressive architecture, and Masonic ideas about Egyptian initiation are joined together in the most profound urban statement in Astana—the Palace of Peace and Reconciliation, ubiquitously known as the Pyramid (Fig. 112).

## Pyramid of Peace

The Pyramid of Astana is dedicated to the renunciation of bigotry and violence, and to the promotion of peace and human equality. Like the entire city, it is endowed with symbolic, mythic, and numerological meaning. The Pyramid is a modern cathedral of world faith and an exemplification of the national character of a country committed to religious accord. A professedly non-denominational structure, this imposing showpiece is Kazakhstan's architectural response to the First Amendment to the United States Constitution. Although perceived by an armada of Internet sleuths as an occult symbol of a Masonic New World Order, the construction of the Pyramid is best understood within the context of Western architectural epistemology. Enlightenment, monumentality, clarity, and homogeneity are the chief aspects of the Pyramid's design, and its architecture is used to generate a physical manifestation of a perfect hierarchical diagram.[360] Just as the city is the blueprint for the new Kazakhstan, the Pyramid is the symbolic blueprint for the permeation of light over darkness.

Designed by Norman Foster, the Pyramid deliberately echoes the simple, austere, and monumental purism of Étienne-Louis Boullée. Foster's Pyramid embodies Boullée's philosophy, in which geometric solids are "symbols of a transcendent order, representing ethical, aesthetic, and religious values, revealing the pre-established harmony between man and the world."[361] For both Foster and Boullée, the symbol of the Pyramid was synonymous with divinity, and beauty was represented through the fundamental principles of mathematical truth. Boullée's architecture combined gargantuan scale and restrained ornamentation with the sublimity of pure geometric forms. His *Cenotaph to Turenne* (1785) presents an immense pyramid on a pedestal as an expression of the supreme wisdom and timelessness of a primitive architectural form. This is especially prevalent in Boullée's famous *Conical Cenotaph*, which maintains the proportions of an equilateral triangle to impart perfect regularity, beauty, and "the aura of immutability" (Fig. 113).[362]

The Pyramid forms the visual terminus of the urban mall, making it a crucial part of Astana's identity. A civic talisman for the promotion of amity and accord, the Pyramid is situated on

**FIG 113** *Cross-section of the Conical Cenotaph* by Étienne-Louis Boullée, ca. 1785.

a small hill in impressive isolation and brilliantly framed along the central axis by two key monuments—the Kazakh Eli Monument and Khan Shatyr. Initially conceived by Nazarbayev, the Pyramid was designed to be one of the most significant icons in Astana. Since it opened in 2006, Foster's masterpiece has been the permanent home of the Congress of Leaders of World and Traditional Religions, an international forum for spiritual leaders founded to promote tolerance and understanding between faiths. The Congress convenes every three years with delegates representing Islam, Christianity, Buddhism, Judaism, Shinto, Taoism, and Hinduism.

The four sides of the Pyramid are oriented toward the four cardinal directions to symbolize, according to Nazarbayev, the friendly embrace of "the representatives of all nations and faiths."[363] At first, the building was designed to mimic the exact dimensions of the Great Pyramid of Cheops and would have been capable of accommodating 80 000 people in its base. However, the plans changed, and the building was ultimately constructed in accordance with the presumed mysticism of the "divine proportion," or Golden Section (a value of 1.618), measuring 61.8 metres along each side of the base, and 61.8 metres in height.[364] Since its discovery by Euclid (ca. 300 BCE), the Golden Section—also known as the Golden Ratio or the symbol $\varphi$—has been associated with magical properties, the music of Mozart, the flight of birds, the spiral shape of galaxies, the proportions of the human body, and the works of artists ranging from Leonardo da Vinci to Salvador Dalí (Fig. 114).[365]

The commissioning of Norman Foster was as important as the completion of the project since it illustrated Kazakhstan's dedication to international cooperation and global outreach. The Pyramid positions the capital as a privileged window to the religious landscape of the world—a concept attested through both interfaith dialogue and expressed in the form of an architectural monolith that is found on nearly every continent of the globe, from the Americas and Africa to Europe and Asia.[366] The building itself is a symbol of religious unity and a beacon for strengthening mutual understanding while abandoning enmity and discord.

Most striking in Foster's architectural programme are the inherent dualities of the building: the contrasts between light and darkness; its belowground and aboveground sections; its interior and exterior.[367] Its caliginous hollow core extends to the very apex of the structure, where it is transformed into a sublime image of visual illumination. Nothing is alienating about the homogeneity of this project, nor is anything notably Kazakh or distinctly cultural. Nazarbayev chose the pyramidal form immaculately as an ecumenical signifier that appeals to the "universal truth" of all religious faiths.[368]

The journey through the Pyramid is marked by a tripartite procession from darkness to light. Foster modelled this after the shared religious view that the "below" equates Hell, the "middle" represents Earth, and the "above" signifies Heaven (Fig. 115). A literary prototype for this scheme was detailed in Abbé Jean Terrasson's influential novel, *Life of Sethos* (1731), which recalls the initiation of the eponymous Egyptian prince into the mysteries of Isis beneath the Great Pyramid. Although a work of fiction, *Life of Sethos* had an enormous influence on eighteenth-century Masonic ritual and was often cited as the authority on ancient Egyptian religion.[369] Mozart and Schikaneder's Masonic opera *The Magic Flute* (1791) was likewise based on the adventures of Sethos, whose trials by Fire (below), Water (middle), and Air (above) were graphically replicated in Jean-Jacques Lequeu's extraordinary designs for a cavernous Masonic lodge called the Gothic House.

The Pyramid is accessed through a tenebrous subterranean foyer clad with dark wood and black granite. Glazed diamond-shaped windows diffuse light into the central atrium hall where darkness is pervasive, but intentionally so, as it is used to arrange a hierarchy of contrasts that ascend from subterranean darkness to progressively brighter light (Fig. 116). The Sufi master, Ibn 'Arabi (1165–1240), used the same metaphor—the gradation of light from a single source—to describe the relationship between the phenomenal world and the absolute being of God.[370] The interplay of light and shade is a vital component of Indo-Islamic architecture as illustrated by the perforated stone screen or *jali*. The sides of the Pyramid are opaque and animated by shifting patterns of coloured light, but the uppermost level reveals the luminescent Congress Chamber. The Chamber is designed to underscore the building's commitment to religious peace by filling the space with maximal lighting, which streams through stained glass imprinted with Doves of Peace and panels representing Kazakhstan's 130 different ethnicities (Fig. 117).

## From Congress to Light

Light is the Pyramid's fundamental element—the quintessence around which the structure is organized, and the ultimate source of the divine in architecture since the earliest of times.[371] The orientation of Egyptian temples corresponded with the processional path of the sun and likewise, in Classical Greece, sanctuaries were aligned to permit the sun's rays to illuminate the cult statue in the inner shrine.[372] By the first century CE, Roman architects of the Pantheon had mastered the physics of light in such a way that at midday on April 21, the anniversary of Rome, a single sunbeam entering the oculus would flood the entire entrance with light, making the perfectly spherical building a sundial for divine rule.[373] Similarly, the octagonal Baptistery of Parma produces dazzling lighting effects that record the traditional feast days of St John the Baptist (June 24) and the Purification of Mary (February 2). For Easter, from March 25 to April 1, a ray of light strikes a painting of the Baptism of Jesus on the upper copula.[374]

Throughout the history of sacred architecture, light simulated the divine presence and symbolized the act of creation. One of the finest examples of the sovereignty of light is found at the Nasir al-Mulk Mosque in Shiraz, Iran, where the morning sun pierces stained glass windows to produce a kaleidoscope of iridescent colours and radiance (Fig. 118). In the Middle Ages, the soaring spaces of ecclesiastical architecture represented a model of the cosmos and reflected Neoplatonic theologies of divine light and geometrical beauty. In the Renaissance, Vincenzo Scamozzi (1548–1616)

**FIG 114** *The Sacrament of the Last Supper* by Salvador Dalí (1904–89), 1955.

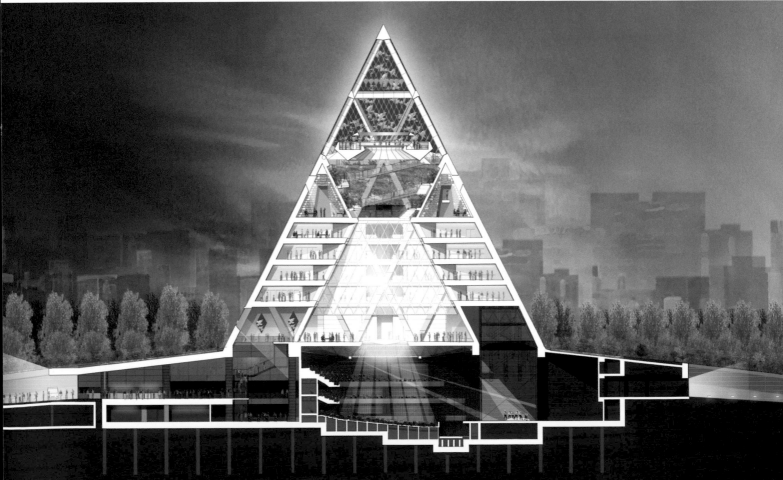

**FIG 115** Elevation and schematic rendering of the Pyramid of Peace and Reconciliation.

**FIG 116** Central hall, Pyramid of Peace.

defined half a dozen types of lighting schemes and proposed a systematic typology of architectural illumination.[375] The brilliant architectural innovator, Sir John Soane (1753–1837), adopted elements of Scamozzi's choreography of light in the design of the Council Chamber for his Freemasons' Hall in 1828 (Fig. 119). Soane's Chamber was arranged to emulate the solemnity of Masonic ritual with a sombre mixture of coloured lighting, sequencing, and décor.[376] The spectacular focal point of Soane's design was a domical lantern that admitted particular segments of light to map the zodiacal constellations onto the floor, further echoing the ceremonial atmosphere of Masonic dramaturgy.[377]

Foster expands on Soane's tradition of splendour and luminosity in the Pyramid, where light unites the order of the building's spaces to the universal mandates of the Congress. Four pillars, dubbed the "Hands of Peace," hold up the Congress Chamber, which houses a round table for religious discussion, surrounded by lush hanging gardens. A connecting ring beam allows the table to function as the oculus, where the advocacy of toleration and unity are expressed at the apex of the Pyramid. The association between the elevation of the Pyramid and the activities of the Congress are attuned by the progressive filtering of sunlight in a manner reminiscent of the stained glass windows in Gothic churches, such as those of the royal chapel of Sainte-Chapelle in Paris (1248), which narrate a complete Christological itinerary from Creation to the Resurrection.

The arcane aspects of architecture appealed to Foster, who once commissioned a Feng Shui geomancer to assist him with the alignment and ventilation of his HSBC headquarters in Hong Kong.[378] Through the reification of light and transparency emphasized by the use of glass and other reflective surfaces, the Pyramid engages with the principles of architectural mysticism. Foster used a comparable approach in his renovation of the Reichstag building in Berlin, where light peering in from the cupola symbolizes the political transparency of the new Federal Parliament of Germany. Similarly, the material transparency of the Pyramid symbolizes the new open identity of Kazakhstan and the necessary conditions required for religious tolerance.[379]

The Congress occupies the atrium, which is focused metaphorically upward into an epiphanic *sanctum sanctorum*. The agendas of the Congress are thus concretized into declarations of peace, unity, stability, and security as they are broadcast from a pinnacle beacon of light. Light not only demarcates the hierarchical importance of the programme, but is also tied symbolically to the Congress's activities and the philosophical organization of the building.[380] To access the Chamber, the delegates must first take lifts up to a garden-like reception space. There, a winding ramp leads up to the topmost floor and the official convening place of the assembly. A broad glass lens set in the floor of the atrium casts light down into the auditorium of the underground Opera house and creates a sense of vertical continuity from the lowest level of the building to the very top. A spectacular open-air performance

More than a progression of futuristic buildings and monumental construction, the architecture of Astana is a type of palimpsest upon which to write a new foundation myth about the peaceful coexistence of the human family.

**FIG 117** Luminous Congress Chamber of the Pyramid of Peace.

**FIG 118** Nasir al-Mulk Mosque in Shiraz, Iran (1876–88).

**FIG 119**  Perspective view of Freemasons' Hall Council Chamber, London, drawn by Joseph Gandy, 1831. Architect: John Soane.

of Verdi's Egyptian opera *Aïda* (1871) was staged in front of the Pyramid in July 2015, complimented by dazzling stage sets by the Italian director, Franco Zeffirelli (Fig. 120).

## Speaking Architecture

In an attempt to preserve a balance between the primacy of rationality and the growing search for truth beyond rational understanding, Ledoux and Boullée introduced a concept called *architecture parlante* (or speaking architecture), which was rooted in the belief that buildings could "speak" their function. By utilizing forms and elements that expressed each building's character, Ledoux endeavoured to capture the true essence of architecture.[381] Speaking architecture also resonates throughout the architecture of Astana as exemplified by the Saryarka Republican Velodrome, which unambiguously communicates its function by its shape—a massive racing helmet. Ledoux's pyramidal Woodcutter's House, cubic Temple of All Virtue (*Panarétheon*), and spherical House of the Agricultural Guards echo the triangle, circle, and square silhouetted by Khan Shatyr Entertainment Centre, the Palace of Independence, and the Nazarbayev Centre, respectively (Fig. 121).

At his utopian Royal Saltworks at Arc-et-Senans in France, Ledoux grafted Masonic principles onto a grand design for social reform.[382] He even prefigured Bayterek and the Pyramid of Peace with his own peculiar social institutions—the Temple of Memory (*Temple de la mémoire*) and the Palace of Reconciliation (*Pacifère*)—both dedicated to universal fraternity and the happiness of humankind. Ledoux's poetic style has had an abiding influence on the development of architecture in Astana, and in many respects Ledoux and Nazarbayev are part of the same architectural revolution and employ the same agencies of social change. Ledoux's design for a Hoopmaker's Workshop was characterized by its circular, barrel-like façade and his Brothel took the form of a giant phallus, while his plan for the Theatre of Besançon was reflected through the "All-Seeing Eye" of the Supreme Being, a pervasive symbol in the iconography of Freemasonry (Fig. 122).

In 2013, Norman Foster completed an All-Seeing Eye of his own with the Nazarbayev Centre as a complement to his majestic glass pyramid. The Nazarbayev Centre distinctly epitomizes Ledoux's stereometric designs and Boullée's grand urban vision in the form of a modern Benthamesque panopticon that peers into the blue sky of the Great Steppe (Fig. 123). Aimed at strengthening national patriotism and civic identity, the Nazarbayev Centre is a non-profit humanitarian and educational institution dedicated to the promotion of international cooperation in the areas of science, culture, politics, and economics. In addition to undertaking research into the history of Kazakhstani statehood and ethnography, the Nazarbayev Centre serves a valuable international role as a beacon broadcasting Kazakhstan's role in the world community.

More than any other building, the Nazarbayev Centre is the complete summation of the country's pan-national mythos and its

**FIG 120**  Outdoor production of *Aïda*, Pyramid of Peace entrance.

**FIG 121** Nazarbayev Centre. Architects: Foster + Partners, 2013.

commitment to global peace, inter-ethnic harmony, and sustainable development. Although this architectural landmark appears to incontrovertibly authenticate the existence of a "New World Order of Eurasian Freemasonry," it is important to note that the All-Seeing Eye was only recently appropriated into the symbolism of Freemasonry to denote the Great Architect of the Universe.[383] Usage of the eye symbol predates the Freemasons, stretching back to the earliest periods of human civilization, beginning with the famous Eye Temple in the ancient city of Tell Brak (ca. 3200 BCE), one of the earliest known sites of organized religion in modern-day Syria. Similarly, the image of the All-Seeing Eye on the back of the Great Seal of the United States has no exclusive relationship to Freemasonry, since it first appeared set within a triangle in a Roman Catholic context as attested by Jacopo Pontormo's painting of 1525, where it serves as a symbol of the Trinity, divine watchfulness, and care over the universe.[384]

## House of Ministries

The House of Ministries stretches for nearly a kilometre across the main axis of the capital, and the two-row arrangement of the building demonstrates an organizing principle of Kurokawa's Master Plan. The astounding length of the building can only be appreciated from a bird's-eye view, and evokes the enormous wingspan of government bureaucracy in the outstretched wings of the mythic Simurgh. Situated right in front of the Presidential Palace, the complex accommodates nearly all govern-

ment ministries. It is a comprehensive temple of state administration—its two gleaming golden columns evoking the twin pillars that stood at the forecourt of Solomon's Temple in Jerusalem. The two pillars, called Jachin (establishment) and Boaz (strength), became recurring motifs in the canon of Western architecture from Würzburg Cathedral (ca. 1215) in Bavaria to Frank Lloyd Wright's milestone of Modern architecture—the Larkin Administration Building in Buffalo (1904; destroyed in 1950). They also hold specific connotations within the mysteries of Freemasonry and are frequently present in Masonic lodge architecture and tracing boards, where they symbolize the Entered Apprentice and Fellow Craft degrees (Fig. 124).

Since its destruction by the Babylonians in 586 BCE, Solomon's Temple has come to represent the *beau ideal* of lost perfection. Its legacy has been assimilated into the designs of the Hagia Sophia in Istanbul (532–37), the Notre-Dame in Paris (1163–1345), and the Sistine Chapel in Rome (ca. 1475–81), whose interior proportions mirror those of Solomon's Temple.[385] In Freemasonry, the Temple represents the culmination of an initiatic science of geometry allegedly descended from Adam and the quintessential model of divine architecture and societal amelioration.[386] The tripartite structure of the Temple—divided into a vestibule, an elongated nave, and a sanctuary (which housed the Ark of the Covenant)—has been extensively commented upon in Judeo-Christian literature. Philo of Alexandria (ca. 25 BCE–50 CE) proposed the configuration of the Temple as a microcosm of the universe and a metaphysical model of

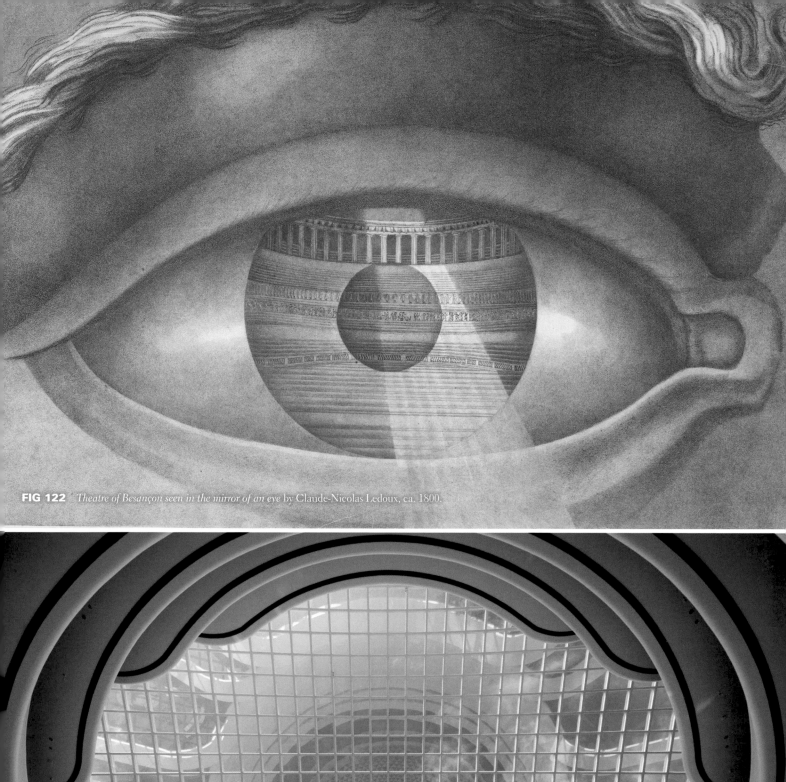

**FIG 122** *Theatre of Besançon seen in the mirror of an eye by Claude-Nicolas Ledoux, ca. 1800.*

**FIG 123** Interior view, Nazarbayev Centre, as a panopticon toward the sky.

**FIG 124** *Second Degree Tracing Board*, featuring the twin pillars of Solomon's Temple. By John Harris (1791–1873), 1844.

human salvation. In Jewish mysticism, it was a celestial abode and the spiritual climax of a treacherous voyage through ascending levels of the divine mystery.[387] This association was elaborated upon in the Qu'ran with Muhammad's "night journey" (Sura 17:1), an ascent to heaven from the site of the Temple, which became a foundational motif in Islamic mysticism.[388] For medieval Christian authors, the three compartments of the Temple constituted the purgative, illuminative, and unitive stages of mystical progress, while Renaissance theorists proposed the Temple was an exemplar of architectural magic.[389]

The design of the yurt also reflects this tripartite magical character, being comprised of the Lower World (inside the door frame), the Middle World (the hearth in the centre), and the Upper World (the place of highest honour opposite the entrance and reserved for elders). Just as the Temple was thought a microcosm of the universe, the yurt brought to mind the cosmos in miniature: the roof was the sky, shangïraq, or "eye of heaven."[390] The hearth, which should never be crossed, was the axis mundi, uniting the Lower, Middle, and Upper Worlds. These worlds are also associated with three musical instruments that embody the traditional beliefs of Kazakh people: the *kobyz*, the *dombra*, and the *sybyzgy*—an open flute that whistles the melody of the Upper World.[391] A similar threefold division was found in ancient Tengrianism and consisted of Heaven, Human, and Earth, which corresponded to the military and political structure of the Turkic Khanate.

The layout and measurements of the Temple have had a profound influence on urban design. In the twentieth century, the perennial images of the original Temple appeared in Otto Wagner's idealized design of the XXII district of Vienna and in Bruno Taut's proposed design of an immense circular Garden City for three million inhabitants. The centrepiece of Taut's chiliastic vision of urban reform was the "City Crown," a crystalline super-temple that symbolized the shared spiritual hopes of society.[392] Taut's utopian longing for the reconstruction of society is analogous to both Masonic perceptions of Solomon's Temple as a vehicle for moral enlightenment, and Nazarbayev's ambition to make Astana the spiritual lighthouse of the world. Inspired by the Temple of Solomon, Taut recommended a suprapolitical utopia, where the citizenry, as in Astana, would come together around a sacred glass urban crown, such as Bayterek. Thus, Astana embodies a version of humanity's future city—a harmonious paradisiacal place in which perfection and purity are symbolized by a communal crystal ball and two glittering golden towers (Fig. 125).

## World Expo

Ledoux and Boullée's *architecture parlante* has been reinvigorated in Adrian Smith and Gordon Gill's designs for Astana's 2017 World Expo, which is dedicated to the development and promotion of sustainable energy. The entire project was conceived as a city within a city, and the government has committed an enormous budget estimated between three

**FIG 125** Golden towers (pillars) of the House of Ministries.

and five billion US dollars.[393] The entire Expo site is a model sustainable eco-city that generates more energy than it uses through a combination of turbines and solar panels integrated into many of its buildings. The central Kazakhstan Pavilion is equipped with a transformative skin that reduces thermal loss and interior solar glare (Fig. 126). As a "symbol of life, around which everything is organized," the Pavilion revivifies Boullée's cenotaph for Isaac Newton (1784), which similarly symbolized nature, perfection, and majesty though a mammoth geometric sphere (Fig. 127). The spherical shape itself is a recurring component of utopian projects, and has appeared in the work of Russian Constructivists and Buckminster Fuller, in Florida's EPCOT, and in the Hangzhou International Conference & Exhibition Centre in China.[394]

Hosting the first ever World Expo in Central Asia marks a turning point in Kazakhstan's pedigree on the international stage. The entire venue has been designed according to the five pillars of Jeremy Rifkin's *Third Industrial Revolution* (2011), which relies on Internet technology and renewable energy to usher in a fundamental reordering of human society. These five pillars are: 1) shifting to renewable energy; 2) converting to energetically self-sufficient buildings; 3) deploying hydrogen storage technologies in every building; 4) using Internet technology to transform the power grid; and 5) transitioning the transport fleet to electric and fuel cell vehicles.[395] The site underwent an extensive evaluation so that each of the Expo's twenty-eight structures would harness the sun, wind, and other elements for optimal energy generation. The buildings incorporate high-performance glazing and maximal solar heat gain in the winter, while providing necessary shade in the summer. Each structure has also been designed to harvest rainwater and according to the architects, the site's "legacy development will be one of the most sustainably built in the world."[396] From 2018 on, the Expo site will house the Astana International Financial Centre and a cutting-edge economic hub for the development of green technologies and investment projects.[397]

The ambitions of Astana's World Expo echo those of the World of Tomorrow, which was first presented at the New York World's Fair of 1939–40. The World of Tomorrow featured a diorama called "Democracity" that depicted a futuristic utopian city that promised ease and prosperity in the form of a semicircular collection of buildings, prefiguring the Shabyt Palace of Arts in Astana. Consisting of a concave ring of shimmering blue glass, the Palace of Arts is a circular temple to the muses and a multidisciplinary institution occupying over 30 000 square metres of space. Taking the form of a monolithic crater, its hollowed-out slanted cone is meant to symbolize the essence of human creativity and the natural elements, while its triangular cross section is inclined toward Independence Square. The impending World Expo signifies Kazakhstan's readiness to be an equal participant in international affairs. Modernity here is utopian and ideological, and a forward-looking Kazakhstani nation is asserting itself as a sustainable urban paradise that embodies what Nazarbayev calls Kazakhstan's "way to the stars" (Fig. 128).[398]

FIG 126    Central Kazakhstan Pavilion at the World Expo grounds, Astana. Architects: Adrian Smith + Gordon Gill, 2015.

FIG 127    Cenotaph to Newton by Étienne-Louis Boullée, 1784.

**FIG 128** Central Kazakhstan Pavilion at the World Expo grounds, Astana. Architects: Adrian Smith + Gordon Gill, 2013.

**FIG 129** *Ossian Receiving the Ghosts of the Fallen French Heroes by A.L.G. de Roussy-Trioson (1767–1824), ca. 1801.*

# EPILOGUE

In the 1760s, James Macpherson (1736–96) published a collection of folk poems that were attributed to Ossian, a semi-mythical Gaelic bard in the vein of Homer. Purporting to be the remains of an ancient Celtic epic, the poems were devoured in twenty-six languages and attracted passionate devotees, including Diderot, Jefferson, Goethe, Robert Burns, and Napoleon, who carried a copy of Ossian's poems on all of his military campaigns (Fig. 129).[399] Despite being unmasked as "the most successful literary falsehood in modern history," Ossian remained an international sensation and had an enormous influence on the Romantic Movement in Germany, the Gaelic Revival in Ireland, and nineteenth-century nationalism in Scotland.[400] In no small measure, the Ossian epic has also impelled this book—not in being a lavish fabrication, but in advancing a pan-national myth compiled from genuine selections and fragments of a nearly forgotten ancient

culture. In addition to preserving the spirit of The Inklings and seventeenth-century Rosicrucianism, this work also carries on the legacy of Mukhtar Auezov (1897–1961), the Kazakh counterrevolutionary scholar who recast the lauded poet Abai into a heroic patriot and the *pater familias* of the modern Kazakhstani state.[401] His epic biography, *The Way of Abai* (1942–56), remains a national treasure, "a kind of Odyssey of the Kazakh people," in which we discover that more than anything else, myth and imagination epitomize the soul of Kazakhstan.[402]

While the Egyptian, Sumerian, Indus, and Yellow River valley cultures regularly take precedence as the progenitors of human civilization, the modern world is also indebted to the Proto-Indo-Europeans who migrated on horseback across the vast steppe and discovered the so-called Cradles of Civilizations. Stretching over 2000 kilometres, the remarkable cultures of the Great Steppe inspired new science, arts, and methods of warfare, and advanced the development of Mesopotamia, Persia, China, India, Byzantium, Poland, and Hungary. As we have seen, where our ancestors thrived was in the heart of Eurasia, where civilization was born, and where the first migratory routes populated the world. It was on this basis that modern Kazakhstan formalized a state rooted in the political, economic, social, and cultural traditions of both the East and the West.

Kazakhstan operates as a quiet global leader in the three areas most needed for the stability and prosperity of the world: religious tolerance, nuclear non-proliferation, and ecological sustainability. These powerful themes form the fruit-bearing seeds of the foundation myth of Astana. Whereas other foundation myths are chiefly insular and xenophobic, in Astana, myth serves as the basis of an inclusive global politic and world society. This book has charted a fascinating journey across forty millennia, using the breathtaking architecture of Astana to summarize the ideas, discoveries, and achievements that have made Kazakhstan an exemplary model for the direction of current affairs. This is the untold story of how President Nazarbayev laid the foundation for a modern civic utopia rooted in the fellowship of multiculturalism, ethnic harmony, and religious accord, and how the architecture and institutions of Kazakhstani statecraft have been used to celebrate the innate genius of humankind. Perhaps no other nation has silently etched so deep a mark in the development of early civilization or been more progressive in laying the groundwork for a peaceful global community.

"The Kazakhstan Way" turns out to be a state of mind, a worldview coterminous with the ideals of freedom and happiness among all nations and people of the world. More than a progression of futuristic buildings and monumental construction, the architecture of Astana is a type of palimpsest upon which to write a new foundation myth about the peaceful coexistence of the human family. On the surface, Astana seems to embody ostentation, nationalistic megalomania, and even Masonic symbolism; however, behind this gilded veil is an urban narrative of substance, meaning, and power. This book began by introducing three key inventions that were responsible for seeding early civilization: the domestication of the horse, the dispersal of Indo-European language, and the invention of the wheel. It is fitting, then, that it concludes by coming full circle to rearticulate three equally important Central Asian advancements essential to our survival in the globalized world: ecological sustainability, religious tolerance, and nuclear disarmament. This dream, this destiny, is enshrined in the architecture of Astana.

Central promenade of Astana.

# BIBLIOGRAPHY

Abazov, Rafis. *Culture and Customs of the Central Asian Republics.* Westport; London: Greenwood Press, 2007.

Abazov, Rafis, and Arystanbek Mukhamediuly. "Kazakhstan Plans to Rewrite Its Innovation Strategy by Hosting EXPO-2017: Will It Work?" *Central Asia-Caucasus Institute Analysts,* Article published September 4, 2013. http://www.cacianalyst.org/publications/analytical-articles/item/12807-kazakhstan-plans-to-rewrite-its-innovation-strategy-by-hosting-expo-2017-will-it-work?.html.

Acharya, Prasanna Kumar. *Architecture of Mānasāra.* London; New York: Oxford University Press, 1933.

Adler, Hans, and Wulf Koepke, eds. *A Companion to the Works of Johann Gottfried Herder.* Rochester: Camden House, 2009.

Aeschylus. *Prometheus Bound.* Edited by Mark Griffith. Cambridge: Cambridge University Press, 1983.

Aitken, Jonathan. *Kazakhstan: Surprises and Stereotypes After 20 Years of Independence.* London: Continuum, 2012.

——. *Nazarbayev and the Making of Kazakhstan.* London: Continuum, 2009.

Akhmetov, Adil. "Migrations of the Ancient Ancestors of American 'Indians' from Asian and their Altaic Origin." *Mangi El* 6:8 (2014): 86–89.

Akishev, Kimal. *Kurgan Issyk: Iskusstvo sakov Kazakhstana (Issyk Mound: The Art of Saka in Kazakhstan).* Moscow: Iskusstvo, 1978.

Akkach, Samer. *Cosmology and Architecture in Premodern Islam: An Architectural Reading of Mystical Ideas.* Albany: State University of New York Press, 2005.

Alberti, Leon Battista. *On the Art of Building in Ten Books.* Translated by Joseph Rykwert, Neil Leach, and Robert Tavernor. Cambridge; London: MIT Press [1450], 1988.

Albo, Frank. "Le Désert de Retz as Masonic Theatre." *Symbolism in 18th Century Gardens: the Influence of Intellectual and Esoteric Currents, such as Freemasonry.* Edited by Andréa Kroon, J.M. Snoek, and M. Scholl. Den Haag: OVN (2006): 197–310.

——. "Masonic Parlante in a Canadian Temple of Democracy: the Manitoba Legislative Building as a Route of Initiation." *Vox Lucis* 28 (2008): 84–130.

——. "Freemasonry and the Nineteenth-Century British Gothic Revival." PhD diss., University of Cambridge, 2012.

Alexander, Catherine, Victor Buchli, and Caroline Humphrey. *Urban Life in Post-Soviet Asia.* London: University College London, 2007.

Alexander, Christopher. *A Pattern Language: Towns, Buildings, Construction.* New York: Oxford University Press, 1977.

——. *The Timeless Way of Building.* New York: Oxford University Press, 1979.

Algar, Hamid. "An Introduction to the History of Freemasonry in Iran." *Middle Eastern Studies* 6:3 (1970): 276–96.

Alimbai, Nursan. "Society and Culture of the Nomads of Central Asia Through Time." *Nomads and Networks: The Ancient Art and Culture of Kazakhstan.* Edited by Sören Stark and Karen Rubinson. Princeton: Princeton University Press, (2012): 153–63.

Alinei, Mario. *Origini delle lingue d'Europa.* Bologna: Mulino, 1996.

——. *Origini delle lingue d'Europa II: Continuità dal Mesolitico all'età del Ferro nelle principali aree etnolinguistiche.* Bologna: Mulino, 2000.

Alinei, Mario, Xaverio Ballester, and Francesco Benozzo. *The Palaeolithic Continuity Paradigm Scientific News,* December 7, 2009, accessed at http://www.continuitas.org/news.html.

Åman, Anders. *Architecture and Ideology in Eastern Europe During the Stalin Era: An Aspect of Cold War History.* Cambridge: MIT Press, 1992.

Anacker, Shonin. "Geographies of Power in Nazarbayev's Astana." *Eurasian Geography and Economics* 45:7 (2013): 515–33.

Anderson, James. *The Constitutions of the Antient and Honourable Fraternity of Free and Accepted Masons…Revised, Continued and Enlarged, with Many Additions by John Entick, M.A.* London: J. Scott, 1767.

Anderson, Richard. *Russia (Modern Architectures in History).* London: Reaktion Books, 2015.

Antelava, Natalia. "Giant Tent to be Built in Astana." *BBC News,* December 9, 2006, accessed at news.bbc.co.uk/2/hi/asia-pacific/6165267.stm.

Anthony, David. *The Horse, the Wheel, and Language.* Princeton: Princeton University Press, 2007.

——. "'The 'Kurgan Culture,' Indo-European Origins, and the Domestication of the Horse: A Reconsideration." *Current Anthropology* 27:4 (1986): 291–313.

Artemyeva, Tatiana. "Utopian Spaces of Russian Masons in the Enlightenment," in *Freemasonry and Fraternalism in Eighteenth-Century Russia.* Edited by Andreas Önnerfors and Robert Collis. Sheffield: University of Sheffield (2009): 63–84.

Aruz, Joan, Ann Farkas, and Elisabetta Valtz Fino, eds. *The Golden Deer of Eurasia: Perspectives on the Steppe Nomads of the Ancient World.* New Haven: Yale University Press, 2006.

Assman, Jan. *Egyptian Solar Religion in the New Kingdom: Re, Amun and the Crisis of Polytheism.* Translated by Anthony Alcock. London; New York: Routledge, 2009.

AstanaGenPlan. *The Master Plan of Astana.* Astana, 2012.

Auezov, Mukhtar. *Abai: A Novel.* Translated by L. Navrozov. Moscow: Progress Publishers, 1968.

Babrius, and Phaedrus. *Fables: Babrius and Phaedrus (Loeb Classical Library No. 436)*. Translated by Ben Perry. Cambridge: Harvard University Press, 1965.

Baehr, Stephen. *The Paradise Myth in Eighteenth-Century Russia: Utopian Patterns in Early Secular Russian Literature and Culture*. Stanford: Stanford University Press, 1991.

Baitanayev, B.A., and Y.A. Yolgin. "Islamic Architecture on the Territory of South Kazakhstan." *Oriente Moderno* 87:1 (2007): 35–52.

Banier, Antoine. *La Mythologie et les Fables Expliquées par l'Histoire*. 3 vols. A Paris: Chez Briasson, 1738–40.

Barczewski, Stephanie L. *Myth and National Identity in Nineteenth-Century Britain*, Oxford: Oxford University Press, 2000.

Barkun, Michael. *A Culture of Conspiracy: Apocalyptic Visions in Contemporary America*. Los Angeles: University of California Press, 2003.

Barruel, Augustin (Abbé). *Memoirs Illustrating the History of Jacobinism*. Translated by Robert Clifford. Fraser: Real-View-Books [1797], 1995.

Barthes, Roland. "The Death of the Author." *Aspen*, no. 5-6 (1967), accessed at http://www.ubu.com/aspen/aspen5and6/threeEssays.html#barthes.

——. "Semiology and the Urban," in *Rethinking Architecture: A Reader in Cultural Theory*. Edited by Neil Leach. London: Routledge, (1997): 158–72.

Basilov, Vladimir, ed. *Nomads of Eurasia*. Translated by Mary Fleming Zirin. Los Angeles; Seattle: University of Washington Press, 1989.

Bater, James. *St. Petersburg: Industrialization and Change*. Montreal: McGill-Queen's University Press, 1976.

Bates, Catherine. *The Cambridge Companion to the Epic*. Cambridge: Cambridge University Press, 2010.

Baudrillard, Jean. *Simulacra and Simulation*. Ann Arbor: University of Michigan Press, 1994.

Bayer, Natalie. "Spreading the Light": European Freemasonry and Russia in the Eighteenth Century. PhD diss., Rice University, 2007.

Beckwith, Christopher. *Empires of the Silk Road: A History of Central Eurasia from the Bronze Age to the Present*. Princeton: Princeton University Press, 2009.

——. *Warriors of the Cloisters: The Central Asian Origins of Science in the Medieval World*. Princeton: Princeton University Press, 2012.

Bekbassar, Nyssanbay. "Astronomical Practices and Ritual Calendar of Euro-Asian Nomads." *Folklore* 31 (2005): 30–120.

Belier, Wouter. *Decayed Gods: Origin and Development of Georges Dumézil's Idéologie Tripartite*. Leiden: Brill, 1991.

Belli, Oktay. "Stone Statues and Balbals in the Turkic World." *Tüba-Ar* 6 (2003): 85–116.

Bellini, Oscar Eugenio and Daglio, Laura. *New Frontiers in Architecture: Dubai Between Vision and Reality*. Vercelli: White Star, 2008.

Beltramini, Guido, and Fulvio Lenzo, eds. *Jefferson and Palladio: Constructing a New World*. Vicenza; Milano: Officina Libraria, 2015.

Bercovitch, Sacvan. *The Puritan Origins of the American Self*. New Haven and London: Yale University Press, 1975.

Berman, Ric. *The Foundations of Modern freemasonry: the Grand Architects – Political Change and the Scientific Enlightenment 1714–1740*. Brighton: Sussex Academic Press, 2012.

Birksted, Jan. *Le Corbusier and the Occult*. Cambridge: MIT Press, 2009.

Bissenova, Alima. "'The Master Plan of Astana: Between the Art of Government and the Art of Being Global." *Ethnographies of the State in Central Asia: Performing Politics*. Edited by Reeves Madeleine, Rasanayagam John, and Beyer Judith, Bloomington: Indiana University Press, (2013): 127–48.

Blackwell, Thomas. *Letters Concerning Mythology*. London: Andrew Millar, 1748.

Blistein, Jon. "Kanye West Criticized for Kazakhstan Performance." *Rolling Stone*. Article published September 4, 2013. http://www.rollingstone.com/music/news/kanye-west-criticized-for-kazakhstan-performance-20130904.

Blumenthal, Ralph "NASA Adds to Evidence of Mysterious Ancient Earthworks." *New York Times*. Article published October 30, 2015. http://www.nytimes.com/2015/11/03/science/nasa-adds-to-evidence-of-mysterious-ancient-earthworks.html.

Boas, Franz. "Migration Of Asiatic Races And Cultures To North America." *Scientific Monthly* 28 (1929): 112–17.

Bogoras, Waldemar. "The Folklore of Northeastern Asia as Compared with that of Northwestern America." *American Anthropologist* 4:4 (1902): 577–683.

Bork, Robert. *The Geometry of Creation: Architectural Drawing and the Dynamics of Gothic Design*. Farnham: Ashgate, 2011.

Bottigheimer, Ruth. *Fairy Tales and Society: Illusion, Allusion, and Paradigm*. Philadelphia: University of Pennsylvania Press, 1986.

Boyce, Mary. *History of Zoroastrianism*. 3 vols. Leiden: Brill, 1975–1991.

Boyer, Christine. *The City of Collective Memory: Its Historical Imagery and Architectural Entertainments*. Cambridge: MIT Press, 1994.

Brasser, Ted J. "The Tipi as an Element in the Emergence of Historic Plains Indian Nomadism." *Plains Anthropologist* 27: 98, Part 1 (1982): 309–21.

Brengues, Jacques, and Monique Mosser. "Le Monde Maçonnique des Lumières." *Histoire des francs-maçons en France vol. 1: 1725-1815*. Edited by Daniel Ligou. Toulouse: Privat (2000): 97–158.

Bridgman, Timothy. *Hyperboreans: Myth and History in Celtic-Hellenic Contacts*. New York: Routledge, 2005.

Brown, Michael et al. "MtDNA Haplogroup X: An Ancient Link between Europe/Western Asia and North America?" *American Journal of Human Genetics* 63 (1998): 1852–61.

Brunn, Stanley. "Fifty Years of Soviet Nuclear Testing in Semipalatinsk, Kazakhstan: Juxtaposed World of Blasts and Silences, Security and Risks, Denials and Memory," in *Engineering Earth: The Impacts of Megaengineering Projects*. Edited by S.D. Brunn. Springer: New York (2011): 1789–1820.

Buchli, Victor. *An Anthropology of Architecture*. New York: Bloomsbury Publishing, 2013.

——. "Astana: Materiality and the City." *Urban Life in Post-Soviet Asia*. Edited by Catherine Alexander, Victor Buchli, and Caroline Humphrey. London: University College London Press, (2007): 49–69.

Buchner, Anthony. "A Survey of Eastern Manitoba Petroforms." *Studies in Manitoba Rock Art I: Petroforms, Miscellaneous Papers 14*. Winnipeg: Manitoba Historic Resources Branch (1987): 21–48.

Buckley, Neil. "ENRC founders made good in Kazakhstan." *Financial Times*. Article published May 3, 2013. https://next.ft.com/content/71a13774-b3e0-11e2-ace9-00144feabdc0.

Burke, James. *Connections*. Boston: Little Brown, 1978.

Buttlar, Adrian. *Der Landschaftsgarten: Gartenkunst des Klassizismus und der Romantik*. Köln: DuMont, 1989.

Cameron, Keith, ed. *National Identity*. Exeter: Intellect, 1999.

Campbell, Joseph. *The Hero with a Thousand Faces*. Princeton: Princeton University Press, 1949.

——. *The Power of Myth*. New York: Anchor Books, 1991.

Campbell, Lyle. "Beyond the Comparative Method." *Historical Linguistics 2001 Selected papers from the 15th International Conference on Historical Linguistics, Melbourne, August 13–17, 2001*. Amsterdam: J. Benjamins (2003): 33–57.

Cannadine, David. "The Context, Performance and Meaning of Ritual: The British Monarchy and the 'Invention of Tradition,' c. 1820–1977." *The Invention of Tradition*. Edited by Eric Hobsbawm and Terence Ranger. Cambridge: Cambridge University Press (1983): 101–64.

Carpenter, Humphrey. *The Inklings: C.S. Lewis, J.R.R. Tolkien, Charles Williams and Their Friends*. London: Allen and Unwin, 1978.

Cassirer, Ernst. *The Philosophy of Symbolic Forms, vol. II: Mythic Thinking*. New Haven: Yale University Press, 1955.

Chase, Richard, *Quest for Myth*. Baton Rouge: Louisiana State University Press, 1949.

"Clinton's Multi Million-Dollar Communist Uranium Deal." January 31, 2008, accessed at www.judicialwatch.org/blog/2008/01/clintons-multi-million-dollar-communist-uranium-deal/.

Clouseau, Inspector Jacques. *The Pentagon within the Earth Pentacle*. Lisakovsk: Baphomet, 1666.

Coleman, Nathaniel. *Imagining and Making the World: Reconsidering Architecture and Utopia*. Bern: Peter Lang, 2011.

——. *Utopias and Architecture*. New York: Routledge, 2005.

Colmo, Christopher. *Breaking with Athens: Alfarabi as Founder*. Lanham: Lexington Books, 2005.

Conrad, David. *Education for Transformation: Implications of Lewis Mumford's Ecohumanism*. Palm Springs: ETC Publications, 1976.

Cooke, Catherine. "Russian Responses to the Garden City Movement." *Architecture Review* 163 (1978): 354–63.

Corbin, Henry. *Temple and Contemplation*. Translated by Philip Sherrard. London: KPI Limited, 1986.

Cummings, Sally. *Kazakhstan: Power and the Elite*. London: I.B. Tauris, 2005.

——, ed. *Symbolism and Power in Central Asia. Politics of the Spectacular*. London: Routledge, 2009.

Curl, James. *Freemasonry and the Enlightenment: Architecture, Symbols, and Influences*. London: Historical Publications, 2011.

Curley, Thomas. *Samuel Johnson, the Ossian Fraud, and the Celtic Revival in Great Britain and Ireland*. Cambridge: Cambridge University Press, 2009.

Dalbai, Adil. "Back to the Future: Spherical World Fair Visions," in *Astana Architectural Guide*. Edited by Philipp Meuser. Berlin: DOM Publishers, 2015.

Dalley, Stephanie, trans. *Myths From Mesopotamia: Creation, The Flood, and Others*. rev. ed. Oxford: Oxford University Press, 2000.

Dalrymple, Theodore. "The Architect as Totalitarian: Le Corbusier's Baleful Influence." *City Journal*. Article published Autumn 2009. www.city-journal.org/html/architect-totalitarian-13246.html.

Danziger, Eve, and Richard Callaghan. "The Southeastern Manitoba Petroforms: Assessment of an Expanded Sample." *Studies in Manitoba Rock Art I: Petroforms, Miscellaneous Papers 14*. Winnipeg: Manitoba Historic Resources Branch (1987): 57–173.

Dave, Bhavna. *Kazakhstan: Ethnicity, Language, and Power*. London; New York: Routledge, 2007.

Davis, Charles. "Architecture and Light: Vincenzo Scamozzi's Statuary Installation in the Chapel of the Palazzo Ducale in Venice." *Annali di architettura* 14 (2002): 171–93.

Day, Christopher. *Places of the Soul: Architecture and Environmental Design as a Healing Art*. Wellingborough: Aquarian, 1990.

de Santillana, Giorgio, and Hertha von Dechend. *Hamlet's Mill: An Essay Investigating the Origins of Human Knowledge and its Transmission Through Myth*. Boston: Gambit, 1969.

de Saussure, Ferdinand. *Course in General Linguistics*. Edited by Charles Bally and Albert Sechehaye. New York: The Philosophical Library [1916], 1959.

DeWeese, Devin. "Sacred History for a Central Asian Town Saints, Shrines, and Legends of Origin in Histories of Sayrām, 18th–19th Centuries." *Revue des mondes musulmans et de la Méditerranée* 89–90 (2000): 245–95.

Dickson, Donald. *The Tessera of Antilia: Utopian Brotherhoods and Secret Societies in the Early Seventeenth Century*. Leiden: Brill, 1998.

Doo, Scooby. *A Gaggle of Three Diamonds.* Giza: Khufu, 2006.

Droste, Magdalena. *Bauhaus 1919–1933.* Köln: Taschen, 1990.

Dubs, Homer, trans. *The History of the Former Han Dynasty.* 3 vols. Baltimore: Waverly, 1938–55.

Dumézil, Georges. *L'Idéologie Tripartite des Indo-Européens.* Bruxelles: Latomus, 1958.

Dundes, Alan, ed. *Sacred Narrative: Readings in the Theory of Myth.* Berkeley; Los Angeles: University of California Press, 1985.

Duriez, Colin. *The Oxford Inklings: Lewis, Tolkien and Their Circle.* Oxford: Lion, 2015.

Dutt, Binode Behari. *Town Planning in Ancient India.* New Delhi: New Asian Publishers, 1977.

Eaton, Ruth. *Ideal Cities: Utopianism and the (Un)Built Environment.* New York: Thames & Hudson, 2002.

Eco, Umberto. *The Book of Legendary Lands.* New York: Rizzoli, 2013.

———. "Function and Sign: The Semiotics of Architecture." *Rethinking Architecture: A Reader in Cultural Theory.* Edited by Neil Leach. London: Routledge, (1997): 173–95.

———. *A Theory of Semiotics.* Bloomington: Indiana University Press, 1979.

Edelstein, Michael, Astrid Cerny, and Abror Gadaev, eds. *Disaster By Design: The Aral Sea and its Lessons for Sustainability.* Bingley: Emerald, 2012.

Edighoffer, Roland. *Rose-Croix et Société Ideale selon Johann Valentin Andreae.* 2 vols. Neuilly-sur-Seine: Arma Artis, 1982–87.

Eliade, Mircea. *A History of Religions Ideas: From the Stone Age to the Eleusinian Mysteries.* Chicago: University of Chicago, 1978.

———. *Images and Symbols: Studies in Religious Symbolism.* Translated by Philip Mairet. London: Harvill Press, 1961.

———. *The Myth of the Eternal Return: or, Cosmos and History.* Translated by Willard Trask. New York: Pantheon Books, 1954.

———. *Patterns in Comparative Religion.* Translated by Rosemary Sheed. Lincoln: University of Nebraska Press, 1958.

———. *The Sacred and the Profane: The Nature of Religion.* Translated by Willard Trask. New York: Harper and Row, 1957.

Elkin, Caroline. "It's Not Easy Going Green: Kazakhstan's Transition to a Green Economy." Honours thesis, Dickinson College, 2015.

Epstein, Klaus. *The Genesis of German Conservatism,* New Jersey: Princeton University Press, 1960.

Erbhard, John. *Brain Landscape: The Coexistence of Neuroscience and Architecture.* Oxford; New York: Oxford University Press, 2009.

Ermolenko, Lyubov. *Srednevekovye kamennye izvaianiia Kazakhstanskikh stepei.* Novosibirsk: Institut arkheologii i etnografi i, 2004.

Euclid. *The Thirteen Books of Euclid's Elements.* Thomas L. Heath. New York: Dover Publications, 1956.

Faggionato, Raffaella. *A Rosicrucian Utopia in Eighteenth-Century Russia. The Masonic Circle of N. I. Novikov.* Translated by Michael Boyd and Brunello Lotti. Dordrecht: Springer, 2005.

Faegre, Torvald. *Tents: Architecture of the Nomads.* London: John Murray, 1979.

Faulkner, Raymond, and Ogden Goelet, trans. *The Egyptian Book of the Dead: The Book of Going Forth by Day.* 20th rev. ed. San Francisco: Chronicle Books, 2015.

Fauve, Adrien. "A Tale of Two Statues in Astana: the Fuzzy Process of Nationalistic City Making." *Nationalities Papers: The Journal of Nationalism and Ethnicity* (2015): 1–16.

Feldman, Burton, and Robert D. Richardson. *The Rise of Modern Mythology, 1680–1860.* Bloomington: Indiana University Press, 1972.

Filarete (Antonio Averlino) *Trattato di Architettura.* 2 vols. Edited by Anna Maria Finoli and Liliana Grassi. Milan: Edizioni il Polifilo, 1972.

Findley, Carter. *The Turks in World History.* New York: Oxford University Press, 2005.

Fisher, Thomas. "Architecture and the Third Industrial Revolution." *Architect Magazine.* Article published January 24, 2014. http://www.architectmagazine.com/practice/architecture-and-the-third-industrial-revolution_o.

Forsten, Benjamin. *Indo-European Language and Culture: An Introduction.* Oxford: Blackwell, 2004.

Foster, Benjamin, trans. *From Distant Days: Myths, Tales, and Poetry of Ancient Mesopotamia.* Bethesda: CDL Press, 1995.

Foucault, Michel, *Security, Territory, Population: Lectures at the Collège de France 1977–1978.* Edited by Michel Senellart. Basingstoke; New York: Palgrave Macmillan, 2007.

Frachetti, Michael. *Pastoralist Landscapes and Social Interaction in Bronze Age Eurasia.* Berkeley: University of California Press, 2008.

Francfort, H.-P., E. Soleilnavoup, J.-P. Bozellec, P. Vidal, E. D'Errico, D. Sacchi, Z. Samashev, and A. Rogozhinskii, "Les petroglyphes de Tamgaly." *Bulletin of the Asia Institute,* 9 (1995): 167–207.

Frankopan, Peter. *The Silk Roads: A New World History.* London: Bloomsbury, 2015.

Gamkrelidze, Thomas, and Ivanov Vjačeslav. *Indo-European and the Indo-Europeans: A Reconstruction and Historical Analysis of a Proto-language and a Proto-culture.* 2 vols. Berlin; New York: Mouton de Gruyter, 1995.

Gaskill, Howard, ed. *The Reception of Ossian in Europe.* London: Thoemmes Continuum, 2004.

Gawęcki, Marek. "New Urbanization of the Steppe. Astana: A Capital Called the Capital." *Studia Historiae Oeconomicae* 31 (2013): 35–56.

Geddes, Patrick. *City Development: A Study of Parks, Gardens, and Culture-Institutes.* Edinburgh, 1904.

Geldern, James von. *Bolshevik Festivals, 1917–1920.* Berkeley: University of California Press, 1993.

Gessen, Keith. "Nowheresville: How Kazakhstan is Building a Glittering New Capital from Scratch." *The New Yorker* 87 (2011).

Gimbutas, Marija. *The Gods and Goddesses of Old Europe: Myths and Cult Images (6500 to 3500 B.C.).* London: Thames & Hudson, 1974.

——. *The Language of the Goddess: Unearthing the Hidden Symbols of Western Civilization.* London: Thames & Hudson, 1989.

Goethe, Johann Wolfgang von. *Sämmtliche Werke*, vol. 2. Stuttgart; Tübingen: Cotta, 1854.

Godwin, Joscelyn and Christopher McIntosh, trans. *Rosicrucian Trilogy: Modern Translations of the Three Founding Documents.* Newburyport: Weiser Books, 2016.

Golden, Peter. *Central Asia in World History.* New York: Oxford University Press, 2011.

——. *An Introduction to the History of the Turkic Peoples: Ethnogenesis and State-Formation in Medieval and Early Modern Eurasia and the Middle East.* Wiesbaden: Otto Harrassowitz, 1992.

Golebiowska-Tobiasz, Aneta. *Monumental Polovtsian Statues in Eastern Europe: the Archaeology, Conservation and Protection.* London: Versita, 2013.

Goodrick-Clarke, Nicholas. *The Occult Roots of Nazism: Secret Aryan Cults and Their Influence on Nazi Ideology.* London: I.B. Tauris, 2003.

Gordon, Colin. *The Age of Attila: Fifth-Century Byzantium and the Barbarians.* Michigan: University of Michigan Press, 2013.

Gottdiener, Mark, and Alexander Lagopoulos, eds. *The City and the Sign: An Introduction to Urban Semiotics.* New York: Columbia University Press, 1987.

Greenberg, Joseph. *Language in the Americas.* Stanford: Stanford University Press, 1987.

Habermas, Jürgen. *The Structural Transformation of the Public Sphere: An Inquiry into a Category of Bourgeois Society.* Translated by Thomas Burger. Cambridge: MIT Press, 1991.

Halbwachs, Maurice. *On Collective Memory.* Chicago: University of Chicago Press, 1992.

Hamblin, William, and David Seely. *Solomon's Temple: Myth and History.* London: Thames & Hudson, 2007.

Hanks, Bryan, and Katheryn Linduff, eds. *Social Complexity in Prehistoric Eurasia Monuments, Metals and Mobility.* Cambridge: Cambridge University Press, 2009.

Hannigan, John. *Fantasy City: Pleasure and Profit in the Postmodern Metropolis.* London: Routledge, 1998.

Hansen, Valerie. *Silk Road: A New History.* Oxford: Oxford University Press, 2012.

Hartley, Charles W., G. Bike Yazicioğlu, and Adam T. Smith, eds. *The Archaeology of Power and Politics in Eurasia: Regimes and Revolutions.* Cambridge: Cambridge University Press, 2013.

Haul, Michael *Das Etana-Epos: ein Mythos von der Himmelfahrt des Königs von Kiš.* Göttingen: Seminar für Keilschriftforschung, 2000.

Herfort, Frank. *Imperial Pomp: Post-Soviet High-Rise.* Bielefeld: Kerber Verlag, 2013.

Herodotus. *The Histories.* Translated by Tom Holland. New York: Penguin Books, 2015.

Herrmann, Wolfgang. *Laugier and Eighteenth-Century French Theory.* London: Zwemmer, 1962.

Hiscock, Nigel. *Symbol at Your Door: Number and Geometry in the Religious Architecture of the Greek and Latin Middle Ages.* Aldershot: Ashgate, 2007.

——. *The Wise Master Builder: Platonic Geometry in Plans of Medieval Abbeys and Cathedrals.* Aldershot: Ashgate, 2000.

Hobbs, Tatiana Skok. "A World-Class City in the Middle or the Steppe: Place Marketing and the Construction of an Image of Place in Astana, Kazakhstan." Master's thesis, University of Ottawa, 2009.

Hobsbawm, Eric, and Terence Ranger, eds. *The Invention of Tradition.* Cambridge: Cambridge University Press, 1983.

Hobson, John. *The Eastern Origins of Western Civilisation.* Cambridge: Cambridge University Press, 2004.

Holmes, Sherlock. *The Case of the Golden Ratio.* Figueres: Fibonacci's Feast, 1955.

Holston, James. *The Modernist City: An Anthropological Critique of Brasília.* Chicago: University of Chicago Press, 1989.

Homan, Michael. *To Your Tents, O Israel!: The Terminology, Function, Form, and Symbolism of Tents in the Hebrew Bible and the Ancient Near East.* Leiden: Brill Publishers, 2002.

Honko, Lauri. *Religion, Myth and Folklore in the World's Epics: The Kalevala and its Predecessors.* New York: Mouton de Gruyter, 1990.

Hoppál, Mihály. "Animistic Mythology and Helping Spirits in Siberian Shamanism." *Circumpolar Animism and Shamanism.* Edited by Takako Yamada and Takashi Irimoto. Sapporo: Hokkaido University Press (1997): 193–206.

——, ed. *Shamanism in Eurasia*, 2 parts. Göttingen: Edition Herodot, 1984.

——. *Shamans and Traditions.* Budapest: Akadémiai Kiadó, 2007.

Horne, Alex. *King Solomon's Temple in the Masonic Tradition.* London: Antiquarian Press, 1971.

Hoskin, Michael. *Tombs, Temples and their Orientations: A New Perspective on Mediterranean Prehistory.* Bognor Regis: Ocarina Books, 2001.

Howard, Ebenezer. *To-morrow: A Peaceful Path to Real Reform.* London; New York: Routledge, [1898] 2003.

Howse, Robert. "Reading between the Lines: Exotericism, Esotericism, and the Philosophical Rhetoric of Leo Strauss." *Philosophy & Rhetoric* 32:1 (1999): 60–77.

Hublin, Jean-Jacques. "The Modern Human Colonization of Western Eurasia: When and Where?" *Quaternary Science Reviews* 30 (2014): 1–17.

Human Rights Watch. *Conflict in the Soviet Union: The Untold Story of the Clashes in Kazakhstan.* New York: Human Rights Watch, 1990.

Incerti, Manuela. "Antiche Geometrie Solari nel Battistero di Parma." *Arte Cristiana* 805 (2001): 293–306.

Isaacs, Rico. "Nomads, Warriors and Bureaucrats: Nation-Building and Film in Post-Soviet Kazakhstan." *Nationalities Papers: The Journal of Nationalism and Ethnicity* (2014): 1–18.

Islam, Muhammad. "The Ideal State/Society of Plato and al-Farabi: A Comparative Analysis." *International Journal of Islamic Thoughts* (2013): 61–80.

Izbitser, Elena. "Wheeled Vehicle Burials of the Steppe Zone of Eastern Europe and the Northern Caucasus, 3rd to 2nd Millennium B.C." PhD diss., Institute for the History of Material Culture, St Petersburg, 1993.

Jablonski, Nina. *First Americans: The Pleistocene Colonization of the New World*. San Francisco: California Academy of Sciences, 2002.

Jacob, Jose. "The Architectural Theory of the *Mānasāra*." PhD diss., McGill University, 2003.

Jacob, Margaret. *Living the Enlightenment: Freemasonry and Politics in Eighteenth-Century Europe*. New York; Oxford: Oxford University Press, 1991.

Jacobs, Jane. *The Death and Life of Great American Cities*. New York: Random House, 1961.

Jacobson, Esther. *The Art of the Scythians*. Leiden; New York: Brill, 1995.

——. *The Deer Goddess of Ancient Siberia: A Study in the Ecology of Belief*. Leiden; New York: Brill, 1993.

James, Edwin. *The Tree of Life: An Archaeological Study*. Leiden: Brill, 1966.

Jarus, Owen. "No, That Ancient Mausoleum Is Not the 'World's 1st Pyramid.'" *Live Science*. Article published August 17, 2016. www.livescience.com/55796-ancient-mausoleum-not-worlds-first-pyramid.html.

Jarzombek, Mark. *On Leon Baptista Alberti: His Literary and Aesthetic Theories*. Cambridge: MIT Press, 1989.

Jencks, Charles. *The New Paradigm in Architecture: The Language of Post-Modernism*. New Haven; London: Yale University Press, 2002.

Jenkyns, Richard. *Classical Literature: An Epic Journey from Homer to Virgil and Beyond*. New York: Basic Books, 2016.

Jewett, Robert, and John Lawrence. *The American Monomyth*. Garden City: Anchor Press, 1977.

——. *The Myth of the American Superhero*. Grand Rapids: W.B. Eerdmans, 2002.

Karimov, Reshad. "Iran's Policy in Caspian Sea Basin and Beyond: The Great Game 2.0." *The Caspian Sea Chessboard: Geo-Political, Geo-Strategic And Geo-Economic Analysis*. Edited by Carlo Frappi and Azad Garibov. Milano: Egea (2014): 129–42.

Kassymova, Didar, Zhanat Kundakbayeva, and Ustina Markus. *Historical Dictionary of Kazakhstan*. Lanham: Scarecrow Press, 2012.

Kaufman, Stuart J. *Modern Hatreds: The Symbolic Politics of Ethnic War*. New York: Cornell University Press, 2001.

Kaufmann, Emil. "Three Revolutionary Architects: Boullée, Ledoux, and Lequeu." *Transactions of the American Philosophical Society* 42:3 (1952): 431–564.

Kelly, Christopher. *Attila the Hun: Barbarian Terror and the Fall of the Roman Empire*. London: Bodley Head, 2008.

Kerry, Paul, ed. *The Ring and the Cross: Christianity and The Lord of the Rings*. Madison: Fairleigh Dickinson University Press, 2011.

Khazanov, Anatoly. *Nomads and the Outside World*. 2nd ed. Translated by Julia Crookenden. Madison: University of Wisconsin Press, 1994.

Khlevniuk, Oleg. *The History of the Gulag: From Collectivization to the Great Terror*. Translated by Vadim Staklo. New Haven: Yale University Press, 2004.

Khrapunov, Viktor. *Nazarbayev—Our Friend the Dictator: Kazakhstan's Difficult Path to Democracy*. Translated by Nicki Challinger. New York: Columbia University Press, 2015.

Kikutake, Kiyonori. "Marine City," *Kokusai Kenchiku* 26 (1959): 36–39.

Kilner, James. "Copper Tycoon Tops Kazakhstan's Rich List." *The Telegraph*. Article published May 15, 2012. http://www.telegraph.co.uk/news/ worldnews/asia/kazakhstan/9268133/ Copper-tycoon-tops-Kazakhstans-rich-list.html.

Kissamedin, G.M. "Image of Crater in the Architecture of 'Shabyt' Palace of Arts and Natural Elements – 2009." *International Academy of Science and Higher Education* (2014): 11–15.

Knoop, Douglas, and Gwilym Jones. *Genesis of Freemasonry: An Account of the Rise and Development of Freemasonry in its Operative, Accepted, and Early Speculative Phases*. Manchester: Manchester University Press, 1947.

Koch, Natalie. "The City and the Steppe: Territory, Technologies of Government, and Kazakhstan's New Capital." PhD diss., University of Colorado, 2012.

——. "The 'Heart' of Eurasia? Kazakhstan's Centrally Located Capital City." *Central Asian Survey* 32:2 (2013[a]): 134–47.

——. "The Monumental and the Miniature: Imagining 'modernity' in Astana," *Social and Cultural Geography* 11, 8 (2010): 769–87.

——. "Urban 'utopias': the Disney Stigma and Discourses of 'False Modernity,'" *Environment and Planning* A 44:10 (2012): 2445–62.

——. "The Violence of Spectacle: Statist Schemes to Green the Desert and Constructing Astana and Ashgabat as Urban Oases." *Social and Cultural Geography* 16:6 (2015): 675–97.

——. "Why Not a World City? Astana, Ankara, and Geopolitical Scripts in Urban Networks." *Urban Geography* 34:1 (2013[b]): 109–130.

Kopbayeva, Diana. "Is Astana a Nationalistic Project? The Role of Kazakhstan's New Capital in Development of the National Identity." *Proceedings of the 1st Annual International Interdisciplinary Conference* (2013): 800–813.

Kopp, Anatole. *Constructivist Architecture in the USSR*. London: Academy Press, 1985.

Köppen, Bernhard. "The Production of a New Eurasian Capital on the Kazakh Steppe: Architecture, Urban Design, and

Identity in Astana." *Nationalities Papers: The Journal of Nationalism and Ethnicity* 41:4 (2013): 590–605.

Krampen, Martin. *Meaning in the Urban Environment*. London: Pion, 1979.

Kronenburg, Robert. *Architecture in Motion: The History and Development of Portable Building*. New York: Routledge, 2014.

Kunanbay, Alma. *The Soul of Kazakhstan*. Edited by Gareth Steen. New York: Easten Press, 2001.

Kurokawa, Kisho. *The Architecture of Symbiosis*. New York: Rizzoli, 1988.

——. *Kisho Kurokawa: Architect and Associates, Selected and Current Works*. Mulgrave: Images Publishing Group, 2000.

——. *Metabolism in Architecture*. London: Studio Vista, 1977.

——. *The Philosophy of Symbiosis*. London: Academy Editions, 1994.

——. *The Study on the Master Plan for the Development of the City of Astana in the Republic of Kazakhstan*. Japan International Cooperation Agency, 2001.

Lallanilla, Marc. "Mysterious Pentagram on Google Maps Explained." *Live Science* (2013). Accessed June 8, 2015. http://www.livescience.com/38623-giant-pentagram-in-kazakhstan.html.

Langer, Susanne. *Philosophy in a New Key*. Cambridge: Harvard University Press, 1942.

Larmour, David H.J., and Diana Spencer, eds. *The Sites of Rome: Time, Space, Memory*. Oxford; New York: Oxford University Press, 2007.

Laruelle, Marlène. "Is Kazakhstan's 'dialogue of civilizations' all about image, or doing some real good?" *The Washington Post's Monkey Cage*. Article published June 27, 2015.

——. "The Orient in Russian Thought at the Turn of the Century." *Russia between East and West: Scholarly Debates on Eurasianism*. Edited by Dmitry Shlapentokh. Leiden: Brill. (2007[b]): 9–38.

——. "Religious Revival, Nationalism, and the 'Invention of Tradition': Political Tengrism in Central Asia and Tatarstan." *Central Asian Survey* 26.2 (2007[a]): 203–16.

——. *Russian Eurasianism: An Ideology of Empire*. Baltimore: John Hopkins University Press, 2008.

——. "Tengrism: In Search For Central Asia's Spiritual Roots." *Central Asia-Caucasus Institute Analysts* 8:6 (2006): 3–5.

Laszczkowski, Mateusz. "Building the Future: Construction, Temporality and Politics in Astana." *Focaal* 60:1 (2011): 77–92.

——. "State Building(s): Built Forms, Materiality and the State in Astana." *Ethnographies of the State in Central Asia: Performing Politics*. Edited by Madeleine Reeves, John Rasanayagam, and Judith Beyer. Bloomington: Indiana University Press (2013): 149–72.

——. "Superplace: Global Connections and Local Politics at the Mega Mall, Astana." *Etnofoor* 23:1 (2011): pp. 85–104.

Laubin, Reginald. *The Indian Tipi: Its History, Construction, and Use*. Norman: University of Oklahoma Press, 1957.

Laugier, Marc-Antoine. *An Essay on Architecture*. Translated by Wolfgang and Anni Herrmann. Los Angeles: Hennessey & Ingalls, [1753] 1977.

Leach, Edmund, ed. *Structural Study of Myth and Totemism*. London: Tavistock, 1968.

Leach, Neil, ed. *Rethinking Architecture: A Reader in Cultural Theory*. London: Routledge, 1997.

Le Camus de Mézières, Nicolas. *The Genius of Architecture; or, The Analogy of That Art with Our Sensations*. Translated by David Britt. Chicago: University of Chicago Press, 1992.

Le Corbusier. *Le Modulor: essai sur une mesure harmonique à l'échelle humaine applicable universellement à l'architecture et à la mécanique*. Boulogne: L'Architecture D'aujourd'hui, 1950.

——. *The Radiant City*. New York: Orion Press, 1964.

——. *Towards a New Architecture*. Translated by Frederick Etchells. London: Butterworth Publishers, 1989.

Ledoux, Claude-Nicolas. *L'Architecture de C. N. Ledoux: Collection qui rassemble tous les genres de batiments employés dans l'ordre social*. Princeton: Princeton Architectural Press [1804], 1983.

Lee, Roberts. *Literary Nationalism in German and Japanese Germanistik*. New York: Peter Lang, 2010.

Le Forestier, René. *Les Illuminés de Bavière et la Franc-Maçonnerie Allemande*, Paris: Hachette, 1914.

Leighton, Lauren. *The Esoteric Tradition in Russian Romantic Literature: Decembrism and Freemasonry*. University Park: Pennsylvania State University Press, 1994.

——. "Pushkin and Freemasonry: 'The Queen of Spades,'" in *New Perspectives on Nineteenth-Century Prose*. Edited by George Gutsche. Columbus: Slavica Publishers (1982): 15–25.

Le Maître, Alexandre. *La Métropolitée, ou, De l'établissement des villes capitales, de leur vtilité passive & active, de l'vnion de leurs parties, & de leur anatomie, de leur commerce, &c*. Amsterdam: Chés Balthes Boekholt pour Jean van Gorp, 1682.

Leong, Albert. *Centaur: The Life and Art of Ernst Neizvestny*. Lanham: Rowman & Littlefoeld Publishers, 2002.

Lethaby, William, *Architecture, Mysticism and Myth*. London: Architectural Press [1892], 1972.

Levin, Isidor. "Etana. Die keilschriftlichen Belege einer Erzählung," *Fabula* 8 (1966): 1–63.

Lévi-Strauss, Claude. *Anthropologie Structurale*. Paris: Plon, 1958.

——. "The Structural Study of Myth." *Journal of American Folklore* 68 (1955): 428–44.

Lewis, C.S. *Selected Literary Essays by C.S. Lewis*. Edited by Walter Hooper. New York: Cambridge University Press, 2013.

Lewis, Geoffrey. *The Turkish Language Reform: A Catastrophic Success*. Oxford: Oxford University Press, 1999.

Lim, Susanna. *China and Japan in the Russian Imagination, 1685–1922: To the Ends of the Orient*. London; New York: Routledge, 2013.

Limpricht, Cornelia. *Platzanlage und Landschaftsgarten als begehbare Utopien: Ein Beitrag zur Deutung der Templum-Salomonis-Rezeption im 16. und 18. Jahrhundert.* Frankfurt am Main: Lang, 1994.

Lin, Zhongjie. *Kenzo Tange and the Metabolist Movement: Urban Utopias of Modern Japan.* London; New York: Routledge, 2010.

Lincoln, Bruce. *Myth, Cosmos, and Society: Indo-European Themes of Creation and Destruction.* Cambridge: Harvard University Press, 1986.

——. *Nikolai Miliutin: An Enlightened Russian Bureaucrat of the 19th Century.* Newtonville: Oriental Research Partners, 1977.

Littleton, Scott, and Linda Malcor. *Scythia to Camelot: A Radical Reassessment of the Legends of King Arthur, the Knights of the Round Table, and the Holy Grail.* Florence: Taylor & Francis, 2013.

Livio, Mario. *The Golden Ratio: The Story of Phi, the World's Most Astonishing Number.* New York: Broadway Books, 2002.

Locher, Mira. *Japanese Architecture: An Exploration of Elements and Forms.* Tokyo: Tuttle Publishing, 2015.

Lodder, Christina. *Russian Constructivism.* New Haven: Yale University Press. 1983.

Lodder, Christina, and Jean-Louis Cohen. *Building the Revolution: Soviet Art and Architecture, 1915–1935.* London: Royal Academy of Arts, 2011.

Love, James. "The Well-Connected Dictator." *Huffington Post.* Article published October 6, 2007 and updated May 25, 2011. http://www.huffingtonpost.com/james-love/the-wellconnected-dictato_b_67423.html.

Luckert, Steven. *Jesuits, Freemasons, Illuminati, and Jacobins: Conspiracy theories, Secret Societies, and Politics in Late Eighteenth-Century Germany.* New York: New York State University, 1993.

Lukacher, Brian. "Joseph Gandy and the Mythography of Architecture." *The Journal of the Society of Architectural Historians* 53 (1994): 280–99.

Lymer, Kenneth. "Petroglyphs and sacred spaces at Terekty Aulie, Central Kazakhstan," in *Kurgans, Ritual Sites and Settlements: Eurasian Bronze and Iron Age.* Edited by J. Davis-Kimball, E.M. Murphy, L. Koryakova and L.T. Yablonsky. Oxford: British Archaeological Reports, BAR International series 890 (2000): 311–21.

——. "Rags and Rock Art: The Landscapes of Holy Site Pilgrimage in the Republic of Kazakhstan." *World Archaeology* 36, No 1 (2004): 158-72.

——. "Shamanistic Rock Art Images from the Republic of Kazakhstan." *Expedition* 46:1 (2004): 16–21.

Lynch, Kevin. *A Theory of Good City Form.* Cambridge: MIT Press, 1982.

Maenchen-Helfen, Otto. *The World of the Huns; Studies in their History and Culture.* Edited by Max Knight. Berkeley: University of California Press, 1973.

Macpherson, Jay. "The Masons and the Great Seal." *Freemasonry on Both Sides of the Atlantic: Essays Concerning the Craft in the British Isles, Europe, the United States, and Mexico.* Edited by William Weisberger, Wallance McLeod, and Brent Morris. New York: Columbia University Press (2002): 557–82.

Maksimova, A., A. Ermolaeva, and A. Mar'yashev. *Naskal'nye izobrazheniya urochishcha Tamgaly.* Alma-Ata: Oner, 1985.

Mallgrave, Harry Francis. *Architect's Brain: Neuroscience, Creativity, and Architecture.* Malden: Wiley-Blackwell, 2010.

Mallory, Jim. *In Search of the Indo-Europeans.* London: Thames & Hudson, 1989.

Mallory, Jim, and Q.D. Adams, eds. *Encyclopaedia of Indo-European Culture.* London and Chicago: Fitzroy Dearborn Publishers, 1997.

Malville, McKim, and Laut Gujral. *Ancient Cities, Sacred Skies: Cosmic Geometries and City Planning in Ancient India.* New Delhi: Indira Gandhi National Centre for the Arts, 2000.

Mannheim, Steve. *Walt Disney and the Quest for Community.* Burlington: Ashgate, 2002.

Manuel, Frank Edward, ed. *Utopias and Utopian Thought.* London: Souvenir Press, 1973.

Markowsky, George. "Misconceptions about the Golden Ratio." *The College Mathematics Journal* 23:1 (1992): 2–19.

Matuzeviciute, M. Giedre, A.V. Logvin, I. Shevnina, A.M. Seitov, J. Fengc, and L. Zhouc. "OSL Dates for the Ancient Geometric Earthworks of Kazakhstan." *Archaeological Research in Asia* 30 (2015): 1–9.

May, Walter, trans. *Manas: The Great Campaign: Kirghiz Heroic Epos.* Bishkek: Kyrgyz Branch of the International Centre, 1999.

Mayor, Adrienne. *First Fossil Hunters: Dinosaurs, Mammoths, and Myth in Greek and Roman Times.* Princeton: Princeton University Press, 2011.

McClung, William. *The Architecture of Paradise: Survivals of Eden and Jerusalem.* Berkeley: University of California Press, 1983.

McKenzie, Kermit E. "Chokan Valikhanov: Kazakh Princeling and Scholar." *Central Asian Survey* 80:3 (1989): 1–30.

Mélikoff, Irene. "Ahmad Yesevi and Turkic popular Islam." *Utrecht Papers on Central Asia* 2 (1989): 83–94.

Meller, Helen Elizabeth. *Patrick Geddes: Social Evolutionist and City Planner.* London; New York: Routledge, 1993.

Mertus, Julie A. *Kosovo. How Myths and Truths Started a War.* Berkeley; London: University of California Press, 1999.

Meuser, Philipp, ed. *Astana Architectural Guide.* Berlin: DOM Publishers, 2015.

Miliutin, Nikolia. *Sotsgorod: The Problem of Building Socialist Cities.* Cambridge: MIT Press, 1974.

Mkrtchyan, Narek. "Astana: a New Post-Soviet Text." *International Journal of Humanities and Social Science* 3:21 (2013): 229–36.

Montgomery, David. "Namaz, Wishing Trees, and Vodka: The Diversity of Everyday Religious Life in Central Asia." *Everyday Life in Central Asia, Past and*

Present. Edited by Jeff Sahadeo and Russell Zanca. Bloomington: Indiana University Press (2007): 355–70.

More, Thomas. *Utopia*. Translated by Clarence H. Miller. New Haven; London: Yale University Press, [1516], 2014.

Morris, Berman. *Wandering God: A Study in Nomadic Spirituality*. Albany: State University of New York Press, 2000.

Mozur, Joseph. *Parables from the Past: The Prose Fiction of Chingiz Aimanov*. Pittsburgh: University of Pittsburg Press, 1995.

Mulder, Fox. *The Cornea of Astana's Panopticon*. Caspian Sea: Four Trees, 2013.

Mumford, Lewis. *The City in History: Its Origins, Its Transformations, and its Prospects*. New York: Harcourt Brace, 1961.

——. "The Fate of Garden Cities." *Journal of the American Institute of Architects* 15 (1927): 37–39.

Mundy, Barbara. *The Death of Aztec Tenochtitlan, the Life of Mexico City*. Austin: University of Texas Press, 2015.

Murphy, Jonathan. "Illusory Transition? Elite Reconstitution in Kazakhstan, 1989–2002." *Europe-Asia Studies*, 58:4 (2006): 523–54.

Nabokov, Peter and Robert Easton. *Native American Architecture*. New York; Oxford: Oxford University Press, 1989.

Naredi-Rainer, Paul. *Salomos Tempel und das Abendland: monumentale Folgen historischer Irrtümer*. Köln: Dumont, 1994.

Nazarbayev, Nursultan. "Building the Future Together." Address of the President of the Republic of Kazakhstan, January 28, 2011. www.akorda.kz/en/addresses/ addresses_of_president/address-of-the-president-of-the-republic-of-kazakhstan-nursultan-nazarbayev-to-the-people-of-kazakhstan-january-28-2011_1341926571.

——. *The Heart of Eurasia*. Almaty: Baspalar Uyi, 2010.

——. *The Kazakhstan Way*. Translated by Jan Butler. London: Stacey International, 2008.

——. "Manifesto: The World. The 21st Century." Speech given March 31, 2016, www.akorda.kz/en/speeches/ external_political_affairs/ext_other_events/ manifesto-the-world-the-21st-century.

——. "A Model for Curtailing Nuclear Proliferation." *The Washington Times*. Article published April 5, 2013. http://www. washingtontimes.com/news/2013/apr/5/a-model-for-curtailing-nuclear-proliferation/.

——. "Prosperity, Security and Ever Growing Welfare of All the Kazakhstanis." Address of the President of the Republic of Kazakhstan, Nursultan Nazarbayev, to the People of Kazakhstan, October 10, 1997. www.akorda.kz/en/addresses/ addresses_of_president/page_address-of-the-president-of-the-republic-of-kazakhstan-nursultan-nazarbayev-to-the-people-of-kazakhstan-october-10-1997_1343986436.

Neef, Christian. "Central Asian Powerhouse. The Kazakhstan Klondike," *Der Spiegel Online*. Article published November 2006. http://www.spiegel. de/international/spiegel/central-asian-powerhouse-the-kazakhstan-klondike-a-447451.html.

Nicoletti, Manfredi, and Luca Nicoletti. *Kazakhstan Central Concert Hall*. Rome: Gangemi Editore, 2011.

Nietzsche, Friedrich. "Myth is Higher than History." *Philosophies of History: From Enlightenment to Postmodernity*. Edited by Robert M. Burns and Hugh Rayment-Pickard. Oxford: Blackwell Publishing, (2004): 146–54.

Olausson, Magnus. "Freemasonry, Occultism, and the Picturesque Garden toward the End of the Eighteenth Century." *Art History* 8.4 (1985): 413–33.

Olcott, Martha Brill. *The Kazakhs*. 2nd ed. Stanford: Hover Institution Press, 1995.

Onians, Richard. *The Origins of European Thought about the Body, the Mind, the Soul, the World, Time and Fate*. Cambridge: Cambridge University Press, 1951.

Önnerfors, Andreas, and Robert Collis, eds. *Freemasonry and Fraternalism in Eighteenth-Century Russia*. Sheffield: University of Sheffield, 2009.

Oosten, Jarich. *The War of the Gods: the Social Code in Indo-European Mythology*. London: Routledge & K. Paul, 1985.

Orazgaliyeva, Malika. "UN Adopts Nuclear-Weapons-Free World Declaration initiated by Kazakhstan." *Astana Times*. Article published December 8, 2015, http://astanatimes.com/2015/12/un-adopts-nuclear-weapons-free-world-declaration-initiated-by-kazakhstan/.

Outram, Alan, Natalie Stear, Robin Bendrey, Sandra Olsen, Alexei Kasparov, Victor Zaibert, Nick Thorpe, and Richard Evershed. "The Earliest Horse Harnessing and Milking." *Science* 323 (2009): 1332–35.

Özgül, Aydin. "Nation Building Policies and Their Impact on the Russian Minority in Post-Soviet Kazakhstan." PhD diss., Middle East Technical University, 2006.

Padovan, Richard. *Proportion: Science, Philosophy, Architecture*. London: E. & F.N. Spoon, 1999.

Paksoy, H. Bülent. *Humans on Mars and Beyond*. CreateSpace Independent Publishing Platform, 2012.

Peirce, Charles. *Writings of Charles S. Peirce: A Chronological Edition*. 6 vols. Edited by Max H. Fisch. Bloomington: Indiana University Press, 1982–2010.

Perego, U.A., A. Achilli, N. Angerhofer, M. Accetturo, M. Pala, A. Olivieri, K.B. Hooshiar, K.H. Ritchie, R. Scozzari, Q.P. Kong, N.M. Myres, A. Salas, O. Semino, H.J. Bandelt, S.R. Woodward, A. Torroni. "Distinctive Paleo-Indian Migration Routes from Beringia Marked by Two Rare MtDNA Haplogroups." *Current Biology* 19:1 (2009): 1–8.

Perelman, Marc. *Le Corbusier: une froide vision du monde*. Paris: Michalon Éditeur, 2015.

Pereltsvaig, Asya, and Lewis, Martin. *The Indo-European Controversy Facts and Fallacies in Historical Linguistics*. Cambridge: Cambridge University Press, 2015.

Pérez-Gómez, Alberto. *Architecture and the Crisis of Modern Science*. Cambridge: MIT Press, 1996.

Philpot, J.H. *The Sacred Tree or the Tree in Religion and Myth*. New York: The Macmillan Company, 1897.

Piggott, Stuart. *Wagon, Chariot, and Carriage: Symbol and Status in the History of Transport*. London: Thames & Hudson, 1983.

——. *Wagon, Chariot, and Carriage: Symbol and Status in the History of Transport*. London: Thames and Hudson, 1992.

Plato. *The Republic*. 3rd ed. Translated by Alexander Lindsay. London: J.M. Dent & Sons, 1923.

Podvig, Pavel, ed. *Russian Strategic Nuclear Forces*. Cambridge: MIT Press, 2001.

Pohl, Michaela. "From White Grave to Tselinograd to Astana: The Virgin Lands Opening, Khrushchev's Forgotten First Reform." *The Thaw: Soviet Society and Culture during the 1950s and 1960s*. Edited by Denis Kozlov and Eleonory Gilburd. Toronto: University of Toronto Press (2012): 269–307.

Poirot, Hercule. *The 47th Proposition of Euclid*. Venice: Pythagoras Publications, 1492.

Polo, Marco. *The Travels of Marco Polo*. Translated by Ronald Latham. London; New York: Penguin Classics [1300], 1958.

Popper, Karl. *Conjectures and Refutations*, London: Routledge & Kegan Paul [1962], 1974.

Potts, Albert. *The World's Eye*. Lexington: University Press of Kentucky, 1982.

Prescott, Andrew. "Some Literary Contexts of the Regius and Cooke Manuscripts." *Freemasonry in Music and Literature, the Canonbury Papers*, vol. 2. London: Canonbury Masonic Research Centre, 2005.

——. "The Earliest Use of the Word 'Freemason.'" *Year Book of the Grand Lodge of the Ancient Free and Accepted Masons of Scotland 2004*. Edinburgh: Grand Lodges of Scotland (2004): 64–67.

Preston, Peter. "How Nursultan Became the Most Loved Man on Earth." *The Guardian*. Article published July 19, 2009, https://www.theguardian.com/books/2009/jul/19/nazarbayev-kazakhstan-jonathen-aitken.

Preziosi, Donald. *Architecture, Language, and Meaning: The Origins of the Built World and its Semiotic Organization*. The Hague: Mouton Publishers, 1979.

——. *Minoan Architectural Design: Formation and Signification*. Berlin: Mouton Publishers, 1983.

Privratsky, B.G. *Muslim Turkistan: Kazak Religion and Collective Memory*. Richmond: Curzon, 2001.

Propp, Vladimir. *Morphology of the Folktale*. Bloomington: Indiana University, 1958.

Puhvel, Jaan. *Comparative Mythology*. Baltimore and London: John Hopkins University Press, 1987.

Quinn, Malcolm. *The Swastika: Constructing the Symbol*. London; New York: Routledge, 1995.

Rabkin, Eric. *Science Fiction: A Historical Anthology*. Oxford; New York: Oxford University Press, 1983.

Rahmsdorf, Sabine. *Stadt und Architektur in der literarischen Utopie der frühen Neuzeit*. Heidelberg: Universitätsverlag C. Winter, 1999.

Ram, Harsha. "Imagining Eurasia: The Poetics and Ideology of Olzhas Suleimenov's AZ i IA." *Slavic Review* 60:2 (2001): 289–311.

Ramírez, Juan, ed. *Dios Arquitecto: J.B. Villalpando y el Templo de Salomón*. Madrid: Ediciones Siruela, 1991.

Rawlinson, George. *The Five Great Monarchies of the Ancient Eastern World; or, The History, Geography, and Antiquities of Chaldae, Assyria, Babylon, Media, and Persia, Collected and Illustrated from Ancient and Modern Sources*, vol. 1. London: John Murray, 1862.

Reichl, Karl. *Singing the Past: Turkic and Medieval Heroic Poetry*. Ithaca: Cornell University Press, 2000.

——. *Turkic Oral Epic Poetry: Traditions, Forms, Poetic Structure*. New York: Garland Publishing, 1992.

Reiss, Mitchell. *Bridled Ambition: Why Countries Constrain Their Nuclear Capabilities*. Baltimore: John Hopkins University Press, 1995.

Renfrew, Colin. *Archaeology and Language: The Puzzle of Indo-European Origins*. London: Jonathan Cape, 1987.

——. *Before Civilisation, the Radiocarbon Revolution and Prehistoric Europe*. London: Jonathan Cape, 1973.

Renna, Thomas. "Bernard of Clairvaux and the Temple of Solomon." *Law, Custom and Social Fabric in Medieval Europe: Essays in Honor of Bryce Lyon*. Edited by Bernard Bachrach and David Nicholas. Kalamazoo: Western Michigan University (1990): 73–88.

Rice, Tamara. *The Scythians*. London: Thames & Hudson, 1957.

Rickey, George. *Constructivism: Origins and Evolution*. New York: G. Braziller, 1995.

Rifkin, Jeremy. *The Third Industrial Revolution: How Lateral Power Is Transforming Energy, the Economy, and the World*. Basingstoke; New York: Palgrave Macmillan, 2011.

Rival, Laura, ed. *The Social Life of Trees: Anthropological Perspectives on Tree Symbolism*. Oxford: Berg, 1998.

Robbins, Christopher. *Apples Are From Kazakhstan: The Land That Disappeared*. New York: Atlas, 2008.

Roberts, John. *The Mythology of the Secret Societies*. New York: Charles Scribner, 1972.

Rosenau, Helen, ed. *Boullée's treatise on architecture; a complete presentation of the "Architecture, essai sur l'art," which forms part of the Boullée papers (MS 9153) in the Bibliothèque Nationale, Paris*. London: A. Tiranti, 1953.

——. *The Ideal City: Its Architectural Evolution in Europe*. London; New York: Methuen & Co., 1959.

Ross, Denison, and Vilhelm Thomsen. "The Orkhon Inscriptions: Being a Translation of Professor Vilhelm Thomsen's Final Danish Rendering." *Bulletin of the School of Oriental Studies* 5:4 (1930): 861–76.

Rowe, Colin. "The Mathematics of the Ideal Villa: Palladio and Le Corbusier Compared." *Architectural Review* 101 (1947): 101–4.

Rowley, Stephen. *Movie Towns and Sitcom Suburbs: Building Hollywood's Ideal Communities*. Basingstoke; New York: Palgrave Macmillan, 2015.

Rozwadowski, Andrzej. "In Search of Shamanic Themes in Eastern Siberian Rock Art," *Shaman* 22: 1 & 2 (2014): 97–118.

——. "Sun Gods or Shamans? Interpreting the 'Solar-Headed' Petroglyphs of Central Asia." *The Archaeology of Shamanism.* Edited by N. Price. London: Routledge (2001): 5–86.

Ruggles, Clive. *Ancient Astronomy: An Encyclopaedia of Cosmologies and Myth.* Santa Barbara: ABC-CLIO, 2005.

——, ed. *Handbook of Archaeoastronomy and Ethnoastronomy.* New York: Springer, 2015.

Ruhlen, Merritt. *The Origin of Language: Tracing the Evolution of the Mother Tongue.* New York: John Wiley & Sons, 1994.

——. "The Origin of the Na-Dene." *Proceedings of the National Academy of Sciences* 95 (1998): 13994–996.

Rykwert, Joseph. *On Adam's House in Paradise: The Idea of the Primitive Hut in Architectural History.* New York: Museum of Modern Art, 1972.

——. *The Idea of a Town: The Anthropology of Urban Form in Rome, Italy and the Ancient World.* Princeton: Princeton University Press, 1976.

——. *The Necessity of Artifice: Ideas in Architecture.* New York: Rizzoli, 1982.

Sabol, Steven. *Russian Colonization and the Genesis of Kazakh National Consciousness.* Basingstoke; New York: Palgrave Macmillan, 2003.

Salingaros, Nikos, A., ed. *Anti-Architecture and Deconstruction.* Solingen: Umbau-Verlag, 2004.

Samashev, Z. "Shamanic Motifs in the Petroglyphs of Eastern Kazakhstan." *Spirits and Stones: Shamanism and Rock Art in Central Asia and Siberia.* Edited by A. Rozwadowski, Poznan: Instytut Wschodni UAM, (2002): 33–48.

Sarsembayev, Azamat. "Imagined Communities: Kazak Nationalism and Kazakification in the 1990s." *Central Asian Survey* 18:3 (1999): 319–46.

Schaer, Roland, Gregory Claeys, and Lyman T. Sargent. *Utopia: The Search for the Ideal Society in the Western World.* New York: The New York Public Library/Oxford University Press, 2000.

Schatz, Edward. *Modern Clan Politics: The Power of 'Blood' in Kazakhstan and Beyond.* Seattle: University of Washington Press, 2004.

——. "The Soft Authoritarian Tool Kit: Agenda-Setting Power in Kazakhstan and Kyrgyzstan." *Comparative Politics* 41, No. 2 (January 2009): 203–22.

Schneider, Donald. *The Works and Doctrine of Jacques Ignace Hittorff, 1792–1867.* 2 vols. New York; London: Garland Publishing, 1977.

Schweizer, Peter. *Clinton Cash: The Untold Story of How and Why Foreign Governments and Businesses Helped Make Bill and Hillary Rich.* New York: Harper, 2015.

Scott, James. *Seeing Like a State: How Certain Schemes to Improve the Human Condition Have Failed.* New Haven: Yale University Press, 1998.

Seaman, Gary. *Ecology and Empire: Nomads in the Cultural Evolution of the Old World.* Los Angeles: Ethnographics, Center for Visual Anthropology, 1989.

Segal, Robert. *Myth: A Very Short Introduction.* Oxford: Oxford University Press, 2004.

Shakespeare, William. *The Tragedy of Richard II.* Edited by Barbara Mowat and Paul Werstine. New York: Washington Square Press, 1996.

Sharp, Dennis. *Nicoletti, Manfredi: Architettura, Simbolo, Contesto = Architecture, Symbol, Context.* Roma: Gangemi, 1998.

Shatskikh, Aleksandra. *Black Square: Malevich and the Origin of Suprematism.* Yale: Yale University Press, 2012.

Shaw, John. "On Indo-European Cosmic Structure: Models, Comparisons, Contexts." *Cosmos* 28 (2012): 57–76.

Shayakhmetov, Mukhamet. *The Silent Steppe: the Story of a Kazakh Nomad Under Stalin.* Edited by Anthony Gardner. Translated by Jan Butler. London: Stacey International, 2006.

Shelekpayev, Nariman. "Kazakh Capitals and the Construction of Kazakh National Identity in the Post-Soviet Period (1991–2011)." Master's thesis. Charles University, Prague, 2013.

Shepard, Wade. *Ghost Cities of China: The Story of Cities without People in the World's Most Populated Country.* London: Zed Books, 2015.

Sher, Yakov. "On the Sources of the Scythic Animal Style." *Arctic Anthropology* 25:2 (1988): 47–60.

Slochower, Harry. *Mythopoesis: Mythic Patterns in the Literary Classics.* Detroit: Wayne State University Press, 1970.

Smith, Anthony D. *Myths and Memories of the Nation.* New York: Oxford University Press, 1999.

Smith, Douglas. *Working the Rough Stone: Freemasonry and Society in Eighteenth-Century Russia.* Dekalb: Northern Illinois University Press, 1999.

Solzhenitsyn, Aleksandr. *The Gulag Archipelago, 1918–1956: An Experiment in Literary Investigation.* Translated by Thomas Whitney. New York: Harper & Row, 1974–78.

Sorkin, Michael. "See You in Disneyland." *Variations on a Theme Park: The New American City and the End of the Public Sphere.* Edited by Michael Sorkin. New York: Hill and Wang (1992): 205–32.

*Soviet Literature.* "Our Contemporaries: Thirty Life Stories. Writers." Moscow: Writers' Union of the USSR, 1977.

Spade, Sam. *Twin Columns of Solomon's Temple.* Astana: Jachin of Ministries, 2007.

Stafford, Fiona, and Howard Gaskill. *From Gaelic to Romantic: Ossianic Translations.* Amsterdam: Rodopi, 1998.

Starobin, Paul. "Sultan of the Steppes." *The Atlantic Monthly,* December (2005): 98-104.

Stausberg, Michael, ed. *Zoroastrian Rituals in Context,* Leiden: Brill Publishers, 2003.

Steinbring, Jack. "The Tie Creek Boulder Site in Southeastern Manitoba." *Ten Thousand Years: Archaeology in Manitoba.* Edited by Walter Hlady. Winnipeg: Manitoba Archaeology Society (1970): 47–75.

Stern, Robert, A.M. *Buildings*. New York: Monacelli Press, 1996.

Sternberg, Leo. "Der Adlerkult bei den Völkern Sibiriens." *Archiv für Religionswissenschaft* 28 (1930): 125–53.

Stewart, Will. "World's First Pyramid… in Kazakhstan: Scientists Discover Tomb Structure was Built 1,000 Years Before Those in Egypt." *Daily Mail*. Article published August 15, 2016. http://www.dailymail.co.uk/news/article-3741937/Scientists-discover-known-pyramid-Kazakhstan-structure-built-1-000-years-Egypt-s-similar-tomb-Djoser.

Stites, Richard. *Revolutionary Dreams: Utopian Vision and Experimental Life in the Russian Revolution 1931–2010*. New York: Oxford University Press, 1989.

Strauss, Leo. *Persecution and the Art of Writing*. Glencoe: Free Press, 1952.

Stronach, David. "The Royal Garden at Pasargadae: Evolution and Legacy." *Archaeologia Iranica et Orientalis: Miscellanea in Honorem Louis Vanden Berghe*. Edited by Leon de Meyer and E. Haerinck. Gent: Peeters Presse (1989): 475–502.

Subtelny, Maria. "The Cult of Holy Places: Religious Practices among Soviet Muslims." *Middle East Journal* 43.4 (1989): 593–604.

Sudjic, Deyan. *Norman Foster: A Life in Architecture*. New York: Overlook Press, 2010.

Suleimenov, Olzhas. *AZ i IA: Kniga blagonamerennogo chitatelia*. Almaty: Zhazushy, 1975.

Surucu, Cengiz. "Modernity, Nationalism, Resistance: Identity Politics in Post-Soviet Kazakhstan." *Central Asian Survey* 12 (2002): 385–402.

Sweeney, Naoíse, ed. *Foundation Myths in Ancient Societies: Dialogues and Discourses*. Philadelphia: University of Pennsylvania Press, 2015.

Sykes, Bryan. *The Seven Daughters of Eve*. New York: W.W. Norton & Co., 2001.

Tafuri, Manfredo. *Architecture and Utopia: Design and Capitalist Development*. Translated by Barbara Luigia La Penta. Cambridge: MIT Press, 1976.

Talamini, Mokslas. Spatial Apparatuses in Central Asia: The Case of Astana. *Lietuvos Ateitis* 3:3 (2011): 53–58.

Tamm, E., T. Kivisild, M. Reidla, M. Metspalu, D.G. Smith, C.J. Mulligan et al. "Beringian Standstill and Spread of Native American Founders." *PLoS ONE* (2007) 2:9: e829. doi:10.1371/journal.pone.0000829.

Tarkhanov, Alexei. *Architecture of the Stalin Era*. New York: Rizzoli, 1992.

Tasmagambetov, Imangali. *The Centaurs of the Great Steppe: The Art Culture of Ancient Nomads*. Almaty: Berel, 2003.

Taut, Bruno. *The City Crown*. Translated and edited by Matthew Mindrup and Ulrike Altenmüller-Lewis. London; New York: Routledge, 2015.

Terrasson, Jean. *Sethos, Histoire ou Vie, Tirée des Monuments, Anecdotes de l'ancienne Égypte. Traduit d'un manuscrit grec*. Paris: Hippolyte-Louis Guérin, 1731.

Tillett, Lowell. *The Great Friendship: Soviet Historians on the Non-Russian Nationalities*. Chapel Hill: The University of North Carolina Press, 1969.

Tintin. *Geometry of the Pheasant Garden*. Karlsruhe: Octagon Press, 1720.

Titov, Alexander. "Lev Gumilev, Ethnogenesis and Eurasianism." PhD diss., London: University College, 2005.

Tod, Ian, and Michael Wheeler. *Utopia*. London: Orbis Publishing, 1978.

Toktogulov, Kadyr. "Kazakhstan Boosts President's Powers." *The Wall Street Journal*. Article published May 13, 2010. http://www.wsj.com/articles/SB10001424052748704247904575240044159679082.

Tracy, Dick. *Square the Circle of the Sun*. Amsterdam: Ritman Library, 1943.

Tredinnick, Jeremy, ed. *An Illustrated History of Kazakhstan: Asia's Heartland in Context*. Hong Kong: Odyssey Books, 2014.

Trevor-Roper, Hugh. "The Invention of Tradition: The Highland Tradition on Scotland." *The Invention of Tradition*. Edited by Eric Hobsbawm and Terence Ranger. Cambridge: Cambridge University Press (1983): 15–42.

Tsing, Anna L. *Friction: An Ethnography of Global Connection*. Princeton and Oxford: Princeton University Press, 2005.

Tyson, David. "Shrine Pilgrimage in Turkmenistan as a Means to Understand Islam Among the Turkmen." *Central Asia Monitor* 1 (1997): 15–32.

Urazova, Dinara. "Green Belt around Astana to be Extended." *Tengri News*. Article published August 28, 2014. https://en.tengrinews.kz/environment/Green-Belt-around-Astana-to-be-extended-254546/.

Vale, Lawrence. *Architecture, Power and National Identity*. New Haven: Yale University Press, 1992.

Valikhanov, Chokan. *Sobranie Sochinenii*, vol. 1. Alma-Ata: Akademii Nauk Kazakhskoi SSR, 1961 [1904].

Ventura, Ace. *The Goose that Laid the Golden Egg*. Akmola: Big Chupa Chups, 2002.

Vidler, Anthony. "The Architecture of Lodges: Ritual Form and Associational Life in the Late Enlightenment." *Oppositions* 5 (1976): 75–97.

——. *Claude-Nicolas Ledoux: Architecture and Utopia in the Era of the French Revolution*. Basel: Birkhäuser. 2006.

——. "The Return to the Origins: Rituals of Initiation in Late Eighteenth century France." *Princeton Journal* 1 (1983): 116–25.

——. *The Writing of the Walls: Architectural Theory of the Late Enlightenment*. Princeton: Princeton Architectural Press, 1987.

Vitruvius, Marcus. *Ten Books on Architecture*. Translated by Ingrid D. Rowland. New York: Cambridge University Press, 1999.

Wainwright, Edward. "Fostering Relations in Kazakhstan." *Reading Architecture And Culture: Researching Buildings, Spaces And Documents*. Edited by Adam Sharr. London: Routledge (2012): 46–61.

——. "Transparency and Obfuscation: Politics and Architecture in the work of Foster + Partners." PhD diss., Cardiff University, 2011.

Walzer, Richard, ed. *Al-Farabi on the Perfect State (Mabādi'ārā'ahl al-madīna al-fādila)*. Oxford: Clarendon Press, 1985.

Wang S., C.M. Lewis, M. Jakobsson, S. Ramachandran, N. Ray, G. Bedoya et al. "Genetic Variation and Population Structure in Native Americans." *PLoS Genet* 3 (2007): e185. doi:10.1371/journal.pgen.0030185.

Ward, Michael. *Planet Narnia: The Seven Heavens in the Imagination of C.S. Lewis*. Oxford: Oxford University Press, 2008.

Ware, Alyn. "ATOM Project Launched at Parliamentary Assembly in Kazakhstan." Global Security Institute. Article published in 2012. http://gsinstitute.org/blogs/event-reports/atom-project-launched-at-parliamentary-assembly-in-kazakhstan.

Watkin, David. "Freemasonry and Sir John Soane." *The Journal of the Society of Architectural Historians* 104 (1995): 402–17.

——. *Sir John Soane: Enlightenment Thought and the Royal Academy Lectures*. Cambridge: Cambridge University Press, 1996.

Wazana, Nili. "Anzu and Ziz: Great Mythical Birds in Ancient Near Eastern, Biblical, and Rabbinic Traditions." *Journal of the Ancient Near East Society* 32 (2009): 111–35.

Weatherford, Jack. *Genghis Khan and the Making of the Modern World*. New York: Crown, 2004.

Wee, Vincent. "Toward a World Without Wars." *The Business Times*. Article published June 3, 2016, www.businesstimes.com.sg/hub/kazakhstan-country-focus/towards-a-world-without-wars.

Wells, Peter, S. *How Ancient Europeans Saw the World: Vision, Patterns, and the Shaping of the Mind in Prehistoric Times*. Princeton: Princeton University Press, 2012.

Wells, Spencer, *The Journey of Man: A Genetic Odyssey*. Princeton: Princeton University Press, 2002.

Wensinck, Arent. *Tree and Bird as Cosmological Symbols in Western Asia*. Amsterdam: Johannes Mueller, 1921.

West, Martin. *The East Face of Helicon: West Asiatic Elements in Greek Poetry and Myth*. Oxford: Clarendon Press, 1997.

——. *Indo-European Poetry and Myth*. Oxford: Oxford University Press, 2007.

Wheeler, Stephen M. *Routledge Urban Reader Series: Sustainable Urban Development Reader*. Florence: Taylor and Francis, 2014.

White, Lynn. *Medieval Technology and Social Change*. Oxford: Oxford University Press, 1962.

White, Ralph, ed. *The Rosicrucian Enlightenment Revisited*. Hudson: Lindisfarne Books, 1999.

Wilber, Donal. *Persepolis: The Archaeology of Parsa, Seat of Persian Kings*. London: Cassell, 1969.

Wilensky-Lanford, Brook. *Paradise Lust: Searching for the Garden of Eden*. New York: Grove Press, 2011.

Wilson, William H. *The City Beautiful Movement*. Baltimore; London: Johns Hopkins University Press, 1989.

Wilson-Jones, Mark. *Principles of Roman Architecture*. New Haven: Yale University Press, 2003.

Wiseman, Boris, ed. *Cambridge Companion to Lévi-Strauss*. Cambridge: Cambridge University Press, 2009.

Wittkower, Rudolph. *Architectural Principles in the Age of Humanism*, London: W. W. Norton & Company, 1949.

——. "Eagle and Serpent. A Study in the Migration of Symbols." *Journal of the Warburg Institute* 2:4 (1939): 293–325.

Wolf, Eric. *Europe and the People Without History*. Berkeley: University of California Press, [1982] 1997.

Wolfel, Richard. "North to Astana: Nationalistic Motives for the Movement of the Kazakh(stani) Capital." *Nationalities Papers* 30 (2002): 485–507.

Woodman, Ellis. "Palace of Peace & Accord, Kazakhstan by Foster and Partners." *Building Design*. Article published September 22, 2006. http://www.bdonline.co.uk/palace-of-peace-and-accord-kazakhstan-by-foster-and-partners/3073828.article.

Wright, Herbert. *Instant Cities*. London: Black Dog Publishing, 2008.

Wu, Nancy, ed. *Ad Quadratum: the Practical Application of Geometry in Medieval Architecture*. Aldershot: Ashgate, 2002.

Yacher, Leon. "Astana, Kazakhstan: Megadream, Megacity, Megadestiny." *Engineering Earth: The Impacts of Megaengineering Projects*. Edited by S.D. Brunn. Springer: New York (2011): 1001–20.

Yates, Francis. *The Rosicrucian Enlightenment*. London: Routledge & Kegan Paul, 1972.

Yessenova, Saulesh. "Nomad for Export, Not for Domestic Consumption: Kazakhstan's Arrested Endeavour to 'Put the Country on the Map.'" *Studies in Russian and Soviet Cinema* 5:2 (2011): 181–203.

——. "The Political Economy of Oil Privatization in Post-Soviet Kazakhstan." *Subterranean Estates: Life Worlds of Oil and Gas*. Edited by Hannah Appel, Arthur Mason, and Michael Watts. Ithaca: Cornell University Press (2015): 291–306.

——. "'Routes and Roots' of Kazakh Identity: Urban Migration in Postcolonialist Kazakhstan." *The Russian Review* 64:4 (2005): 661–79.

——. "Soviet Nationality, Identity, and Ethnicity in Central Asia: Historic Narratives and Kazakh Ethnic Identity." *Journal of Muslim Minority Affairs* 22:1 (2002): 11–38.

Zabirova, Aigul. "The Latest Urbanization Processes in Kazakhstan: A Case Study of Astana." Paper presented at Third Annual Conference of the Central Eurasian Studies Society, Madison, Wisconsin, October 18, 2002.

Zakharov, I.A., M.V. Derenko, B.A. Maliarchuk, I.K. Dambueva, C.M. Dorzhu, and S.Y. Rychkov. "Mitochondrial DNA Variation in the Aboriginal Populations of the Altai-Baikal Region: Implications for the Genetic History of North Asia and America." *Annals of the New York Academy of Sciences* 1011 (2004): 21–35.

Zhansagimova, Dina. *Kazakhstan – Culture Smart!: The Essential Guide to Customs and Culture*. London: Kuperard, 2013.

# ENDNOTES

**A NOTE ON WORD CHOICE**

The term "Kazakh" as used in this work refers to the ethnic group which descended from Turkic and Mongol tribes, as well as the official language of the state. "Kazakhstani," on the other hand, is broader, being both the culturally inclusive demonym for the citizens of the Republic of Kazakhstan, and the nation's adjectival form (meaning "pertaining to Kazakhstan").

1  Founded in 1776 by Adam Weishaupt (1748–1830), a professor of canon law at the University of Ingolstadt. The Illuminati sought to undermine the Roman Catholic hegemony ruling Bavaria and replace it with an enlightened liberal republic. Today, more than two hundred years since being officially dissolved in 1785, the Illuminati have matured into a countercultural obsession and their subversive machinations and apparent global influence are found everywhere from the symbolism of multinational corporations to the hip-hop industry. Le Forestier (1914), Epstein (1960), Roberts (1972), Luckert (1993), Barruel (1995), and Barkun (2003).

2  The terms "Astana" + "Freemasonry" or "Astana" + "Illuminati" result in nearly 100 000 hits on Google.

3  Stewart (2016).

4  Jarus (2016). Key members of the Saryarka Archaeological Institute responsible for the find include: Valeriy Loman, Igor Kukushkin, Eugene Dmitriev, and Victor Novozhenov.

5  Lallanilla (2013).

6  See Blumenthal (2015), who advances the dubious claims of Dmitriy Dey.

7  Matuzeviciute, et al (2015) employed Optically Stimulated Luminescence samples for dating.

8  Jacob (2003) 190. The *Mānasāra* is a fifth- to seventh-century authoritative treatise of Vāstu Śāstra, a traditional Indian system of architecture that pertains to principles of design, layout, measurements, ground preparation, space arrangement, and sacred geometry. See Acharya (1933), Dutt (1977), Malville and Gujral (2000), and Quinn (1995).

9  There is also Kazakhgate, yet another conspiracy theory, involving James Giffen's bribery scheme. For a critical treatment of the affair, see Yessenova (2015).

10  Hermetic Code Tours and Albo (2008).

11  Chase (1949), Dundes (1985), The classic works on locating science in myth is Santillana and von Dechend (1969) and Popper for whom "science is myth-making just as religion is" (1974) 127.

12  Segal (2004) 91–112.

13  For an indispensable collection of primary texts and commentary on mythographical scholarship from 1680 to 1860, see Feldman and Richardson (1972).

14  Nietzsche (2004) 150.

15  Aitken (2009 and 2012), Cummings (2005 and 2009), Herfort (2013), Meuser (2015), Pohl (2012), Talamini (2011), Wright (2008), Yacher (2011), and Zabirova (2002).

16  Fauve (2015) 1, Murphy (2006), and Schatz (2009).

17  Lewis (2013) 265.

18  Carpenter (1978) and Duriez (2015).

19  Kerry (2011) and Ward (2008).

20  The term "Central Asia" has no cultural roots or definite boundaries and is employed in this book to cover the region stretching from the Caspian Sea in the west to China in the east and from Afghanistan in the south to Russia in the north.

21  Although it should be noted that according to the *World Fact Book*, Uzbekistan is the thirteenth-largest natural gas producer in the world.

22  Shepard (2015).

23  On paradisiacal architecture, see Manuel (1973), McClung (1983). On Walt Disney's utopian approach to city planning and the experimental community of EPCOT, see Mannheim (2002).

24  Banier (1738–40); Blackwell (1748); Feldman and Richardson (1972) 86–93 and 99–111; Lukacher (1994) 280–99 and (2006) and Lethaby (1972).

25  The "invisible" fraternity claimed to be in possession of salvific occult knowledge and their apocryphal manifestos—*Fama Fraternitatis* (1614), *Confessio Fraternitatis* (1615), and *The Chemical Wedding of Christian Rosenkreuz* (1616)—were penned as clever hoaxes that united medicine, philosophy, art, religion, mathematics, and the mystical progressions of spiritual alchemy. Yates (1972), Edighoffer (1982–87), Dickson (1998), and Godwin and McIntosh (2016).

26  For the prehistory and legacy of the Rosicrucians, see White (1999).

27  Anthony (2007), Golden (2011), Hanks and Linduff (2009), West (1997, 2007), and Hobson (2004), the latter of whom argues that the rise of the West after 1492 was a result of appropriating more technically and socially advanced Eastern innovations.

28  Berman (2000) 6, 43, and 81.

29  Although Astana is presently heated by coal, in 2012 Kazakhstan had executed a series of sustainable initiatives that included having 50 percent of the country's electricity derived from cleaner sources; a 40 percent reduction in its carbon emissions; 30 percent of its waste converted into

green energy; and implementing a stable long-term basis for green investment and innovation.

30 Campbell (1991).

31 Hublin (2014) 1–17.

32 Wells (2002) 114.

33 Brown (1998), Jablonski (2002), Tamm (2007), and Zakharov (2004).

34 Wang (2007).

35 Perego (2009). See also Sykes (2001) wherein all modern Europeans descend from seven mitochondrial haplogroups referred to as "clan mothers."

36 Greenberg (1987), Ruhlen (1994, and 1998). Most historical linguists, however, reject Greenberg and Ruhlen's method of mass comparison to establish genealogical relationships between languages. See Campbell (2003) and William Poser at: http://itre.cis.upenn.edu/~myl/languagelog/archives/003036.html.

37 Akhmetov (2014).

38 The pioneer of modern anthropology, Franz Boas (1858–1942) was one of the first to offer a systematic analysis of mythologies and migrations linking ancient Central Asia and the indigenous cultures of North America. See Boas (1929). On the comparisons between the folklore of northeastern Asia and northwestern America, see Bogoras (1902).

39 Wittkower (1939) 303.

40 For more recent scholarship on the subject, see Subtelny (1989) and Montgomery (2007).

41 Valikhanov (1961) 113.

42 McKenzie (1989). Privratsky posits an "architectural theory of religious behavior and persistence," claiming that "Islam for the Kazakhs is a religion of sacred space before it is a religion of sacred narrative, or of religious law." Privratsky (2001) 58.

43 Hoppál (1997) 193–206, Lymer (2000, 2004), and Tyson (1997). Similar traditions are found around the world, including India, Israel, Ireland, and Scotland, where Celtic pilgrimage sites, called "clootie wells," are decorated with strips of cloth, or "clooties," to demarcate a blessed tree or a sacred healing well.

44 For an archaeological analysis of Tamgaly, see Francfort (1995), and Maksimova (1985).

45 Buchner (1987), Danziger and Callaghan (1987), and Steinbring (1970). Turtle formations and boundary stones are also ubiquitous in the Övörkhangai and Töv provinces in Mongolia.

46 A shamanistic interpretation of petroglyphs is provided by Rozwadowski (2001, 2014).

47 On the sources of Scythian animal style, see Sher (1988).

48 Bekbassar (2005). On shamanic motifs in the petroglyphs of Eastern Kazakhstan, see Samashev (2002).

49 Citation is from the subtitle of the book. For another astute reexamination of the worldview and patterns of prehistoric societies, see Wells (2012).

50 In particular, see Gimbutas (1974, 1989), Mallory (1989), and Renfrew (1973, 1987). For a revisionist view of the subject of Indo-European origins, see Pereltsvaig and Lewis (2015), where the authors argue that linguistic analysis, as opposed to evolutionary biology, should be used to account for the genesis and spread of languages.

51 In light of new archaeological material from eastern Kazakhstan, Frachetti (2008) shows how the Bronze Age nomadic communities played a decisive role in shaping formative networks of exchange across Eurasia.

52 Outram, et al (2009) 1332–35.

53 Alinei (2009).

54 James Burke (1978) 52–54 and Lynn White (1962) 1–38 both saw the development of the stirrup as a crucial innovation influencing the social development of medieval Europe.

55 For the earliest wheeled transport, see Piggott (1983 and 1992), and Izbitser (1993) for the most authoritative account of steppe vehicle burials.

56 Anthony (1986) and (2007) 300–339.

57 The precise geographic homeland (Urheimat) of Proto-Indo-European remains hotly debated and divided into four main camps: Pontic-Baltic (Mesolithic), Anatolia (Early Neolithic), Central Europe-Balkans (Neolithic), and Pontic-Caspian (Chalcolithic), or the so-called "Kurgan Hypothesis." See Forsten (2004) and Mallory (1997). Other, less accepted models point to the Indian subcontinent, the Armenian Highlands, or the Paleolithic Continuity Paradigm, advanced by Alinei (1996 and 2000), which traces the genesis of the language to the Upper Paleolithic period.

58 Concerning migration in the history of the Eurasian steppe, see Seaman (1989).

59 For a summary of these innovations, see Anthony (2007) 458–66.

60 See Herodotus 4:1–82 and Aeschylus, Prometheus Bound 802 ff.

61 According to Marco, his father and uncle, Niccolò (1230–94) and Maffeo Polo (1230–1309) travelled through what is now southern Kazakhstan from Bukhara north of the Tien Shan through to Dadu, what is present day Beijing. Polo [1300] (1958) 12, 35.

62 According to Herodotus, Histories IV.13–16, Aristeas of Proconnesus wrote of the Hyperboreans in a lost poem called Arimaspea (ca. 650 BCE) about a journey of the Issedones who were believed to have lived in the Kazakh Steppe. Bridgman (2005) 29–32, and Eco (2013) 224–30.

63 Wilensky-Lanford (2011) 96–97. There are several accounts of the resting place of Noah's Ark in Central Asia, including the Sayram Su mountains in southeastern Kazakhstan. DeWeese (2000).

64 This close association led Nazarbayev to propose an alternative name for Kazakhstan as Ula Dala Eli, or the Country of the Great Steppe.

65 On the importance of the Silk Roads in the development of the global political economy, see Wolf (1997).

66 Hansen (2012) provides new archaeological light on the Silk Roads and Frankopan (2015) offers bold reassessment that challenges Eurocentric history.

67 Bissenova (2013) 138, Gawęcki (2013), Hobbs (2009) 123, and Laszczkowski (2011).

68 Buchli (2013) 99 for whom the "spectacle of postmodernism" in Astana is designed to create a "new nationalist subjectivity as opposed to a universalist Soviet one."

69 Other buildings where blue is a distinctly prominent colour include: the Parliament of the Republic of Kazakhstan; the National Museum; the Astana International Airport; the Central Election Commission Headquarters; the Academy of Public Administration; the Astana Railway Station; the Moscow Business Centre; the Northern Lights Apartment Complex; the Millennium Park Apartment Complex; the Keruen Shopping Mall; the Talan Towers; and the Museum of the First President of the Republic of Kazakhstan.

70 Kül-Tegin was likely preoccupied with divine legitimacy having slain his older brother in civil war after their father died, and ruling until his own death in 731. Many of his battles were waged in southeastern Kazakhstan, although his monuments (and homeland) were in Mongolia. I am indebted to Michael Hancock for this observation.

71 The east side of the monument I and II E 3: "When the blue sky above [Tengri] and the dark earth below were made, then were made between them both the sons of men. Over the sons of men set themselves [as rulers] my forbears Bumin kagan and Istämi kagan, and having set themselves [as rulers] they governed and kept in order the Turkish peoples' kingdoms and polity." See Ross and Thomsen (1930) 864.

72 Laruelle (2006) 3.

73 See Laruelle (2007ᵃ) where she explores the ways in which Tengrianism is politically deployed in the service of post-Soviet nationalisms in Kyrgyzstan, Tatarstan, Bashkortostan, Buryatia, and Kazakhstan.

74 Paksoy (2012) 57–70 makes an outrageous case for Tengrianism as being ideally suited for the future governance of Mars.

75 Largely financed by the Kingdom of Qatar, an extravagant mosque is soon to be opened in Tajikistan to accommodate 150 000 worshippers.

76 "Altai, the Golden Cradle of the Turkic World" is the name of an international forum on Turkic ethnography and heritage held every two years in Kazakhstan.

77 Tredinnick (2014) 60–67.

78 The Scythians likely inherited these technologies from their prehistoric ancestors, although most of what we know about them is from their neighbours, the Greeks and Persians. On the stylistic and iconographic tradition of the Scythians and their outstanding contribution to metallurgy, see Jacobson (1995).

79 Laruelle (2007ᵇ) 28–29.

80 Lim (2013) 167. On early Soviet identity creation in its various republics, see Tillett (1969).

81 Herodotus *Histories* I:200–214.

82 The Golden Man showcases the great wealth and status of the elite echelons of Scythian society. Akishev (1978).

83 Tasmagambetov (2003) 249–324.

84 Ibid. 22.

85 Babylonians and Persians list Saka and Gimirrai; Greek sources cite Saka, Cimmerian, and Scythian; in Hebrew, they are identified as Ashkuz and Gimirri; and Assyrian, Ashkuza. It was only in the last century that archaeologists began to suggest that the Saka and Scythians were associated at all. Four groups of Scythians are recorded on Darius I's massive Behistun Inscription: the Saka beyond the [Caspian] Sea, the Saka with pointed hats, the Saka beyond Sogdiana, and the Saka that drink soma.

86 Rice (1957).

87 Herodotus 4:2, Beckwith (2009) 85.

88 See Dubs (1938–55) and Aruz (2006) 147.

89 Also known as the Yuezhi or Xiongnu—the predecessors of the Huns who later threatened the Eastern and Western halves of the Roman Empire. The scarcity of sources has inspired much debate on whether these various names apply to the same group of people or a collection of related (or unrelated) peoples.

90 See Kelly (2008) for the history of Attila as an astute military commander who exploited the weaknesses of the Roman Empire and the reedition of Gordon's classic *Age of Attila* (2013).

91 The opaque history of the Huns relies on only a handful of Greek and Latin sources. For instance, the medieval chroniclers of the Árpád kings of Hungary (ca. 1000–1301) claim their ancestry from Attila, whom they paint in a positive light as a hero rather than a villain.

92 On the world of the Huns, their history, and their culture, see Maenchen-Helfen (1973).

93 For a comprehensive survey of the trajectory of Turkic peoples from steppe, to empire, to nation-state, see Carter (2005) and Golden (1992).

94 See Ross and Thomsen (1930) for an English translation with commentary.

95 It is important to note that the reception of Genghis Khan in Kazakhstan is not unilaterally positive. Weatherford (2004) provides a revisionist assessment of the charismatic Mongol warrior and unifier.

96 The date of 1465, from which modern Kazakhstan recently celebrated its 550 years of existence in 2015, derives from this historical work and personal memoir written by the Kashmiri ruler, Haydar Dughlat (1499–1551).

97 Folk etymology suggests that the Hordes took their name from the Kazakh word for "one hundred" (*Jüz, Zhüz*), but the term also reflects local Sufi traditions, as *Jüz* is Arabic for "group, part."

98 Cameron (1999) 4, and Kaufman (2001) 25.

99 Mertus (1999) and Goodrick-Clarke (2003).

100 Various official reasons have been used for moving the capital, including the risk of earthquakes and pollution in the region of Almaty. Anacker (2013) 523–26 and Wolfel (2002) 495–98. Nazarbayev provides his own personal and strategic decisions for moving the capital in (2008) 298–305 and (2010) 62–71. For an exploration on the contrasts in national self-identification between Almaty and Astana, see Shelekpayev (2013).

101 Mkrtchyan (2013) 233.

102 Nazarbayev (2008) 301.

103 On Neo-Eurasianism in Kazakhstan, see Laruelle (2008) 171–201.

104 Laruelle (2008) 141 and Titov (2005) 42–89.

105 Puhvel (1987) 4 defines his "monogenesis" approach to comparative Indo-European mythology as "tracing the mythical matter of disparate societies back to a common ancestry."

106 Most expressively stated by Gumilyov, Eurasianism has at its heart the question of Russian identity at the crossroads between Europe and Asia. His support of Kazakh, Tatar, and other Turkic identities sparked a massive wave of Gumilyov fervour throughout Central Asia. Indeed, visitors to Astana can study at the L.N. Gumilyov Eurasian National University, which was founded by Nazarbayev in 1996, foreshadowing the transfer of state power into the steppe away from Almaty.

107 The international flavours of Uzbek, Korean, Georgian, and Japanese cuisine are further represented along Astana's Restaurant Alley.

108 Most of the scholarship on the architecture of Astana has been circumscribed to political motivations: Surucu (2002), Koch (2010, 2012, 2015), Kopbayeva (2013), Köppen (2013), and Laszczkowski (2013).

109 Basilov, ed. (1989) 55–65.

110 In private correspondence with Professor Abazov on June 19, 2016. I am indebted to him for referring me to the work of Islam (2013) on Al-Fārābī and the ideal state.

111 See Strauss (1952) 9–18, Howse (1999) 60–77, and Colmo (2005).

112 See Beckwith's provocative study (2012), which illustrates how key innovations from Central Asia, like the recursive argument method, "revolutionized medieval Europe and gave rise to the culture of science in the West."

113 As cited in Nazarbayev (2010) 8. For Al-Fārābī's original text with commentary, see Walzer (1985).

114 Kazakhstan adopted a Green Economy policy in 2013 for the efficient use of natural resources, and in 2014, construction began on a "Green Quarter" residential and office complex in Astana that incorporates advanced technologies aimed at reducing water and energy consumption by 20 percent. Elkin (2015).

115 From the speech at the meeting with Board members of the Assembly of People of Kazakhstan, October 18, 2002. http://www.kazakhembus.com/content/discover-kazakhstan-0.

116 Famously stated by Churchill in 1943 in response to the bombed Houses of Parliament.

117 Bercovitch (1975).

118 For the importance of foundation myths in identity construction and the building of cities in the ancient world, see Sweeney (2015). On the foundation myths and rituals of Rome that pertain to city planning, see Rykwert (1976) 27–153.

119 Yessenova (2002).

120 Findley (2005) 38–39.

121 Oosten (1985).

122 The Greek precursor to Lincoln's grand Indo-European pattern is Richard Onians (1951), who asserted an underlying system in Classical conceptions about the mind, soul, and fate in correlation with views of anatomy, physiology, and human behaviour.

123 See Lawrence and Jewett's companion work (2002) on the historical and religious roots of the American superhero myth and its threat to traditional democracy.

124 For Beckwith, the Central Eurasian Cultural Complex refers specifically to the comitatus, a group of hero-warriors who adventure alongside their chosen king-leader, as in the case of Beowulf or Tamerlane. The classic definition is Germanic in origin, but Beckwith suggests it is much older and more widespread.

125 The title announced in Kazakhstan's upper house of Parliament on June 3, 2010.

126 Bates (2010), Jenkyns (2016), and Honko (1990).

127 Reichl (2000) 12–43. Reichl's analysis of oral epic poetry in Central Asia shows its typological similarity to the heroic poetry of medieval Europe.

128 In Kazakhstan, it is common to call poetic storytellers zhyrau (zhyr means "epic story"), whereas bakhshi is equated with shamans per se. Zhyraus served Khans as advisors and composed memoirs and epics about them.

129 See Herder's treatise of 1778 Über die Wirkung der Ditchtkunst auf die Sitten der Völker in alten und neuen Zeiten (On the Effect of Poetry on the Mores of the Peoples in Ancient and Modern Times) in Adler and Koepke (2009) 195.

130 As Abazov states, many Kazakh intellectuals, such as the poet Ilias Zhansugirov, (1894–1938) became nation-builders by appropriating "local folklore, myth, legends, and epics, portraying them as components of the 'true' people's culture." Abazov (2007) 93–94.

131 See Benjamin's essay of 1936 The Narrator in Bottigheimer, ed. (1986) 238.

132 May (1999).

133 On the politics of kin-based clan divisions in post-Soviet Kazakhstan, see Schatz (2004).

134 Yessenova (2005). In addition to establishing relations among patrilineal units of extended families, *shejýre* also provides a genealogical map that extends in certain cases from what is known as the "poetico-mythical" era to the modern period. See Alimbai (2012) 156–61.

135 Zhansagimova (2013) 49.

136 Initially published in Russian as *Morfologiia Skazki*. See Propp (1958).

137 Lévi-Strauss (1955 and 1958).

138 Analysis on Lévi-Strauss's structural study of myth is provided by Leach, ed. (1968) and for a companion to his life and works, see Wiseman, ed. (2009).

139 Nazarbayev's State of the Nation Address on January 28, 2011.

140 Hobsbawm and Ranger, eds. (1983) 1–14.

141 Trevor-Roper (1983) 15–42.

142 Cannadine (1983) 101–64.

143 Barczewski (2000).

144 Littleton and Malcor (2013).

145 On the subject of nation-building and Kazakhstan films, see Isaacs (2014), and Yessenova (2011) for an insightful study of *The Nomad as* state-sponsored "image-making" propaganda.

146 Isaacs (2014) 7.

147 Yacher (2011).

148 Tsing (2005), and Bissenova (2013) 127.

149 On the collective memory of cities experienced by citizens, see Boyer (1994).

150 Vale (1992) 346.

151 Erbhard (2009), and Mallgrave (2010).

152 For an introduction to urban semiotics, see Gottdiener and Lagopoulos (1987), and Krampen (1979), who explored the mechanics by which meaning is injected into the urban environment.

153 de Saussure (1959) 108–9. For a general introduction to Saussurean urban semiotics, see Gottdiener and Lagopoulos (1987) 1–21.

154 Preziosi (1979) applies structuralism to identify the formal and functional aspects of an "architectonic code" in Minoan palaces (ca. 1500 BCE). See also his companion work, Preziosi (1983).

155 On the "language" of Post-Modernism and witty pronouncements against International Style, Brutalism, and Deconstructivism, see Jencks (2002) and Salingaros (2004). Essentially, Post-Modernism revokes design pretensions of scientific rationality and progress in favour of pluralism, eclecticism, and sensuous references to past architectural ornamentation.

156 Buchli (2013).

157 Day (1990).

158 Structuralism influenced Alexander's theories of environmental "pattern language" in architecture, building and urban design (1977).

159 Barthes (1997) 158.

160 Initially published as *La mort de l'auteur*, a pun on Sir Thomas Malory's compilation of Arthurian legend stories, *Le Morte d'Arthur* (1485). See Barthes (1967).

161 Eco (1979) 84–86.

162 Eco (1997) 179–81.

163 Stern (1996) 15.

164 Buchli (2007) 54.

165 Peirce (1982–2010) II: 53–54.

166 See Buchli (2007) 52–55 for his careful interpretations of the *shangïraq* as both an index and metonymic exemplar of Kazakh identity.

167 On yurt symbolism and assembly, see Kunanbay (2001) 91.

168 Rykwert (1976) 45–48.

169 Eliade (1978) 43.

170 Founded by Kazimir Malevich (1878–1935) in 1915, Suprematism is an avant-garde art movement characterized by abstract geometric forms and the "supremacy of pure artistic feeling." Suprematism was fundamentally opposed to Constructivism, the other contemporary Russian design

philosophy that had a profound impact on the language of Astana. See Shatskikh (2012).

171 On the archaeological record of Eurasia and the role of politics in the history and prehistory of the region, see Hartley, et al, eds. (2013).

172 Sudjic (2010) 246.

173 Kunanbay (2001) 86.

174 Laugier's account of the Primitive Hut was one of the most influential architectural theories of the eighteenth-century. The famed Jesuit priest presents the invention of architecture as the arrangement of four perpendicular branches supporting horizontal beams and a leafy-pitched roof. Rykwert (1972) 43–49.

175 Herrmann (1962), and Vidler (1987) 7–22.

176 For an examination of the function, form, and symbolism of ancient tents in the Hebrew Bible and the Ancient Near East, see Homan (2002).

177 Corbin (1986) 220–23.

178 Akkach (2005) 180–81.

179 Kunanbay (2001) 87.

180 Nabokov and Easton (1989) 164.

181 Laubin (1957) 108–9; 241. On the evolution of tipis and Plains Indian nomadism, see Brasser (1982) 309–21.

182 Goethe (1854) 179.

183 Campbell (1949). The Museum of the First President of the Republic of Kazakhstan in Astana includes complete genealogical records of Nazarbayev's ancestry, alongside archival documents, gifts from foreign dignitaries, and historical memorabilia. See Aitken (2009) 5, where Nazarbayev's birth is connected to "promising portents of destiny and mysticism" from Shaprashti tribesmen.

184 Aitken (2009) and Khrapunov (2015).

185 On the architecture of ancient Persia, see Wilber (1969).

186 Nylander (1979) 354–55. For a detailed history of archaeological exploration of Persepolis, see Mousavi (2012).

187 See the multidisciplinary virtual reconstruction project, http://persepolis3d.com/, which brings to life the grandeur and complexity of ancient Persian urban planning and design.

188 For a detailed study of St Petersburg's wider historical significance, see Bater (1976).

189 On the Brothers Grimm and German fairy tale nationalism, see Lee (2010) 27–50.

190 Aitken (2009) 14, 20, 26.

191 Aitken (2009) 119 and on Yassawi, see Mélikoff (1989).

192 Nazarbayev (2010) 41, 44–50, 53–54.

193 On Thomas Jefferson, a self-taught architect, his buildings, and admiration for Palladio in constructing American society, see Beltramini and Lenzo, eds. (2015).

194 Koch (2012) 123. Le Maître (1682) highlighted three crucial functions of a capital: authority, exchange, and the concentration of national values; whereas for Foucault (2007) 14, suggested that a capital must "diffuse throughout the territory all that is necessary to command people with regard to their conduct and ways of doing things." I am indebted to Koch (2013ᵃ) for this reference.

195 Nazarbayev once told a journalist: "I am the architect of Astana … I am not ashamed to say that." See Woodman (2006).

196 After apprenticing under the celebrated Kazakh architect, Kaldybay Montakhayev, Abilda went on to develop a design philosophy that established a marriage between the past and future, traditional building and modern technology. Meuser (2015) 63.

197 Aitken (2009) 238.

198 Blistein (2013), Preston (2009), and Starobin (2005) 98 characterized Nazarbayev as a "vainglorious despot" who presides over a "human rights wasteland" as a "brilliant wheeler-dealer, formidable orator, tireless toiler—and consumer of local vodka."

He has also been listed among the pantheon of personality cults around the globe and immortalized in cinema, fairy tales, statuary, and performance arts. Western media, Human Rights Watch, and former government officials have played no small part in attempting to tarnish his public image by denouncing him as "an incorrigible dictator" of a police state, lumping him with a clutch of brutish "-stan" country tyrants. Human Rights Watch (1990), Buckley (2013), Khrapunov (2015) 169, Kilner (2012), Love (2011); see Schweizer (2015) Chapter Two: "The Transfer: Bill's Excellent Kazakh Adventure"; and the media watchdog group, Correct the Record, which debunks Schweizer's allegations of collusion linking Nazarbayev and the Clinton Foundation with a uranium mining contract in Kazakhstan, http://correctrecord.org/clinton-cash-debunked/.

199 Toktogulov (2010).

200 Aitken (2012) 76 cites 752 tests, but the more common number is 456. See https://www.ctbto.org/nuclear-testing/the-effects-of-nuclear-testing/the-soviet-unionsnuclear-testing-programme/.

201 See http://www.un.org/en/events/againstnucleartestsday/.

202 Brunn (2011) 1800.

203 Secretary of State, James Baker, also played a significant role in Kazakhstan surrendering its nuclear missiles. Reiss (1995) 138–82. Mozur (1995) 110 credits the cherished Kyrgyz novelist, Chingiz Aitmatov, for playing a major role in Kazakhstan's denuclearization.

204 See http://www.theatomproject.org/en/. See also Ware (2012), Nazarbayev (2013), and Orazgaliyeva (2015).

205 Wee (2016).

206 Nazarbayev (2016).

207 Nazarbayev (2008) 296 and Nazarbayev (2010) 123.

208 Nazarbayev (1997).

209 Mayor (2011) 40–44 makes a compelling case that the winged snow leopard, or griffin, was actually based upon the Scythians's first-hand

accounts of discovering the bones of the dinosaur Protoceratops, which had four legs, a nasty-looking beak, and a bony frill at the back of the skull, mistaken for wings.

210 Article 7 of the Constitution of the Republic of Kazakhstan outlines that the state language shall be Kazakh, while state institutions and local self-administrative bodies shall officially adopt Kazakh and Russian on equal grounds.

211 In an interview with the BBC. Antelava (2006).

212 Salopov, "President Nazarbayev's Personal Capital." *Kommersant*, October 28, 1997.

213 Nazarbayev (2010) 40–41, 45.

214 Translation provided by Michael Hancock.

215 Mumford (1961) 575.

216 Aitken (2009) 235.

217 Koch (2012) 1.

218 Nazarbayev (2010) 38–39.

219 French sociologist, Émile Durkheim (1858–1917), first posited the sacred-profane dichotomy, but the theory was further elaborated by Eliade (1954) 12–17 and (1957) 20–57.

220 Nazarbayev (2008) 273.

221 See Nazarbayev's poignant account of the legendary tale in (2008) 273–4.

222 Foster (1995) 103–4.

223 Attributed to Lu-Nanna, the king of Ur (2150–03 BCE), the Etana epic was known in antiquity by its incipit: "They Planned a City." On the Etana epic in light of world folklore, see Haul (2000), and on the proliferation of Etana fairy tales, including a Russian version known as "The Duckling," see Levin (1966).

224 Nazarbayev (2008) 313.

225 Aitken (2012) 104.

226 For Nazarbayev's own account of the myth and the symbolic meaning of Bayterek Tower, see (2010) 225–31.

227 Barthes (1997) 166.

228 On Hittorf's works, including analyses of his architectural achievements and the interrelations between his pursuits as an architect, an archaeologist, and a theorist, see Schneider (1977).

229 The obelisk was originally positioned outside the temple of Ammon at Luxor and then gifted to France in 1833 by Muhammed Ali, Khedive of Egypt.

230 Aitken (2009) 10. Pushkin was initiated in Lodge Ovid No. 25, Kischinev in 1821. Concerning Puskin's use of numerology, thaumaturgy, and Masonic elements in his short story the "Queen of Spades," see Leighton (1982) 15–25, and Leighton (1994) 131–94.

231 Compare with the pseudoscientific Sun Language Theory developed in Turkey and advocated by Atatürk in the 1930s, which proposed that all human languages originated from proto-Turkic speakers. For a complete history of Turkish language reform, see Lewis (1999).

232 Ram (2001) 301–2. On the linguistic connection between the *dingir* and *tengri*, see Rawlinson (1862) 78 and Eliade (1958) 64.

233 Suleimenov (1975) 229 as cited in Ram (2001) 301.

234 Wazana (2009).

235 See *Egyptian Book of the Dead*, Spells 39 and 108, which deal with solar battles against Apophis in Faulkner (2015), and on Egyptian solar religion, see Assman (2009).

236 On the founding of Tenochtitlán by Huitzilopochtli, see Mundy (2015), where the author also explores the colonial evolution of Mexico City and the indigenous landscapes and contributions that underpin the modern capital.

237 Wittkkower (1939).

238 Gamkrelidze and Vjačeslav (1995) 764.

239 Ibid. See also Tasmagambetov (2003) 20–21 and 44. For a fascinating study of the deer within the iconography of the early nomads of Siberia and Central Asia from the Neolithic period to the early Iron Age, see Jacobson (1993).

240 Dumézil's trifunctional hypothesis was elaborated in numerous books and articles between 1930 and 1986, although principally modified in (1958). For a detailed study of the reformulation and reinterpretation of Dumézil's theories, see Belier (1991).

241 On the sacred tree in religion and myth, see Philpot (1897), and for anthropological perspectives of tree worship, see Rival, ed. (1998).

242 Wensinck (1921) explores the cosmological symbolism of trees and birds in Western Asia, and James (1966) provides an archeological study of the Tree of Life from the ancient Near East, Iran, India, the Aegean, Greece, Rome, Syria, Europe, and in Judeo-Christian iconography.

243 Starobin (2005) 99.

244 See also Mkrtchyan (2013) 230.

245 Nazarbayev (2010) 26.

246 Nazarbayev provides his own account of the discovery in (2010) 105–6.

247 Kassymov, Kundakbayeva, and Markus (2012) 234.

248 Nazarbayev (2010) 15–16, 111, 234.

249 Ibid. 258.

250 I am indebted to Saulesh Yessenova for this semantic annotation.

251 The name Astana derives from the same Iranian root that renders the English word "state" and "stand." The "-stan" countries have the same word—as Kazakhstan is the "land of the Kazakhs." The threshold of a yurt was also traditionally called the Astana—likely because that was where one stood to greet another. Analysis provided by Michael Hancock in private correspondence.

252 As cited in Buchli (2007) 46.

253 Buchli (2007) 66, n. 5. See Miliutin (1964) for his own thoughts on socialist city planning. Many of the principles of Le Corbusier's Functional City were laid down by the *Congrès Internationaux d'Architecture Moderne* (CIAM) founded in 1928 and in the Swiss architect's Athens Charter, published in 1943.

254 AstanaGenPlan (2012) 46–47.

255 Pohl (2012) 269.

256 Alexander and Buchli (2007) 8.

257 On Communist utopian architecture and urbanism, see Stites (1989) 190–204.

258 Åman (1992) explores the relationship between Stalinist architecture (or Socialist Realism) and political ideologies in Poland, Czechoslovakia, Hungary, Romania, Bulgaria, and former East Germany.

259 Larmour and Spencer (2007) 342, and Anderson (2015) 151.

260 Tarkhanov (1992) 116–80.

261 Meuser (2015) 158.

262 See Hoppál, ed. (1984), which investigates all aspects of Eurasian shamanism, including songs, drums, meditation, and concepts of the soul.

263 Hoppál (2007) 78. On the symbolism of the eagle in the religious thought and mythology of Siberian shamanism, see Sternberg (1930) 146ff.

264 Golebiowska-Tobiasz (2013) 44.

265 On the medieval stone statues of Kazakhstan's steppes, see Belli (2003) and Ermolenko (2004).

266 Rickey (1995) explores the origins and evolution of Constructivism.

267 On Russian avant-garde architecture between 1922 and 1935, see Lodder and Cohen (2011).

268 Geldern (1993) 197.

269 On Russian Constructivism, see Kopp (1985), and Lodder (1983).

270 Shayakhmetov (2006) provides a gripping first-hand account of the scale of suffering under Stalin's rule of Kazakhstan.

271 Robbins (2008) 106. Since the breakup of the Soviet Union, Kazakhs have transformed this monumental shrine from a Soviet museum to a symbol of national sovereignty and spiritual rebirth. See Privratsky (2001).

272 For a comprehensive and penetrating history of the Gulag, see Khlevniuk (2004).

273 See Edelstein, Cerny, and Gadaev, eds. (2012) for the deliberate policy decisions resulting in the Aral Sea's disappearance and the damaging results in soil salinization, water pollution, and toxic sands, which have impacted the entire bioregion and beyond.

274 Podvig (2001) 463.

275 The official website of President Nazarbayev cites that Astana was awarded the title in 1999. See http:// www.akorda.kz/en/republic_of_ kazakhstan/astana. But according to the UNESCO website, Astana received Honourable Mention in 1998–99, behind Hanoi, Vietnam. See portal.unesco.org/culture/en/ev.php-URL_ID=2550&URL_DO=DO_ TOPIC&URL_SECTION=201.html.

276 Laszczkowski (2011), Neef (2006), Wolfel (2010) 489.

277 Anacker (2013) 519–20, Bissenova (2013) 128, and Wainwright (2011) 163.

278 More coined the term *utopia* in 1516, providing the ambiguous meaning of the Greek words, *eu-topos* (no place) and *ou-topos* (good place). See More [1516], translated by Miller (2014).

279 Plato 6.500e, translated by Lindsay (1923) 220.

280 On architecture and utopia, see Coleman (2005 and 2011), Eaton (2002), Manuel and Edward, eds. (1973), Schaer (2000), Tafuri (1976) and Tod and Wheeler (1978).

281 For a thorough examination of the relationship between literary utopias and the urban and architectural projects of the Renaissance, see Rahmsdorf (1999) and Rosenau (1959).

282 Alberti's *De Re Aedificatoria* (1450) offers a detailed study of architecture and explores a wide array of subjects, from history of town planning to the philosophy of beauty. See Alberti (1988), translated by Rykwert.

283 Jarzombek (1989) 117.

284 Eaton (2002) 241 reaches this conclusion in her work on ideal cities and utopian urbanism.

285 Stronach (1989) 475–502.

286 Fuller's dome would have spanned diameter of two miles and, among other things, would have allowed for the elimination of automobile traffic.

287 On the City Beautiful Movement and its proponents, see Wilson (1989).

288 Baudrillard (1994). Influenced by the semiotic theories of de Saussure and Barthes, Baudrillard's sharp critique of contemporary society (in particular, seduction, virtual reality, and the first Gulf War) explores the implications of a historically understood version of structural semiology.

289 In 1966, Disney produced a documentary entitled EPCOT in which he outlined the basic principles and designs of his model community.

290 Sorkin (1992) 205–32.

291 Mannheim (2002).

292 The prolific urban planner, James Rouse, described Disneyland as the "greatest piece of urban design in the United States today," while the historical geographer, Richard Francaviglia, called Main Street, U.S.A., "one of the most successfully designed streetscapes in human history." Rowley (2015) 115–50.

293 Anderson (2015) 71–73, see also Cooke (1978) for Russian responses to Howard's Garden City Movement.

294 Conrad (1976) 96.

295 Shakespeare, *Richard II* 2.1.45–50.

296 Former mayor of Astana, Adilbek Zhaksybekov, as cited in Anacker (2013) 519.

297 Although picturesque, the shallow Ishim has contributed to the unpleasant proliferation of mosquitoes, which thrive in stagnant waters.

298 Kurokawa (1977). On Metabolism and urban utopianism in modern Japan, see Lin (2010).

299 Köppen (2013) 597.

300 See Kurokawa (1994) for his philosophy of symbiosis in architecture and urban planning.

301 Ibid. 75.

302 Kurokawa (2000) 216.

303 Kikutake (1959) 36–39.

304 Vitruvius's famous passage on the proportions of man, *Ten Books on Architecture* III.1.3.

305 Le Corbusier (1927) 95 contra Kurokawa (1994) 23.

306 Clearly set out in James Stevens Curl's forthcoming book, *Making Dystopia: The Strange Rise and Survival of Arcitectural Barbarism* (2017). As Dalrymple (2009) puts it, "Le Corbusier was to architecture what Pol Pot was to social reform." See also Perelman (2015).

307 Geddes (1904), and on Geddes as a social evolutionist and city planner, see Meller (1993).

308 AstanaGenPlan (2012) 178–85. The proposal for the 22.4-kilometre North-South Astana Light Metro would link the city's main line station with Astana International Airport.

309 Wheeler (2014) traces the history of sustainable community development and explores urban design, transportation, ecological planning, economic development, social and environmental justice, as well as green architecture and building.

310 Urazova (2014). On the Green Belt initiative, see Nazarbayev (2010) 247–53.

311 For an ethnography of Brasília and a powerful critique of the utopian premises of its design, see Holston (1989). On the failed attempts of imperialistic state planning and the imposition of administrative order on nature and society, see Scott (1998).

312 Hannigan identifies four additional characteristics of the "Fantasy City": it "operates *day and night*, in the same spirit as the Nevada casinos"; 2) it is *modular*, mixing and matching themed restaurants, megaplexes, and museums; 3) it is *solipsistic*; "isolated from surrounding neighborhoods physically, economically and

culturally"; and 4), it is *postmodern*, "insomuch as it is constructed around technologies of simulation, virtual reality and the thrill of the spectacle." See Hannigan (1998) 2–4.

313 On the new frontiers of architecture in Dubai, see Bellini and Daglio (2008).

314 AstanaGenPlan (2012) 158–65.

315 Bissenova (2013) 137.

316 On premodern Islamic cosmology, mysticism, and architecture, see Akkach (2005).

317 On the Sufi character of Kazakh religious expression, see Privratsky (2001) 15–16.

318 Ibid. 178. On the Islamic architecture and mausolea for southern Kazakhstan, see Baitanayev and Yogin (2007).

319 I am indebted to Valeriy Loman for this valuable information. See also Anthony (2007) 441–43.

320 Kurokawa (2001) II.3.18.

321 See Finoli and Grassi (1972) for a critical edition of all of the surviving Filarete manuscripts.

322 Kurokawa (1988) 18.

323 On the elements and forms of traditional Japanese architecture, see Locher (2015).

324 For a complete literary and archaeological history of Zoroastrianism, including contributions to Hellenistic thought, Judaism, Christianity, Mithraism, and Central Asia, see Boyce (1982).

325 http://strategy2050.kz/en/page/geometry.

326 Stites (1989) 40 and 88.

327 Stausberg, ed. (2003) analyzes Zoroastrian rituals amid a broad range of disciplines, as well as historical and geographical perspectives.

328 Karimov (2014) 130.

329 Droste (1990) 32.

330 Wittkower (1949) 101–54 shows how Alberti's Santa Maria Novella in Florence (1470) employed Pythagorean ratios of numerical

harmony (*eurhythmia*) to implement the laws of nature in the divinization of architecture. Geometric principles of Palladio's villas, palaces, public buildings, and church façades are discussed on pages 57–100.

331 Le Corbusier (1988) 72, and Padovan (1999) 321. See Le Corbusier (1950) for his codification of an anthropometric scale of proportions, and Rowe (1947) for Le Corbusier's use of Palladian mathematics in his Villa Stein at Garches.

332 Birksted (2009). For a discussion of how much Theosophy and esotericism influenced "the dark side of the Bauhaus," see Rykwert (1982) 44–49.

333 Nicoletti's works and vocabulary of architecture derived from nature and geometry are discussed in Sharp, ed. (1998) 7–27.

334 Attempts to recover the principles of medieval Gothic architecture continue to be a major source of scholarly debate. Albo (2012), Bork (2011), Hiscock (2000 and 2007) and Wu, ed. (2002).

335 "On a finite straight line construct an equilateral triangle." See Euclid, translated by Heath (1956) 241 and Albo (2012) 78 and 100–2.

336 Phaedrus, *Fables* IV.2.4–6.

337 Kaufmann (1952) first coined the phrase "revolutionary architect" in reference to Ledoux and Boullée.

338 See Ledoux's monumental opus *L'Architecture considérée sous le Rapport de l'Art, des Moeurs et de la Législation* (Architecture considered under the relation of art and legislation) published in 1804 and translated into English in 1983 and Boullée's *Architecture, essai sur l'art* (Essay on the Art of Architecture) of 1788 and translated into English in 1953.

339 Attributed to Samuel Hemming (1767–1832), this standard definition has been part of the English Fellow Craft degree since the early nineteenth century. Carr, ed. (1967) 377.

340 Additionally: Alexander Sumarokov (1717–77), Vasilii Maikov (1728–78), Mikhail Kheraskov (1733–1807),

Vladimir Lukin (1737–94), Alexei Rzhevskii (1737–1804), Nikolay Novikov (1744–1818), Alexander Radishchev (1749–1802), and Nikolay Karamzin (1766–1826).

341 Other aspects of the Paradise Myth included the co-opted imagery and symbols of the Orthodox Church, the idea of rebirth, and the notion of Russia as a "happy garden state."

342 Baehr (1991) 90–111 emphasizes the distinction between the Russian Paradise Myth and its Masonic counterpart in which masons themselves (and not the Tsar) would collectively bring about the restoration of the world. For the significant role Freemasonry played in the formulation of a wide range of utopian themes in Russian culture and intellectual thought, see Artemyeva (2009) 63–84.

343 Though Freemasonry never entered Central Asia, Bayer (2007), Smith (1999), Faggionato (2005), and Önnerfors and Collis, eds. (2009) have shown how Masonic lodges played an integral part of an emerging civil society in eighteenth-century Russia. The Bukharan reformist intellectual and statesman, Ahmad Dānish (1827–97), "regarded masonry as an instrument for the obliteration of all social distinctions." See Algar (1970) 279.

344 Yates (1972) 209.

345 In particular, Pius IX's *Multiplices Inter* (1865) and Pope Leo XIII's *Humanum Genus* (1884).

346 The sociologist and critical theorist, Jürgen Habermas, referred to this phenomenon as the bourgeois "public sphere." Habermas (1991) 35.

347 Jacob (1991) 15.

348 On the origins of Freemasonry, see Berman (2012), Curl (2011) 1–70, Knoop and Jones (1947), and Roberts (1972) 17–57.

349 Prescott (2004) 64–67.

350 Prescott (2005) 43–77.

351 On the Scottish origins of modern Freemasonry, see Stevenson (1988).

352 Curl (2011) 308.

353 For a thorough examination of the architecture of Freemasonry, see Curl (2011), on the Temple, specifically: 71–96.

354 Brengues and Mosser (2000) 130. Notable architects include: Jean-Baptiste de Puisieux (1679–1776), Jean-François-Thérèse Chalgrin (1739–1811), Alexandre-Théodore Brongniart (1739–1813), Jacques Cellérier (1742–1814), Bernard Poyet (1742–1824), Jean-Baptiste Rondelet (1743–1829), Pierre Rousseau (1751–1829), Antoine Vaudoyer (1756–1846), and the architect of the city of Paris, Pierre-Louis Moreau-Desproux (1727–93).

355 In his quixotic study, *The Genius of Architecture; or, The Analogy of That Art with Our Sensations* (1780), Le Camus de Mézières offered a sensationalist exploration of architecture that supplied the theoretical underpinning for the formal explorations of Ledoux and Boullée. See (translated) Le Camus de Mézières (1992) 17 and 160.

356 Vidler (1976) 94.

357 Vidler (1983) 120.

358 The literature on this subject is enormous. A snapshot of the critical works are: Albo (2006), Buttlar (1989), Curl (2011) 175–245, and Olausson (1985).

359 Le Forestier (1970) 1026. The most important architectural theorist and Freemason of the late Enlightenment, Quatremère de Quincy (1755–1849), considered that the temples of Thebes and Karnak housed underground subterranean vaults. Vidler (1987) 98.

360 This reading of the building is largely indebted to the scholarship of Wainwright (2011) 164–211, and Wainwright (2012) 46–61.

361 Pérez-Gómez (1996) 137.

362 Boullée, translated by Rosenau (1953) 82.

363 From the official website of the Pyramid at http://astana-piramida.kz/.

364 Meuser (2015) 128. Despite its presumed ancient heritage, the "divine proportion" was coined in Fra Luca Pacioli's book *De Divina Proportione* of 1498 and the "Golden Section," or *goldener Schnitt,* appears for the first time in Martin Ohm's *Die reine Elementar-Mathematik* of 1835.

365 For a mannered approach to the subject, including debunking many of the myths associated with the Golden Section, see Livio (2002) and Markowsky (1992) 2–19.

366 Teotihuacan, Cholula, and Uxmal in Mesoamerica; Saqqara, Giza, and Dahshur in Egypt; Argolis and Güímar in Greece and Spain; Thanjavur, Borobudur, and Xi'an in India, Indonesia, and China, not to mention several modern examples from Paris to Kazan.

367 Wainwright (2012) 48–52.

368 Wainwright (2011) 208.

369 Curl (2011) 157–58; and Terrasson (1731).

370 Akkach (2005) 33–36.

371 For an overview of how ancient monuments such as Chichén Itzá, Ankor Wat, the Pyramids of Giza, and Stonehenge related to celestial motions, see Ruggles (2005).

372 Ruggles (2015) provides the definitive sourcebook on cosmologies, calendars, orientations, and alignments of sacred architecture from the Neolithic period to Renaissance Christendom.

373 Wilson-Jones (2003) 182–97.

374 Incerti (2001) 293–306.

375 Davis (2002) 171–93.

376 See Watkin (1995) 402–17, Watkin (2006) 123–24, 170–71, and 183–84.

377 Albo (2012) 102–3.

378 Sudjic (2010) 166.

379 Wainwright (2012) 59.

380 Wainwright (2011) 207–11.

381 See Ledoux [1804] (1983) and Vidler (2006).

382 Vidler (1987) 101.

383 Macpherson (2002) 557–82.

384 For a well-illustrated survey of the symbolism of the Eye, see Potts (1982).

385 Ramírez (1991) 1–50.

386 Anderson (1767) 3. On Freemasonry and Solomon's Temple, see Curl (2011) 71–96, Hamblin and Seely (2007) 175–90, Horne (1971), and Limpricht (1994) 71–145.

387 Corbin (1986) 263–390.

388 Hamblin and Seely (2007) 131–64.

389 Renna (1990) 76–77 and Wittkower (1949) 102–7.

390 Faegre (1979) 92 and Kronenburg (2014) 24–26.

391 Kunanbay (2001) 189.

392 See Taut [1919] (2015) and Naredi-Rainer (1994) 188–89.

393 Abazov and Mukhamediuly (2013).

394 Dalbai (2015) 172–83.

395 See Fisher (2014) and Rifkin (2011) for Rifkin's theory of a shared clean energy grid that will transform culture and production.

396 See http://smithgill.com/work/expo-2017/.

397 See http://www.aifc.kz/.

398 Nazarbayev (2008) 273–95.

399 Stafford and Gaskill (1998) 153–57.

400 Curley (2009) 1. On the reception of Ossian in Europe, including Scotland, Wales, Ireland, France, Germany, Sweden, Finland, Czechoslovakia, Hungary, Poland, Russia, Spain, Italy, and Portugal, see Gaskill (2004).

401 On the sociopolitical and nationalist views of early twentieth-century Kazakh intellectuals, see Sabol (2003).

402 *Soviet Literature* (1977) 47.

403 The Sumerian *Tale of Etana* is your beginning.

# INDEX

*Italicized page numbers indicate references to figures.

# ILLUSTRATION CREDITS

Adrian Smith + Gordon Gill Architecture, 251 (top), 252–53, inside back cover

Aibek Akhanov, 118, 148–49, 196–97, 210–11

Alamy Stock Photography. 32, 39 (top), 43, 54–55, 81 (bottom), 82 (top), 109, 110, 113, 123 (bottom), 134, 136–37, 150, 163, 188 (top), 212, 218–19

Alexander Bachimov, 172

Astana Mayor's Office, 68, 82 (bottom), 128–29, 154, 176–77, 202–6, 215

Bibliotheca Philosophica Hermetica, Amsterdam, 29

Bibliothèque nationale de France, Paris, 63, 228, 245 (top), 251 (bottom)

Bilal Arslan, 46–47, 168–69

Bridgeman Art Library, London, 224 (bottom)

Buketov Karaganda State University, 12

Central State Museum of the Republic of Kazakhstan, Almaty, 40

Christopher Herwig, 164–65

Collection of Edwin Binney, 131 (bottom)

David Köster, 8, 120–21

DigitalGlobe, Inc., 15–17

Disney Enterprises, Inc., 179

Dmitry Chistoprudov, 10, 30, 90–91, back cover

Dmitry Chulov, 157

DRA&U, 175

Elmar Akhmetov, 18–23, 64

Evgeny Tkachenko, 132–33

Galleria Nazionale delle Marche, Urbino, 171 (top)

Gallerie dell'Accademia, Venice, 184

Gavin Hellier, 81 (top), 200–201, 227

George Washington Masonic Memorial, photography by Arthur W. Pierson, 221

Gerd Ludwig/National Geographic Creative, 143

Gleb Kramchaninov, 193

Grand Lodge of the District of Columbia, photography by Paul D. Dolinsky, 222–23

Hungarian National Gallery, Budapest, 60

ITAR-TASS Photo Agency, 147

Jane Sweeney, 235

Jim Sanders, 36 (top)

Karla Nur, 240–41

Katie Spiker 123 (top)

Krym Altynbekov, 57

Landeskunde Baden-Württemberg, 85

Lebedev Physics Institute (FIAN), Moscow, 166–67

Lucy Harrison, cover

MAE (Kunstkamera), 72–73

Musée national des châteaux de Malmaison et de Bois-Préau, 254

Museo de Arte de Ponce, Ponce, Puerto Rico, 78

Museum of Fine Arts, Boston, 52–53

National Gallery of Art, Washington D.C., 231 (top)

NASA/Carla Cioffi, 126–27

Nigel Young/Foster + Partners, 100, 102–3, 105, 216, 231 (bottom), 232, 242–43, 245 (bottom)

Nihad Ademi, author's portait, interior jacket

Nina Mingioni, 6–7, 44, 49, 76–77

Nutthavood Punpeng, 158–59

Oleg Ivastov, 183

Pavel Tenyakov, 187

Petar Milošević, 199 (bottom)

Pennsylvania Academy of the Fine Arts, Philadelphia, 224 (top)

Polish Military Institute of Geography, Warsaw, inside front cover

Press Office of the President, Astana, 106

Ramil Galeev, 94–95

Ray and Dianna Harryhausen Foundation and Tate, London, 24

Ryan Koopmans, 58–59, 209, 248–49

Santa Maria del Fiore, Florence, 71

Satellites Pléiades, Airbus Defence and Space, 180

Shchusev Museum of Architecture, Moscow, 160

Shutterstock, 82 (top), 88, 92–93, 97, 117, 144, 188 (bottom), 190–91, 236–37, 257

Sir John Soane's Museum, London, 238

Skidmore, Owings & Merrill LLP, 194

State Hermitage Museum, photography by Vladimir Terebenin, 50

Studio 44 Architects, 98–99

Susan Portnoy, 140

Trustees of the British Museum, London, 39 (top), 124, 131 (top)

Txema Magdalena, 67

Valentin Guidal, 199 (top)

Valeriy Loman, 35

Vancouver Lodge of Education and Research, 246

Vatican Museums, Rome, 39 (bottom)

VG Bild-Kunst, Bonn, Germany, 114

Vladimir Trofimchuk, 139

Walters Art Museum, Baltimore, 171 (bottom)

Wikimedia Commons, 36 (bottom)

Zachary Cofran, 153

# OFFICIAL RULES OF
# THE ASTANA CHALLENGE

### Contest Sponsor: Parkview Inc.

All participants in the Astana Treasure Hunt (the "Challenge") will be deemed
to have accepted, and be bound by, the following rules and conditions:

**ELIGIBILITY:** The Challenge is open to any individual over 18 years of age who has a copy of *Astana: Architecture, Myth, & Destiny* (the "Book") and has submitted his/her solution at www.astanamyth.com. Frank Albo (the "Author"); Cliff Johnson, (the "Creator"); Vidacom Publications (the "Publisher"); Hayden Sundmark (the "Designer"); and Parkview Inc. (the "Sponsor"); as well as their respective attorneys, agents, employees, and immediate family (related or not), heirs, and assigns are ineligible to participate in the Challenge.

**GUIDELINES:** Concealed within the Book are secrets and mysteries (the "Clues") that, once solved, reveal a hidden message (the "Solution"). The first person, or group of persons (the "Sleuth"), to deduce the Solution in its exact wording, must follow the Instructions (see below) to become the verified "Winner" and claim the Prize (see below).

**RULES:** The Sponsor reserves the right in its sole discretion to disqualify any Sleuth who: (a) tampers with the participation in, or operation of, the Challenge; (b) violates any rules of the Challenge; or (c) acts in a disruptive manner and offends, threatens, or harasses any Sleuth participating in the Challenge. The Challenge will run until the Solution has been submitted and the Winner has been verified, or until December 31, 2018 (the "Closing Date"), whichever occurs sooner. Submissions made through agents or third parties are invalid.

**INSTRUCTIONS:** The Sleuth must submit his/her answer through the website or by email to solution@astanamyth.com. The Winner will be required to complete, sign, and return an affidavit of eligibility and liability, as well as a release within fifteen (15) days of being contacted by a representative of the Challenge. During that time, the Winner will also be required to satisfy the Sponsor that his/her Solution resulted from his/her own analysis and skill, and without the use of any prohibited conduct or confidential information. Permission to announce the Winner's name must be provided in writing to the Sponsor before being awarded the Prize. The Winner may also be asked to participate in publicity, except where prohibited by law.

**NOTIFICATION:** The Solution has been safely stored and will only be revealed once the Winner has been verified, at which point the Challenge will be deemed terminated. If the Winner does not accept the Prize or does not respond to the Sponsor's notification, the Prize will be deemed forfeited, and the next Sleuth who has submitted the Solution will be contacted. The above procedure will be followed until a Winner has been determined.

**PRIZE:** The Sleuth, whom the Sponsor in its sole discretion has declared the Winner, will be awarded two (2) Business Class tickets from Amsterdam to Astana, seven (7)-day luxury hotel accommodations in Astana, and a cash prize of US $5000. If the Sleuth consists of more than one participant, each must comply with the above requirements, agree in writing to share the Prize and release the Sponsor from any liability in connection therewith. The Sponsor takes no responsibility for dividing the Prize and has no obligation to award it until the Sponsor receives such written agreement and release.

**DISCLOSURES:** The Sponsor shall have complete discretion over the interpretation of the rules and reserves the right to refuse to award the Prize to anyone who the Sponsor determines is in breach of these rules and conditions or otherwise fails to establish their eligibility. The decision of the Sponsor regarding the Winner and all matters related to the Challenge are final. If a Winner is not declared by the Closing Date, the Sponsor may decide in its sole discretion to extend the Challenge and will post the extension at www.astanamyth.com.

**LIABILITY:** The Sponsor is not responsible for misdirected, lost, delayed, altered, or illegible submissions. The Prize may not be transferred or assigned without the Sponsor's written consent. All expenses for participating in the Challenge are the sole responsibility of the Sleuth. By participating in the Challenge, each Sleuth releases the Author, Creator, Publisher, Designer, and Sponsor from any and all liability for any loss, harm, damages, cost, or expense, including, without limitation, property damage, personal injury and/or death, arising out of participation in the Challenge or the acceptance, use or misuse of the Prize. Participation in the Challenge and all matters relating thereto is governed by the laws of the Province of Manitoba without reference to choice of law rules, and the Courts situated in that Province shall have exclusive jurisdiction over all disputes relating to the Challenge.

Aerial perspective of the World Expo 2017 site, Astana.